"We have needed a book like this on eschatology for some time. Now we have it! John Hammett writes with his typical excellence. He is biblically faithful, theologically rigorous, and pastorally sensitive. He is comprehensive and clear. And, he is incredibly fair and gracious with opposing views. I am delighted to commend its widest use."

—**Daniel L. Akin**, president, Southeastern Baptist Theological Seminary

"I was blessed to have Dr. Hammett as one of my professors for Systematic Theology in seminary. The biblically attuned, conceptually careful, spiritually sensitive approach he has demonstrated in class for decades is on display in *The Source of Hope*. This is a helpful introduction to the fundamentals of Christian eschatology and will be beneficial for student and professor alike."

—**Matthew Emerson**, dean of theology, arts, and humanities, Oklahoma Baptist University

"In a world that is mired in despair and anxiety, a fresh reminder of our source of hope in the return of Christ is much needed. Argued from a biblical, historical, global, theological, and practical vantage point, Hammett provides the reader a clear summary of the varying positions on challenging eschatological doctrines, while giving ample warrant for his own views. While it is unlikely you will agree with every conclusion in this volume, the author provides an irenic and convictional approach to the various issues."

—**Jeremy M. Kimble**, professor of systematic and applied theology, Cedarville University

"Hammett has provided a valuable resource for the church. This book flows from three decades of study and teaching and is presented in a fair and irenic tone. This work will prove to be a trustworthy guide that will offer instruction and hope for the next generation."

—**Ben Merkle**, Dr. M. O. Owens Jr. Chair of New Testament Studies, Southeastern Baptist Theological Seminary

"John Hammett's book on eschatology deserves to be read widely. It is remarkably clear and understandable without being simplistic. Hammett also faithfully explains and defends the central end time truths that all believers who trust in God's Word confess. At the same time, he is charitable and fair in evaluating controversial views. I also loved the practical application sections that helped readers see why these teachings are important for everyday life. Highly recommended!"

—**Thomas Schreiner**, James Buchanan Harrison Professor
of New Testament Interpretation,
The Southern Baptist Theological Seminary

"John Hammett provides contemporary Christians with the text we have long needed, a comprehensive entry-level introduction to Eschatology. *The Source of Hope* provides a wealth of information regarding the biblical bases, historical expressions, and contemporary debates for the major loci within the doctrine of last things. Hammett's latest contribution should become the first text consulted not only by experts in the field but by novices interested in a wise and balanced approach to primary concepts and to controverted opinions alike."

—**Malcolm B. Yarnell III**, research professor of theology,
Southwestern Baptist Theological Seminary

THE SOURCE OF HOPE

THE SOURCE OF HOPE

AN INTRODUCTION TO ESCHATOLOGY

JOHN S. HAMMETT

B&H
ACADEMIC®
BRENTWOOD, TENNESSEE

The Source of Hope: An Introduction to Eschatology

Published by B&H Academic®
Brentwood, Tennessee

ISBN: 978-1-0877-5616-5

Dewey Decimal Classification: 236
Subject Heading: ESCHATOLOGY \ END OF THE WORLD \ DEATH

Printed in the United States of America
30 29 28 27 26 25 VP 1 2 3 4 5 6 7 8 9 10

CONTENTS

PREFACE

I am very grateful to the folks at B&H Academic for their invitation to write this book. In truth, I have wanted to have such a book since the fall of 1996, when I began teaching Systematic Theology at Southeastern Baptist Theological Seminary. I continually wanted to be able to direct students to one book that would introduce them to all the major issues in eschatology. While there are many good books on individual topics in eschatology, a comprehensive introduction was lacking. As a result, I spent a significant amount of time over the past twenty-five or so years researching these topics and writing summaries for students in the form of lecture notes for seminary classes and doctoral seminars. Thus, the opportunity to write this book is especially meaningful.

Even though this book is releasing at the end of my teaching career, which will limit my opportunities to use it in a classroom setting, I am glad to leave it for the present and future generations of students and others who may benefit from it. In recognition of the past generation of students at Southeastern whose questions have challenged me and whose interest has encouraged me, I dedicate this book to them collectively. May it point them, and all who read it, to the source of hope.

ABBREVIATIONS

BDAG	*A Greek-English Lexicon of the New Testament and Other Early Christian Literature*, by W. Bauer, F. W. Danker, W. F. Arndt, and F. W. Gingrich, 3rd ed. (Chicago: University of Chicago Press, 2000)
BECNT	Baker Exegetical Commentary on the New Testament
CSB	Christian Standard Bible
EBC	The Expositor's Bible Commentary
EBTC	Evangelical Biblical Theology Commentary
ESV	English Standard Version
Institutes	*The Institutes of the Christian Religion*, by John Calvin; ed. J. T. McNeill; trans. and indexed F. L. Battles, LCC, 2 vols. (Philadelphia: Westminster, 1960)
JETS	*Journal of the Evangelical Theological Society*
LCC	Library of Christian Classics
NICNT	New International Commentary on the New Testament
NIDNTT	*The New International Dictionary of New Testament Theology*, ed. L. Coenen, E. Beyreuther, and H. Bietenhard; English translation ed. C. Brown, 4 vols. (Grand Rapids: Zondervan, 1975–86)
NIGTC	New International Greek Testament Commentary

NIV	New International Version
NPNF1	*Nicene and Post-Nicene Fathers, First Series*
TWOT	*Theological Wordbook of the Old Testament*, ed. R. L. Harris, G. L. Archer, and B. Waltke, 2 vols. (Chicago: Moody, 1980)
ZECNT	Zondervan Exegetical Commentary on the New Testament

CHAPTER 1

An Introduction to Eschatology

Why a Book on Eschatology?

Immanuel Kant, perhaps the most important philosopher of the Enlightenment, said in his *Critique of Pure Reason*, "All interest of my reason (the speculative as well as the practical) is united in the three following questions: (1) What can I know? (2) What should I do? (3) What may I hope?"[1] The contemporary philosopher Peter Kreeft says the three cardinal Christian virtues of faith, love, and hope correspond to these questions.[2] The first question—"what can I know?"—is the key question in the field of epistemology. Faith in God's Word answers the epistemological question. It gives us what we may most certainly know. "What should I do?" is the

[1] Immanuel Kant, *Critique of Pure Reason*, trans. and ed. Paul Guyer and Allen Wood (Cambridge, UK: Cambridge University Press, 1998), 677.

[2] Peter Kreeft, *Heaven: The Heart's Deepest Longing* (New York: Harper Collins, 1980), 11.

question of ethics. Love to God and neighbor sums up our ethical duty. The last question—"what may I hope?"—is addressed by the doctrine of eschatology. Eschatology is our source of hope.

Hope is our great need due to the realities of the world in which we live. We are surrounded by injustices and tragedies every day, and every life that begins ends, sooner or later, in death. We wonder, Will things always be this way? Craig Hill says, "At heart, all eschatologies are responses if not quite answers to the problem of evil."[3] Despite all appearances, the doctrine of eschatology says there is a future for which we may dare to hope. And as eschatology deals with last things, things not yet seen, hope is the pervasive theme of eschatology, as hope is the Christian response to things promised but not yet seen (Rom 8:24). For example, one recent book on eschatology is simply called *The Christian Hope*;[4] another is structured to include the word "hope" in the title of every chapter of the book;[5] still another studies Paul's eschatology under the rubric of "the hope of glory."[6]

But the hope held out to us in eschatology is "a daring hope,"[7] even called by one an "insane expectation that what is lost will be given back."[8] For some, the fact that we have been waiting for the central event of eschatological hope, the return of Jesus, for two thousand years has caused some to doubt the viability of Christian hope. But this objection to the hope held out by eschatology goes all the way back to the scoffers mentioned in the New Testament itself (2 Pet 3:3–4). The Enlightenment turned away

---

[3] Craig C. Hill, *In God's Time: The Bible and the Future* (Grand Rapids: Eerdmans, 2002), 4.

[4] Brian Hebblethwaite, *The Christian Hope* (Grand Rapids: Eerdmans, 1984).

[5] John E. Phelan Jr., *Essential Eschatology: Our Present and Future Hope* (Downers Grove: IVP Academic, 2013). From chapter 1, "Hope and Promise," to chapter 10, "Hope for the Church," every chapter links eschatology to hope.

[6] Constantine R. Campbell, *Paul and the Hope of Glory: An Exegetical and Theological Study* (Grand Rapids: Zondervan Academic, 2020).

[7] Jerry L. Walls, "Introduction," in *The Oxford Handbook of Eschatology*, ed. Jerry L. Walls (Oxford: Oxford University Press, 2008), 6.

[8] David Bentley Hart, *The Beauty of the Infinite: The Aesthetics of Christian Truth* (Grand Rapids: Eerdmans, 2003), 392.

from eschatology and looked to human potential as the source of hope.[9] By employing the resources of reason and science, enlightened thinkers thought they could bring in a future utopia apart from divine intervention. But this Enlightenment confidence in human ability and potential was severely shaken in the twentieth century by two world wars, the Holocaust, nuclear weapons, and global terrorism.

The twentieth century saw a sharp uptick in interest in eschatology, such that one theologian calls the twentieth century, "the century of eschatology."[10] This was especially so in evangelical theology with the rise of dispensationalism, a form of biblical interpretation that championed a version of eschatology made popular by the 1970 publication of a book by Hal Lindsey, *The Late Great Planet Earth*, and even more widely publicized by the twelve volumes of the Left Behind series of books by Tim LaHaye and Jerry Jenkins, which sold more than 80 million copies between 1996 and 2004.[11]

Yet even this widespread interest in eschatology has had its problems and detractors. Some have tried to correlate world events and politics with their eschatological charts, with minimal success;[12] still others have claimed that they had figured out the date for the return of Christ or the end of the world.[13] Like all the others who thought they had figured out things that

[9] "The Enlightenment-crafted projections of humanity's future were bereft of distinctively Christian eschatology." Walls, "Introduction," 8.

[10] Christoph Schwöbel, "Last Things First? The Century of Eschatology in Retrospect," in *The Future as God's Gift: Explorations in Christian Eschatology*, ed. David Fergusson and Marcel Sarot (Edinburgh: T & T Clark, 2000), 217.

[11] Walls cites one source that claims *The Late Great Planet Earth* was "*the* best-selling nonfiction book of the entire decade of the 1970s." Walls, "Introduction," 10.

[12] For examples of eschatological interpretations of events in Israel, see Walls, "Introduction," 14. In commenting on the difficulty of entangling biblical interpretation and international politics, he adds, "It is easy to lose sight of the fact that eschatology is concerned with ultimate issues, not penultimate ones." (14).

[13] Edgar C. Whisenant self-published *88 Reasons Why the Rapture Will Be in 1988* and never repented of his error. Radio preacher Harold Camping prophesied the end of the world twice in 2011, first on May 21, then October 21. Finally, before he died in 2013 he came to repent of his attempts to forecast this date, calling his

Jesus said only the Father knows (Mark 13:32), they were mistaken and gave eschatology a bad name. Others note the widespread disagreements within evangelical thought on matters like the rapture, tribulation, and millennium and conclude that eschatology has little clear value and practical importance.

But if hope is essential to healthy human living, and eschatology is the source of hope, then eschatology should be of interest, not only to every Christian, but even to every human. Moreover, as John Polkinghorne states, "Christian belief must not lose its nerve about eschatological hope. A credible theology depends upon it."[14] Here are some ways in which eschatology is crucial to Christian thought, life, and ministry.

Eschatology is connected to numerous major and far-reaching biblical themes that clearly touch pressing questions of today. Michael Bird, echoing ethicist Richard Hays, notes seven such themes. The church needs eschatology, he argues, to carry Israel's story forward to its consummation, to show that the cross is a saving event for the world (Col 1:20), to give a critique to pagan culture by our proclamation of Jesus as ultimate Lord of all (Phil 2:10–11), to resist triumphalism and complacency by our understanding that judgment begins with the household of God (1 Pet 4:17), to affirm the goodness of the body by our affirmation of the resurrection of the body, to ground our mission in the coming of the kingdom, and to speak with integrity about suffering and death because there is coming a *telos* that will put all suffering in proper perspective (Rom 8:19; 2 Cor 4:17).[15]

---

statements "sinful." See Robert D. McFadden, "Harold Camping, Dogged Forecaster of the End of the World, Dies at 92," *New York Times*, December 18, 2013, https://www.nytimes.com/2013/12/18/us/harold-camping-radio-entrepreneur-who-predicted-worlds-end-dies-at-92.html.

[14] John Polkinghorne, *The God of Hope and the End of the World* (New Haven, CT: Yale University Press, 2002), 149.

[15] Michael F. Bird, *Evangelical Theology: A Biblical and Systematic Introduction* (Grand Rapids: Zondervan, 2013), 241–43, drawing upon Richard B. Hays, "'Why Do You Stand Looking Up Toward Heaven?' New Testament Eschatology at the Turn of the Millennium," in *Theology at the Turn of the Millennium*, ed. L. G. Jones and J. J. Buckley (Oxford: Blackwell, 2001), 123–29.

Moreover, eschatology also has great practical value for the Christian life. We already mentioned hope, but Paul tells us that if we have hope in Christ only for this life, "we should be pitied more than anyone" (1 Cor 15:19). Jesus promises us tribulation in this world and reward only eschatologically (John 16:33; Matt 5:12). The hope of heaven is not "pie in the sky by and by when we die" but a light that shines on our path now, even and especially in the darkest times. Moreover, meditation on last things is not morbid, but spiritually healthy. In the most widely read devotional book of all time, *The Imitation of Christ*, Thomas à Kempis recommends meditation on death: "You are truly blessed if you keep the hour of your death before you and prepare yourself for it."[16] The unbeliever is enslaved by the fear of death, but Christ frees us so that we can look at death unafraid (Heb 2:14–15; 1 Cor 15:54–57).

Eschatology is also crucial for numerous areas of contemporary ministry. Terrorist attacks, gun violence and mass shootings, and pandemics have made people freshly aware of what we usually try to avoid or ignore—namely, the uncertainty of life and the certainty of death. Such awareness opens doors for ministry. For the pastor or counselor, dealing with death, funerals, and the bereaved demands a firm grasp of heaven, hell, and associated questions. As Russell Moore perceptively states, "A Christian's eschatology does not consist in his prophecy charts but in his funeral service. At a funeral the church is perhaps at its most theological."[17] Eschatology is vital to this area of ministry.

Eschatology is also an important area for the teaching ministry of the church. In the last 150 years, eschatology has been more studied than at any prior period in church history,[18] and it has been the subject of a plethora

---

[16] Thomas à Kempis, *The Imitation of Christ*, ed. Claire Fitzpatrick, new illus. ed. (New York: Catholic Book, 1977), 53–54.

[17] Russell D. Moore, "Personal and Cosmic Eschatology," in *A Theology for the Church*, rev. ed., ed. Daniel L. Akin (Nashville: B&H, 2014), 671.

[18] See the claim of James Orr that eschatology was the primary topic for doctrinal development in the twentieth century in, James Orr, *The Progress of Dogma* (Grand Rapids: Eerdmans, 1952), 20–28.

of books, articles, and conferences. While there is much good material that has been produced, eschatology has also often been the subject for speculative and sensational treatments that have led some into unwarranted fanaticism. Knowledge of eschatology helps a pastor or leader keep others from such extremes.

Finally, in terms of missions, eschatology is important because there is a link between eschatology and the completion of the Great Commission. There are verses hinting that one reason why Christ has not returned is that he is waiting for all to hear (Matt 24:14; 2 Pet 3:9). Based on this verse and others, there is a widespread eschatological belief that "the end of time will be accompanied by widespread preaching of the gospel to all nations."[19] Eschatology has been a powerful motivation for missions, both in the past and today.

For all these reasons, we think the time is ripe for a fresh articulation of the doctrine of eschatology, the source of hope, for a battered and deeply divided world greatly in need of a hope that nothing in this world can give. In the remainder of this chapter, we will give an overview of eschatology as a whole and then a preview of the topics we will address in this book.

What Is Eschatology?

With the Greek word for "last" forming the first part of the word "eschatology" (*eschatos*), it is often referred to as the doctrine of last things.[20] Eckhard Schnabel draws out what he sees as the implications of "last" for the definition of eschatology as follows: "Used in a strict sense, *eschatology* refers to prophecies, events, and developments that are close to and

---

[19] Timothy C. Tennent, *Theology in the Context of World Christianity: How the Global Church Is Influencing the Way We Think about and Discuss Theology* (Grand Rapids: Zondervan, 2007), 222.

[20] Two major reference works, *Evangelical Dictionary of Theology* and *Dictionary for Theological Interpretation of the Bible*, have no entry for eschatology but have substantive articles under "Last Things" and "Last Things, Doctrine of."

connected with, the last period of history before the end."[21] Anthony Hoekema sees the typical definition of eschatology as including not just things connected to the last period of history, but future things more generally. He says, "Customarily, it [eschatology] has been understood as referring to events which are still to happen, both in relation to the individual and to the world."[22]

Since eschatology deals with events "still to happen," it has a strong future orientation, especially as traditionally understood. For example, the title of every chapter in the book *Eschatology: Biblical, Historical, and Practical Approaches* begins with the phrase "The Doctrine of the Future."[23] This future orientation will be the approach taken in this book. We will address events still future for the individual, such as one's physical death, existence in the intermediate state, eventual bodily resurrection and judgment, and the final states of heaven and hell. We will include future events that will involve not only individuals but the cosmos, such as the tribulation, return of Jesus, general resurrection, final judgment, and possible millennial experience. Thus understood, eschatology is seen as both personal and cosmic.[24] Moreover, this future orientation is not just temporal, but also teleological,[25] as our hope is not grounded in the future *per se* but the future in which God's purposes reach their *telos*.

Others acknowledge the future focus implied by *eschatos* ("last") but see the last things as the consummation of a larger pattern and think we

---

[21] Eckhard Schnabel, *40 Questions about the End Times* (Grand Rapids: Kregel Academic, 2011), 9.

[22] Anthony A. Hoekema, *The Bible and the Future* (Cambridge, UK: Eerdmans, 1979), 1.

[23] D. Jeffrey Bingham and Glenn R. Kreider, eds., *Eschatology: Biblical, Historical, and Practical Approaches* (Grand Rapids: Kregel Academic, 2016). For example, the title of the first chapter is "The Doctrine of the Future and Canonical Unity: Connecting the Future to the Past."

[24] As in Russell D. Moore, "Personal and Cosmic Eschatology," *A Theology for the Church*, 671–721.

[25] Walls, "Introduction," 4.

may speak of the fulfillment of earlier stages of the pattern as also eschatological.[26] For example, some see the hope of the coming of the kingdom of God as central to Old Testament eschatology.[27] But with the first advent of Jesus, the kingdom becomes not just future, but also present. Some call this "realized eschatology," but in evangelical circles the more often used term is "inaugurated eschatology."[28] Hoekema thinks "inaugurated" does better justice to the twin truths that (1) "the great eschatological event of the Old Testament had taken place in the coming of Jesus Christ and the establishment of his kingdom" and (2) that "there remain many eschatological events that have not yet been realized."[29]

We agree with those who argue that eschatology in its most complete sense encompasses both things already realized and things still to come.[30] We definitely agree with those who argue that eschatology has present relevance,[31] and will point out a number of such points of present relevance in chapters to come. But one book cannot cover everything, and much of what we call "inaugurated eschatology" is incorporated in standard treatments of Christology. This book will focus on the traditional topics associated with future eschatology.

---

[26] F. F. Bruce and J. J. Scott, Jr., "Last Things," in *Evangelical Dictionary of Theology*, 3rd ed., ed. Daniel J. Treier and Walter A. Elwell (Grand Rapids: Baker Academic, 2017), 477; Stephen R. Spencer, "Last Things, Doctrine of," in *Dictionary for Theological Interpretation of the Bible*, ed. Kevin J. Vanhoozer (Grand Rapids: Baker Academic, 2005), 438.

[27] George Eldon Ladd, *The Presence of the Future: The Eschatology of Biblical Realism* (Grand Rapids: Eerdmans, 1974), 52.

[28] Bruce and Scott, "Last Things" (479), credit the influential work of G. E. Ladd in the widespread adoption of "inaugurated" to describe how the kingdom had come in Jesus but had not reached its full and final consummation.

[29] Hoekema, *Bible and the Future*, 17.

[30] Hoekema insists, "full-orbed biblical eschatology must include both what we might call 'inaugurated' and 'future' eschatology." Hoekema, *Bible and the Future*, 1.

[31] "Everything done in the church is, or should be, done in light of the presence of the kingdom of God in Jesus's ministry, message, death, and resurrection." Phelan, *Essential Eschatology*, 13.

What Lies Ahead

Some books approach eschatology by sketching the eschatological teaching in each section of the Bible.[32] Others trace the historical development of eschatology in the history of the church.[33] Still others seek to gain insight by comparing Christian eschatology with that of other world religions and a number of different Christian traditions.[34] While we will certainly give attention to biblical teaching, historical developments, and other traditions, the purpose and focus of this book is theological—we want to ask what Christians should believe about the major events that lie within the field of future eschatology based on biblical teaching.

Following this introductory chapter, chapters 2 and 3 will deal with the last things in a person's life on earth. Chapter 2 will focus on biblical teaching concerning death, but will also address related issues, such as near-death experiences and the movement called transhumanism,[35] which seeks to make death optional for people. Chapter 3 will ask the question which has occupied the minds of many through the ages: What lies beyond death? We will look at biblical terms like *Sheol*, *Hades*, and "paradise" and examine the issue of what is called the intermediate state (the state in which a human exists in the time between the death of their body and the resurrection of their body).[36]

---

[32] See Part 2 of Bingham and Kreider's *Eschatology*, 107–262, with chapters on each section of the Bible from Moses and the Pentateuch to Hebrews and the General Epistles.

[33] See Part 3 of Bingham and Kreider's *Eschatology*, 265–430; Hebblethwaite, *The Christian Hope*.

[34] See Part IB and Part II, 113–342 of Walls, *Oxford Handbook of Eschatology*.

[35] See Carol Zaleski, "Near-Death Experiences," in *Oxford Handbook of Eschatology*, 614–28. See Jacob Shatzer, *Transhumanism and the Image of God: Today's Technology and the Future of Christian Discipleship* (Downers Grove: IVP Academic, 2019).

[36] For the debate on the so-called intermediate state, see John W. Cooper, *Body, Soul & Life Everlasting: Biblical Anthropology and the Monism-Dualism Debate* (Grand Rapids: Eerdmans, 2000).

With chapter 4, we move beyond the last things for individuals to things that pertain to the cosmos as a whole, with a chapter on the rapture and tribulation. The relation of these two events will call for special attention. Most evangelical scholars agree that there will be a time of intense tribulation before the second coming of Christ, but some see the rapture of the church as an event separate from and before the Second Coming and as an event that will take place either before or sometime during this period of intense tribulation. We will examine the various positions that relate this sign of tribulation to the event of the rapture, such as pretribulation, prewrath, or posttribulation.[37]

This will lead naturally to the topic of chapter 5, the second coming of Christ. Some would argue that this is the central event of eschatology. It is called our "blessed hope" (Titus 2:13) and is by far the most frequently mentioned future eschatological event in the New Testament. Chapter 5 will survey biblical teaching on the Second Coming by asking four questions: What is the Second Coming? When will the Second Coming occur? Why is there a Second Coming (what is the purpose or reason for it)? and What should our response be?

Chapter 6 returns to personal eschatology, with two events that pertain to every individual: the resurrection of the body and judgment. These are both said to happen after Christ's return (1 Thess 4:16; Matt 25:31–34). What is not as clear is whether or not there will be the inauguration of a millennial kingdom at Christ's return. We will deal with the various millennial positions in chapter 7.[38]

Chapters 8 and 9 will deal with eternal destinies—the former chapter dealing with heaven and the latter with hell. Both these traditional eternal

---

[37] These three views are presented in Alan Hultberg, ed., *Three Views on the Rapture: Pretribulation, Prewrath, or Posttribulation* (Grand Rapids: Zondervan, 2010). Two less popular views—midtribulation and partial rapture—will also be considered in chapter 4.

[38] There are many books on the various millennial positions. Two helpful collections are Robert G. Clouse, ed., *The Meaning of the Millennium: Four Views* (Downers Grove: InterVarsity, 1977) and Darrell L. Bock, ed., *Three Views on the Millennium and Beyond* (Grand Rapids: Zondervan, 1999).

destinations have been the subject of considerable debate in recent years, with numerous authors arguing that we should think of heaven primarily in terms of the new creation, much like this creation but renewed, purified, and emptied of all the effects of sin, and others arguing that heaven will be mostly about being in God's presence. The debates surrounding hell have been primarily over the nature of the punishment received by the lost: Will it be eternal conscious punishment or punishment that ends with their complete annihilation? A secondary debate concerns those who will be in hell, with attempts to extend the boundaries of salvation beyond those who place explicit faith in Christ to those with faith in the revelation they have received to sincere adherents of other major religions to absolutely everyone.[39] The book will conclude with a summary of how each of these elements of eschatology is connected to our theme of hope.

Methodology and Approach

The theological methodology utilized in this book may be compared to a pyramid. The foundational layer of this pyramid is biblical teaching. For each of the future events of eschatology we address, we will begin by asking what Christians should believe based on biblical teaching. In doing this, we are following the traditional evangelical and Protestant principle of *sola Scriptura*, in which Scripture is privileged as the sole normative source for theology.

However, we recognize our fallibility and limitations in interpreting Scripture and believe that theology is best done in community. In the providence of God, we have a chronological community of twenty centuries of brothers and sisters who have reflected on the Scriptures and a global community of brothers and sisters who are engaged in the study of the Scriptures today. Both can aid us in our task of biblical interpretation. Thus,

---

[39] Introductions to these debates can be found in Michael E. Wittmer, *Four Views on Heaven* (Grand Rapids: Zondervan, 2022) and Preston Sprinkle, ed., *Four Views on Hell* (Grand Rapids: Zondervan, 2016).

the second level in our methodology pyramid is historical and global illumination. We will look at the traditional understandings of these various eschatological events bequeathed to us by earlier brothers and sisters, and the newer understandings coming from the global church,[40] and use them to check our understandings of Scripture for blind spots due to our own historical context. Moreover, historical developments often raise questions not explicitly addressed in Scripture. For example, developments in medical technology that can keep a heart beating and lungs breathing indefinitely raise the question of how we define death. Here we seek to respond to such questions by carefully applying biblical principles.

Once we have sought to understand biblical teaching as thoroughly as possible, with the aid of the community of interpreters, we offer a systematic theological formulation of the event in question, giving how Scripture calls us to understand this event. This is the third layer in our theological methodology. Yet here we want to speak with a balance of conviction and humility. Not all doctrines are taught with equal clarity in Scripture; not all theological formulations have become part of the enduring fabric of consensual Christianity down through the centuries. Even among those equally committed to the inerrancy of Scripture, there have been differences of opinion as to what the inerrant Scriptures teach on a particular issue. This has been particularly true of many issues in eschatology. This calls for what has become known as "theological triage."[41]

To the doctrinal formulations we offer on the various aspects of eschatology, we may assign one of four levels, reflecting the depth and degree of clarity of biblical teaching on this topic, the breadth of agreement among Christians historically on this topic, and its intrinsic importance to Christian life and ministry. Level 1.0 would be reserved for **essential** biblical

---

[40] Such as the chapter on eschatology entitled "Eschatology: Jonathan Edwards and the Chinese Back to Jerusalem Movement" in Tennent, *Theology in the Context of World Christianity*, 221–48.

[41] See Gavin Ortlund, *Finding the Right Hills to Die On: The Case for Theological Triage* (Wheaton: Crossway, 2020).

teachings. These are matters that are abundantly clear in biblical teaching, have been widely affirmed by the church throughout history, and are essential to being a Christian. These are doctrines that should command the adherence of all Christians. These would be matters like the second coming of Jesus or the resurrection of the body.

On some doctrines, a level of 2.0 seems appropriate. These would be standard **evangelical** beliefs that seem well-founded biblically but are disputed by some segments of Christianity and are not essential elements of the gospel. Level 2.0 doctrines in the field of eschatology are somewhat fluid today. For example, the second coming of Jesus, considered as a Level 1.0 doctrine above, is only affirmed by 79 percent of Christians in the U.S.,[42] while it is considered one of the "points of agreement" among evangelicals,[43] making it what some might consider a Level 2.0 doctrine. At the same time, a doctrine like the eternal conscious punishment of the lost was once at least a Level 2.0 doctrine, but in recent years some segments of evangelicalism have adopted a position called conditional immortality, believing that the lost suffer for a just but finite time and then cease to exist. We will discuss and evaluate this movement among evangelicals in a later chapter. For now, it illustrates the fluid nature of evangelical eschatological beliefs.

A third level of doctrines, Level 3.0, may be identified as **denominational** beliefs. These beliefs tend to be mostly in the area of ecclesiology, but there have been some denominations that have affirmed the position of premillennialism as a denominational distinctive. Most have left the millennium and several other related beliefs about the rapture and tribulation as Level 4.0 doctrines, **personal** beliefs.[44]

---

[42] Russell Heimlich, "The Second Coming of Jesus," Pew Research Center, April 21, 2009, https://pewresearch.org/religion/2009/04/09/christians-views-on-the-return-of-christ/.

[43] Joe Carter, "Jesus Is Coming Back When?" The Gospel Coalition, March 8, 2012, https://www.thegospelcoalition.org/article/jesus-is-coming-back-when/.

[44] For example, the Evangelical Free Church of America had included for decades an affirmation of the premillennial return of Jesus in their statement of faith. But in

There are strong differences of opinion among individuals as to which beliefs are essential, evangelical, denominational, or personal, with those devoted to dispensational eschatology often assigning a higher value to its distinctive tenets than others would. Some attempt at theological triage among the doctrines associated with eschatology seems very valuable, and such an attempt will be made in this volume.

The capstone in our theological methodology will be practical application. Theology is incomplete if not integrated fully into Christian life and ministry. While there will be significant individual variation in terms of how eschatological beliefs impact one's life and ministry, there will be suggestions for practical application with relation to each of the beliefs discussed below.

One final distinctive of this book should be apparent from the descriptions above but should perhaps be made explicit. This volume privileges breadth of coverage over depth. Each of the topics to which we devote a mere chapter has been the subject for multiple full-length books. Our treatment will be necessarily less exhaustive. But we think the benefit of giving pastors, church leaders, young people, and all students of the Scriptures a single volume that will introduce them to all the major issues in the field of eschatology is well worth sacrificing the depth found in other books. Such books are mentioned in the footnotes and included in the bibliography found after the conclusion of this volume for those who do want to engage in deeper study.

August 2019, at their annual meeting, the denomination voted to delete the term "premillennial" from their statement of faith and no longer maintain it as a "denominational distinctive." See Daniel Silliman, "EFCA Now Considers Premillennialism a Non-Essential," *Christianity Today*, August 23, 2019, https://www.christianitytoday.com/news/2019/august/ecfa-drops-premillennialism-evangelical-free-church-teds.html.

CHAPTER 2

Death: The Final Frontier

Introduction

Space is not the final frontier—death is. It is the land to which we must all go but none can visit in advance. For most people throughout human history, death has been a mystery, a puzzle, a grief. Tim Keller calls it "the Great Interruption . . . the Great Schism . . . the Great Insult" and "our Great Enemy."[1] It casts its shadow over all of life as the inescapable end to which every life must eventually come and raises a question as to the meaningfulness of life. Is this life all there is? Is death the absolute end? Still today, it is an awkward topic, one that makes most people feel uncomfortable and even fearful. It is one of the few taboo subjects for conversation in polite American society.[2] Indeed, Scripture says the devil uses the fear of death as an instrument of enslavement (Heb 2:14–15), and contemporary American

[1] Timothy Keller, *On Death* (New York: Penguin, 2020), 1–2.

[2] Hans Schwarz, *On the Way to the Future: A Christian View of Eschatology in the Light of Current Trends in Religion, Philosophy, and Science*, rev. ed. (Minneapolis: Augsburg, 1979), 13. Schwarz says, "Death is an impolite word," and refers to many euphemisms we use to avoid the reality of death.

society clearly reflects our desperate attempts to ward death off and pretend it is not coming, that we aren't getting older. Yet, despite the discomfort death occasions for many, it should hold no fear for Christians. Rather, careful understanding of death is important to us for a variety of reasons.

First, death as the inevitable storm that will eventually come can cause people to look to their foundation and ask if it is rock or sand (Matt 7:24–27). Can it stand the storm of death? The inescapable reality of death can lead one to a search for true and lasting life and thus be used by God to lead one toward salvation. Second, passing through death is required of every believer, and preparation for that can spark profound areas of personal growth.[3] Third, death is an important time for ministry. Both counseling bereaved persons and leading funerals are important aspects of ministry and may be for some people the only time they will be open to hearing the message of life. Fourth, death is important for evangelism, for an important part of the gospel appeal is the need to prepare for death (see John 3:16; Rom 6:23). Finally, death has been the subject of several recent controversies that raise important theological, ethical, and practical concerns. A proper understanding of death will give us a basis from which to address these controversial issues. Death demands our theological attention. We start, as always, with Scripture.

A Biblical Understanding of Death

A biblical definition of death is needed, because whereas modern medicine increasingly views humans solely in physical terms, the Bible views humans more holistically. The Bible has a surprisingly high view of the body, but it does not view the body as possessing life in itself. Life and death are more than merely bodily phenomena.

---

[3] Anthony A. Hoekema, *The Bible and the Future* (Grand Rapids: Eerdmans, 1979), 84–85. Hoekema argues that even now Christians can anticipate some blessings from death. It will "bring an end to sinning" and will mean entering into the full riches of eternal life (85).

Old Testament Teaching on Death

Genesis 2:7 is a pivotal verse for defining life. The body is viewed here as inert apart from a special gift of God that imparts life. Only after God breathes life into the body is the man viewed as "a living being." It is worth noting that the phrase "breath of life" is used of animals in Gen 6:17. It simply denotes creatures that are living. Moreover, the word for "being" in the phrase "living being," is *nephesh*, often translated "soul." It too can be used for something in animals as well as humans (Gen 1:21). While this term bears several senses in the Old and New Testament and can be used of something that is distinctive to humans and that survives the death of the body, the most common and important sense of *nephesh* is as the seat of life.[4] That which makes a human a living being, as opposed to a dead one, is the presence of *nephesh*, which is a non-physical reality (though Lev 17:11 associates life with blood, which is medically accurate).[5] But this life is not distinctive to humans; animals too possess life. What is distinctive about human life is its association with something called spirit (*ruaḥ*).

How does this help us in understanding death? First, it helps us understand the basic meaning of death in the Old Testament. Death occurs when that which animates the physical body departs. That non-material reality can be called the soul (*nephesh*) or the spirit (*ruaḥ*), and we see both associated with death in the Old Testament. Genesis 35:18 uses the phrase

---

[4] For the multiple meanings of the term "soul" and other terms relating to the human constitution, see John S. Hammett and Katie J. McCoy, *Humanity*, Theology for the People of God, ed. David S. Dockery, Nathan A. Finn, and Christopher W. Morgan (Brentwood, TN: B&H Academic, 2023), 273–316. See also H. Wheeler Robinson, *The Christian Doctrine of Man* (Edinburgh: T & T Clark, 1911); Hans Walter Wolff, *Anthropology of the Old Testament*, trans. Margaret Kohl (Philadelphia: Fortress, 1974) John W. Cooper, *Body, Soul, and Life Everlasting: Biblical Anthropology and the Monism-Dualism Debate* (Grand Rapids: Eerdmans, 2000).

[5] See the discussion of the Hebrew understanding of blood, especially in the sacrificial system, in Leon Morris, *The Apostolic Preaching of the Cross* (Grand Rapids: Eerdmans, 1955), 108–17.

translated as "with her last breath," to describe the death of Rachel. A literal translation would be "her soul was going forth." The same idea is seen in 1 Kgs 17:21–22, where *nephesh* is translated as "life," and death is seen as *nephesh* departing and life is *nephesh* returning. But elsewhere death is seen as separating spirit (*ruaḥ*) and body (Eccl 12:7). That which had animated the body had departed, something termed soul or spirit. The body is dead. But what about the destiny of that nonmaterial part? Does it suffer death? What is spiritual death?

There are hints in the Old Testament that death has implications beyond the physical. For example, God warns Adam in Gen 2:17 that he will surely die the day he eats of the tree. Some argue that "the day" is simply a way of emphasizing the certainty of death rather than immediacy (and so the NIV simply translates it as "when"). But it is also possible to see spiritual death as immediate and the path to physical death begun;[6] that is, the moment Adam and Eve sinned they became subject to physical mortality and made physical mortality part of the reality for all humans after them (Rom 5:12–14). Spiritual death also seems to be in view, because humans are a totality, both spiritual and physical, making it likely that spiritual and physical death should not be thought of as separate, but as one involving the other.[7] The idea of spiritual death seems also implied by the description of humans as dead in trespasses and sin (Eph 2:1), and in need of a new birth, a birth of the spirit (John 3:6). That is, the spirit as the capacity for relationship with God died. It remains within human nature, but as a capacity needing a new birth. The reality of spiritual death is made explicit in the New Testament, but it is at least hinted at in the Old Testament.

---

[6] "Upon eating the forbidden fruit, they do not immediately fall over and die from something like cardiac arrest. But they do die. They die spiritually, and their bodies also begin to experience the gradual decay that leads ultimately to their physical deaths." Christopher W. Morgan with Robert A. Peterson, *Christian Theology: The Biblical Story and Our Faith* (Nashville: B&H Academic, 2020), 12.

[7] Leon Morris, *The Wages of Sin* (London: Tyndale, 1955), 10. See also Hoekema, *The Bible and the Future*, 82–83.

In addition to defining death, the Old Testament gives teaching on the origin of death. The first mention we find of death in the Old Testament is Gen 2:16–17, where it is seen as the certain consequence of sin. Death is threatened as the penalty for sin in Gen 2:17; it is pronounced in Gen 3:19 as the consequence of and judgment for sin, and eternal life in the garden is denied to Adam and Eve in Gen 3:22 because of their sin. Does that mean that Adam and Eve were created immortal and would not have died had they not sinned?

After a judicious weighing of the evidence, Millard Erickson suggests the concept of "conditional immortality as the state of Adam before the fall"; that is, "given the right conditions, he could have lived forever."[8] This could explain the concern expressed in Gen 3:22 that if Adam and Eve ate from the tree of life, they would live forever. Under the right conditions they could have become immortal. Perhaps if they had not succumbed to the temptation of the serpent, they could also have been granted immortality. But there are several considerations that count against the idea that they were created immortal. First, Scripture predicates immortality of God alone (1 Tim 6:16). Second, immortality is described as something to be sought (Rom 2:7), something Christ brings to light through the gospel (2 Tim 1:10), and something that will be given to us at the resurrection of the body (1 Cor 15:53). The idea of the immortality of the soul is a separate question that we will consider in the next chapter, but immortality as the state of Adam and Eve before the fall seems very unlikely.

The importance of the teaching that the origin of human death came through sin is that death is not natural for human beings. It was not part of God's original intention for humans at creation. Whether we would have been granted immortality had we resisted temptation or whether God would have sustained our life in some other way is a question not answered by Scripture, because the reality is, we sinned, and death came as the judgment on sin. Because of sin, death is now inevitable, and due to the corruption

---

[8] Millard F. Erickson, *Christian Theology*, 3rd ed. (Grand Rapids: Baker Academic, 2013), 559.

of the body, it can even be welcomed as the end of pain and suffering. But it is always unnatural, and still, it remains the final enemy (1 Cor 15:26).

One surprise for many Christian readers of the Old Testament is its ambiguous attitude toward death. There is a significant difference between the attitude toward death in the Old and New Testament. Passages like Ps 88:10–12 or Isa 38:18–19 do not ring with the assurance in the face of death we find in the New Testament. This is not due to any error in the Old Testament, but due to the historical nature of progressive revelation and the centrality of Christ and his resurrection victory over death. It was given to Christ to bring "life and immortality to light through the gospel" (2 Tim 1:10). Thus, the Old Testament teaching on death and especially what lies beyond death is shadowy and vague. As we will see in chapter 3, the hope of an afterlife is there, but it is not made clear. Thus, there is a measure of ambiguity toward death in the Old Testament. It is presented both as an enemy (Pss 49:14; 55:4) and a friend (Job 3:13, 17), both as separation from God and others (Pss 6:5; 88:5) and as reunion with one's "people" or "ancestors" (Gen 25:8; Num 20:24; Gen 47:30).[9]

As a result, most of the Old Testament reflects the idea that God's blessings come to his people in this life. The hope and confidence of the psalmist was that he would "see the LORD's goodness in the land of the living" (Ps 27:13); the promise to those who honor their father and mother is long life, not eternal life (Ex 20:12). There is a stronger emphasis on earthly prosperity, as opposed to spiritual riches in heaven. Calvin describes the difference in this way:

> The Lord of old willed that his people direct and elevate their minds to the heavenly heritage; yet, to nourish them better in this hope, he displayed it for them to see and, so to speak, taste, under earthly benefits. But now that the gospel has more plainly and clearly revealed the grace of the future life, the Lord leads our

[9] Philip S. Johnston, *Shades of Sheol: Death and Afterlife in the Old Testament* (Leicester, UK: Apollos, 2002), 27–34.

> minds to meditate upon it directly, laying aside the lower mode of training that he used with the Israelites.[10]

The key point to remember is that God did not give clear teaching on the afterlife to Old Testament believers; that fact gives the Old Testament an ambiguous attitude toward death. C. S. Lewis believes that the average Old Testament believer did not know they were going to heaven when they died, and he thinks that was a good thing. It shows us that God is worth worshipping just because he's God, apart from the gift of eternal life.[11]

Finally, two key terms from the teaching on death in the Old Testament are "universal" and "unique." By the first word we mean that death comes to all. Joshua 23:14 describes death as going "the way of the whole earth." It is not that God does not have power over death; the fact that God translated Enoch and Elijah into his presence without passing through death is sufficient to show that. But from Gen 3:22 onward, it was clear that God did not intend for humans to live forever in our present fallen condition. That death was the transition point into a newer and fuller life was a truth brought to full light later. But for now, death comes to all.

This should encourage those who work as pastors and counselors to not be in awe of medical doctors. Despite all our medical advances and technology, the death rate is still the same: 100 percent. So, when the doctors have done all they can, we ask them to step aside and allow us to tell their patients about the One who has overcome the power of death.

By unique, we mean that death comes only once. Death was seen as final in the Old Testament. The hope of survival in any form at all was present but dim, and the idea of reincarnation was absent. Second Samuel 14:14 compares death to water being spilled on the ground, "which can't be recovered." This should give us pause in evaluating the experiences of those who "died" and were then resuscitated. Did they truly "die"? We will

---

[10] John Calvin, *Institutes*, II.xi.I (1:450).

[11] C. S. Lewis, *Reflections on the Psalms* (New York: Harcourt Brace, 1958), 39–42.

examine this point in more detail later. Both these points, the universality and uniqueness of death, are more explicitly taught in the New Testament (Rom 5:12; Heb 9:27), but they are clearly implied in Old Testament teaching as well.[12]

We have already alluded to the ambiguity in the Old Testament concerning any hope for life beyond death. For the most part, death, while an occasion of sadness, was often accepted. Death was at times seen as "a natural and peaceful event,"[13] if one died old and full of years and left behind a godly legacy (Gen 25:8). There could be a good death, the death of the righteous (Num 23:10). Death is part of life, for which there is an appropriate time (Eccl 3:2).

But there were other circumstances in which death was viewed much more negatively. Sometimes death, especially when premature or untimely, was seen as the punishment for sin. Thus, to be "cut off" sometimes can refer to excommunication from the people of God (possibly Lev 17:9–10) but can also definitely refer to physical death as the punishment for sin (Lev 20:1–5).[14] Similarly, long life (Ps 91:16) or restoration to health (Isa 38:16–17, 20) could be regarded as salvation and forgiveness. Another negative aspect of death, especially of an untimely death, was that it cut one off from Yahweh and ended one's opportunity to praise him (Ps 88:5, 10; Isa 38:10–11, 18).

But alongside this negative, pessimistic attitude toward death and what lies beyond, there was also a developing idea, shadowy but definitely present, that death was not the absolute end of existence. Some texts in the Old Testament suggest that Sheol is the world of the dead, in which both the righteous and unrighteous continue in a shadowy, dreary existence (Ps 6:5).

---

[12] For more detail on Old Testament teaching on death, see Johnston, *Shades of Sheol*, 23–46; Paul R. Williamson, *Death and the Afterlife: Biblical Perspectives on Ultimate Questions*, New Studies in Biblical Theology 44 (London: Apollos, 2018), 22, 38–39.

[13] Johnston, *Shades of Sheol*, 26.

[14] Elmer Smick, "*kārat*," *TWOT*, 1:457. Of the word for "cut off," Smick says, "It is sometimes difficult in a given context to know whether the person(s) who is 'cut off' is to be killed or only excommunicated."

We will examine the exact nature of Sheol in the next chapter, but the idea we want to examine now is a much more positive attitude toward death, involving deliverance from Sheol and life in God's presence. This idea seems to have been fueled by two convictions.

One such idea was that the fellowship a believer enjoys with God is so strong that not even death can destroy it. This is seen most often in the Psalms (see 16:10–11; 23:6; 49:15). Second was the conviction that God is just. But justice is not always vindicated in this world. If judgment to bring justice does not occur in this world, and yet must be carried out to vindicate God's justice, a future life is necessary, in which the scales will be balanced and justice served. The writer of Ecclesiastes seems to want to affirm such a future life, but has no clarity (see 3:19–21; 12:6–7). The psalmist talks of final destiny (73:17) and is more confident in affirming a continuation of his fellowship with God (73:23–24).

Passages such as those cited above, along with a few clear passages on resurrection (Dan 12:2; Isa 26:19), and the idea brought out by Jesus that God is the God of the living (Matt 22:23–32) give a basis for the belief, embraced by the Pharisees but not the Sadducees, in the resurrection of the dead. In fact, a recent article suggests the "seeds of resurrection hope" are implicitly present in images and stories even as early as the book of Genesis.[15] But for more explicit teaching, we turn to the New Testament.

New Testament Teaching on Death

Two main words summarize what the New Testament adds to our understanding of death: "clarification" and "victory." The New Testament clarifies much that was implied or ambiguous in the Old Testament. Jesus, along with the Pharisees, believed that the Old Testament affirmed a belief in resurrection and an afterlife (Matt 22:23, 31–32), but the clearest proof of an afterlife was his own resurrection. For Paul, the reality of Christ's

---

[15] Mitchell L. Chase, "The Genesis of Resurrection Hope," *JETS* 57, no. 3 (2014): 467–80.

resurrection was the key to hope beyond the grave (1 Cor 15:14, 20–24). And since we are united with Christ, our true life is already hidden with God in him, and we will be with him, even beyond the grave (John 14:3; Phil 1:23; Col 3:3).

The New Testament also clarifies that death is the separation of the spirit (or soul; Rev 6:9) from the body (Luke 8:55; 23:46) and that death takes both physical and spiritual forms. And if physical death may be defined as the separation of spirit and body, spiritual death may be defined as separation of the whole person from God. This separation is not a physical matter, for God is omnipresent. Rather, it is a separation from a right relationship with God.

A final area of clarification in the New Testament concerns the universality and uniqueness of death. As all sin (Rom 3:23), all are appointed to die, but only to die once. God may have inspired the writer of Heb 9:27 to include that verse specifically to refute the idea of reincarnation.

But the newest note in the New Testament teaching on death is that of victory. Death is no longer accepted but viewed as an enemy because it is a reminder and consequence of sin (1 Cor 15:56). Yet it is an enemy whose sting has been removed and an enemy that has been defeated and will be ultimately destroyed (1 Cor 15:26). Jesus is identified as the one who holds the keys of death (Rev 1:18) and liberates those held in bondage by their fear of death (Heb 2:14–15). For a time now, it still has the power to hurt. At Lazarus's grave, Jesus did not just weep; he was moved with anger (John 11:33, 38: the verb *embrimaomai* connotes anger) at the ravages of this invader. But while we grieve, we do not grieve as those who have no hope (1 Thess 4:13), for we know that nothing, not even death, can separate us from Christ, and in him we too have victory over death (Rom 8:37–39).

Contemporary Questions about Death

In the second half of the twentieth century, a variety of cultural, intellectual, medical, and even political forces converged to raise a variety of difficult questions about death that are still the subject of debate. The first comes from the rise of the scientific study of death.

The Scientific Study of Death

For most of history, death has occurred within the home, with family around a loved one. Some families even pass down stories of visions of heaven that faithful saints of God had in their last moments—visions they shared as powerful witnesses to family members present with them. But with the advent of modern medicine, the picture began to change. Death began to occur more often in hospitals than homes. This change presented both difficulties and opportunities. The difficulty was that such an environment was often felt to be lonely and impersonal for the patients. They were tended to, but not listened to, when often they needed to talk about the death they knew was coming. This situation also presented an opportunity for researchers to talk to several dying individuals and study their experience of approaching death. They found most patients willing and some even eager to talk with them.

One such opportunity was taken by Elisabeth Kübler-Ross, and her findings were presented in a best-selling book published in 1969, *On Death and Dying*.[16] In that book, Dr. Kübler-Ross calls for a more thoughtful, attentive, human response to the dying that includes inviting and listening to them talk about what they are feeling. The book consists largely of interviews with dying patients and presents a now classic analysis of the stages people go through in facing death and dying: denial and isolation, anger, bargaining, depression, and acceptance. She found that patients go through these stages with remarkable consistency but reach acceptance most quickly and completely when helped by someone who listens non-judgmentally as they talk their way through the stages.

---

[16] Elisabeth Kübler-Ross, *On Death and Dying* (New York: Macmillan, 1969). Interestingly, the subtitle is *What the Dying Have to Teach Doctors, Nurses, Clergy and Their Own Families.*

There is much practical value here for those who work with the dying, and for counselors especially. Theologically, however, it is problematic in a few key areas. First, though she is more descriptive than prescriptive, some of her recommendations lack or oppose a Christian approach to death. For example, she says, "Once the patient dies, I find it cruel and inappropriate to speak of the love of God."[17] Rather, she advises to allow family members to express their anger and grief. But this is a both/and situation. We can accept them unconditionally and listen to whatever they say and still helpfully and sensitively bring the love and presence of God into the situation.

Second, our concern as believers is not primarily to help people come to an acceptance of death but an acceptance of the One who can take them through death to life. In this light, I believe that what Kübler-Ross offers people may, in the end, be to their detriment. Perhaps death should be scary; perhaps God intended it to be so to move us to seek him. It is interesting that Kübler-Ross's shortest chapter is on bargaining, for the bargaining is most often with God, and here she notes that the bargaining stage seems to bring in chaplains more often than the other stages.

Of course, Kübler-Ross seeks to be objective and takes a tolerant, non-evaluative stance toward religion at most points. As such, she is characteristic of the pluralistic view of modern America. However, she does offer one interesting assessment, which includes a sad indictment of the powerlessness of the faith of most people to help them in facing death:

> We can say here, however, that we found very few truly religious people with an intrinsic faith. Those few have been helped by their faith and are best comparable with those few patients who were true atheists. The majority of patients were in between, with some form of religious belief but not enough to relieve them of conflict and fear.[18]

[17] Kübler-Ross, 156.

[18] Kübler-Ross, 237.

The work of Kübler-Ross merits attention for several reasons. First, it is a seminal work in its field and has some value and insights. Second, it began the scientific study of death that developed into the second area we will discuss, the study of what are called near-death experiences. Third, it is an excellent example of the modern attempt to apply therapeutic, psychological solutions to spiritual problems. Such studies seem to ignore the important and pressing questions dying people ask: Is there an eternal destiny beyond death? Am I going to heaven or hell? Instead, it focuses on interesting but less important questions, such as the stages people go through in approaching death and how to help them come to a healthy, psychological resolution. The assumption seems to be that we have no access to truth on the big questions, so all we can do in the study of death and dying is to evaluate its effect on the patient's earthly life and offer no help on the ultimate questions raised by death and dying.

Near-Death Experiences

The second arena in which death has been much discussed in the contemporary context has been linked to what are called near-death experiences. While there are some accounts of those thought to be dead who were revived from the nineteenth and early twentieth century, the study of those judged to be dead by some medical standard and later revived has been largely the result of advances in medical technology in the latter parts of the twentieth and now into the twenty-first century. Most often, the "death" has been a cessation of the heartbeat, with revival or resuscitation coming through a variety of CPR measures.

The reports of such experiences have become so common that there is now an international association and website devoted to the study of them.[19] They date the origin of such studies to the 1975 work of

[19] See https://iands.org/ for the website of the International Association for Near-Death Studies, with headquarters in Durham, North Carolina.

Raymond A. Moody, *Life After Life.*[20] In it, he draws from research on those who have had such experiences and gives a number of elements common to many, but not all, of the accounts. Some of the most striking elements of such accounts are the experience of being out of the body, the encounter with a being of light, and the sensation people have of reviewing their lives, before being called back to this life. One nearly universal effect of such an experience, according to Moody, is that "almost every person has expressed to me the thought that he is no longer afraid of death." The reason for this lack of fear, Moody concludes, is "that after his experience a person no longer entertains any doubt about his survival of bodily death."[21] Beyond the loss of fear of death, Carol Zaleski adds other "transforming effects," such as "renewed dedication to one's core beliefs, and a sense of mission or purpose," as common elements in near-death accounts.[22]

More recently, Christians have written books narrating such experiences as trips to heaven, where they met loved ones and can now testify to the reality of heaven. Baptist pastor Don Piper, after suffering a horrendous auto accident, recounts spending ninety minutes in heaven before he was revived. Todd Burpo recounts the experiences of his son Colton in *Heaven Is for Real.*[23] Less well-known are accounts of what are called "distressing NDEs." Maurice Rawlings is an evangelical Christian as well as a surgeon. He reports patients who had near-death experiences that were scary and involved seeing hell, entering hell, or being pulled down by demons. He notes that such experiences were reported immediately after resuscitation,

---

[20] Now in a 40th anniversary edition, Raymond A. Moody, *Reflections on Life After Life* (New York: Harper Collins, 2015) has sold more than 13 million copies. For more on how Moody came to be interested in and to investigate this phenomenon, see Carol Zaleski, "Near-Death Experiences," in *The Oxford Handbook of Eschatology*, ed. Jerry L. Walls (Oxford: Oxford University Press, 2008), 614–17.

[21] Moody, *Life After Life*, 68–69.

[22] Zaleski, "Near-Death Experiences," 618.

[23] Don Piper, *90 Minutes in Heaven: A True Story of Death and Life* (Grand Rapids: Revell, 2004); Todd Burpo and Lynn Vincent, *Heaven Is for Real: A Little Boy's Astounding Story of His Trip to Heaven and Back* (Nashville: Thomas Nelson, 2010).

while the fear was still fresh, and were later not remembered by the patient. He suggests that one reason why the reports of Moody and others are so uniformly positive is that the negative experiences are either not remembered or not reported.[24] Carol Zaleski suggests another reason: "Because negative near-death experiences have far less appeal to our culture, they remain, for the most part, anomalous and undigested."[25] The International Association for Near-Death Studies receives accounts of both positive and negative experiences, though they say the negative experiences are the minority.[26]

In any case, the overwhelming majority of people who have had such experiences describe them as some of the most profound and important experiences of their lives. Obvious questions jump to mind upon reading such accounts. Are such individuals hallucinating, lying, or dreaming? What are we to make of their experience? Did they die?

As to the last question, it depends on one's definition of death. Their heartbeat stopped and they lacked detectable vital signs, but, considering Heb 9:27, which teaches that we die once, we might hesitate to call their experience death. Carol Zaleski argues, "Near-death experiencers were never fully dead. Death is a state from which, but for a miracle, no one returns."[27] What about the miracles of those raised from death in the Bible? How could they die and be resurrected if we die only once? There may be a distinction between what we observe as death and death in the plan of God. The accounts of Lazarus and others may be taken as exceptions that show God's sovereignty over death, not as disproving Heb 9:27.

A second question is, are the experiences described genuine out-of-body experiences? The evidence seems to be fairly strong for this. Patients

---

[24] Maurice Rawlings, *Beyond Death's Door* (Nashville: Thomas Nelson, 1978), 64–65.

[25] Zaleski, 622.

[26] "What Is a Near-Death Experience?" International Association for Near-Death Studies, Inc., accessed October 1, 2012, http://iands.org/about-ndes.html. The Association believes at least several million people in the United States alone have had near-death experiences.

[27] Zaleski, 619.

report seeing their body and have afterward stated what various doctors did while they were clinically unconscious. In view of Paul's experience in 2 Cor 12:1–6, there certainly seem to be no grounds for seeing such experiences as a theological impossibility. Christian theology has long maintained that there is an immaterial aspect as well as a material aspect in humanity. Normally the two (we may call them body and soul) exist as a unity, but we affirm that they can exist apart for a time in the unnatural state of death. Perhaps the unity can be temporarily interrupted in the experiences we are describing.

The most important question is of course how we are to explain and evaluate them. It seems that one common response among evangelical leaders is concern that such experiences may be elevated above biblical teaching and cause people to be deceived.[28] Moody strongly objects:

> It seems to me that the best way of distinguishing between God-directed and Satan-directed experiences would be to see what the person involved does and says after his experience. God, I suppose, would try to get those to whom he appears to be loving and forgiving. Satan would presumably tell his servants to follow a course of hate and destruction. Manifestly, my subjects have come back with a renewed commitment to follow the former course and to disavow the latter.[29]

---

[28] John MacArthur thinks such experiences may be hallucinations (see "Heaven Is Real: Hallucinations Are Not," Grace to You, April 28, 2014, https://www.gty.org/library/blog/B140428/heaven-is-real-hallcnations-are-not); Douglas Groothuis, *Deceived by the Light* (Eugene, OR: Wipf & Stock, 2002) examines popular accounts that seem to reflect deception; David Jones has similar concerns, noting that none of those resuscitated in Scripture give us a description of what they experienced during their near-death experience (see Justin Taylor's presentation of Jones's outline giving a description and evaluation of near-death experiences: "A Biblical and Theological Analysis of Near Death Experiences," The Gospel Coalition, April 24, 2014, https://www.thegospelcoalition.org/blogs/justin-taylor-a-biblical-and-theological-analysis-of-near-death-experiences/).

[29] Moody, *Life After Life*, 108–9.

But Moody does not understand the nature of the biblical tempter, who masquerades as "an angel of light," and his servants, who masquerade as "servants of righteousness" (2 Cor 11:14–15). Love, by itself, is not evidence that something is of God. Do those who have such experiences come back loving God more fervently, following Jesus Christ more zealously?

Carol Zaleski offers a more guarded assessment: "In traditional language, a near-death experience is a kind of private revelation, which can neither provide its own warrant nor interpret itself. It may be help or hindrance, gift from God or device of the enemy." She contrasts the near-death experience of A. J. Ayer, whose atheistic outlook led him to interpret it as "an essentially physiological event," with the near-death experience of Richard John Neuhaus, who interpreted his experience in the light of his "Christian formation" and was able to integrate it into his "life of faith."[30]

For this author, there seems to be no reason to accuse Christians of lying who report near-death experiences that include visions of heaven nor to deny the reality of the experiences of others who report out-of-body experiences. But there is reason for concern over how some interpret their experiences. Did they really see what awaits them beyond death? I am struck by the lack of any use of the word "holy" to describe the being met in any of the reports or of the place they visited. If these individuals got close to heaven and met a being who was God or even was sent by God, holiness surely should have been a major impression. Moreover, for those who are unbelievers, if they interpret their experience as meaning that beyond death they will not face the judgment of God, their experience will have been much more of a hindrance than a help, much more of a device of the enemy than a gift of God. Such interpretations encourage universalistic beliefs (namely, that all people go to the same place after death), which is surely one of Satan's main strategies in this time. Within a Christian framework, such experiences could be interpreted as trips to an intermediate destination, after which judgment would have occurred.[31]

---

[30] Zaleski, "Near-Death Experiences," 622–25.

[31] This is the suggestion of Rawlings, *Beyond Death's Door*, 64–65.

What of the reports of Christians who claim to have visited heaven? As I said, none of the accounts I have read seem to reflect the holiness of God, and that is a valid concern, but I am willing to allow the possibility that God has granted some believers a genuine preview of heaven. What I am concerned about is allowing such narratives to replace the teaching of Scripture, or even seeing such accounts as necessary to "prove" the Bible. We have already been given clear teaching about what lies beyond death by Jesus. What need do we have to hear from others who may be prone to err or be deceived, or deliberately deceive?[32]

Euthanasia, Assisted Suicide, and End-of-Life Care[33]

Suicide has, of course, been present throughout human history but has been generally regarded as one form of homicide, and thus a violation of the sixth commandment. In older, traditional Catholic theology, it was categorized as a mortal sin, which must be properly confessed to be forgiven. Since by its nature one is not living afterward to confess it, suicide condemned one to hell, which was seen as the automatic penalty for dying with an unconfessed mortal sin on one's conscience. Protestants (as well as modern Catholics)[34] have repudiated the understanding of suicide as the unforgivable sin,[35] but have seen it as a sin, nonetheless.

---

[32] Alex Malarkey, who with his dad Kevin Malarkey, wrote *The Boy Who Came Back from Heaven* (Carol Stream, IL: Tyndale House, 2011), later confessed he had made the whole thing up.

[33] For more on all the topics discussed in this section, see chapter 10, "Euthanasia, Physician-Assisted Suicide and Care for Persons at the End of Life," in J. P. Moreland and Scott Rae, *Body & Soul* (Downers Grove: InterVarsity, 2000).

[34] "We should not despair of the eternal salvation of persons who have taken their own lives. By ways known to him alone, God can provide the opportunity for salutary repentance." *Catechism of the Catholic Church* (Rome: Urbi et Orbi Communications, 1994), 550.

[35] I like the wise comment I heard from a pastor preaching the funeral service of one who had committed suicide: "It is not how we die, but how we lived, that determines our eternal destiny."

Physicians, bound by their Hippocratic Oath to preserve rather than destroy life, have historically steadfastly opposed assisting in suicide or performing so-called mercy killings or euthanasia. But over the past forty years, physician-assisted suicide has become a topic of debate and even approved as law in some states in the United States and even whole countries in Europe.[36] Some even favor a more active type of euthanasia, in which a physician or other person actively takes a person's life rather than just assisting someone in suicide.

What is driving these movements? Theoretically, the desire is to prevent needless suffering and pain. But this response overlooks the fact that modern medicine has given us tools to control pain such that earlier generations never possessed. Why should euthanasia and related ideas have such appeal now? Have we suddenly become more merciful?

Some would respond that modern medicine has created more problems than it has solved. It can keep a human body functioning long after the quality or meaning of life has gone. In times past, it is claimed, death claimed older people sooner, before their ability to meaningfully participate in life ended. But today, flu and pneumonia, once called "the old person's friend," can be effectively treated with antivirals and antibiotics. Diseases like Alzheimer's and dementia can leave the shell of a person walking around long after the personality of a person has vanished. Radiation, chemotherapy, and other debilitating procedures can lengthen the last stages of life and prolong the pain of dying. Machines can even keep the heart and lungs functioning long after the brain has died.

Some of the concerns expressed are legitimate. The creation of heart-lung machines and other methods of CPR have forced medical practitioners to reconsider how to define death. The older definition of the cessation of

---

[36] As of October 2022, physician-assisted suicide is legal in ten countries and eleven states in the U.S. See Avivah Wittenberg Cox, "A Designed Death—Where and When the World Allows It," *Forbes*, October 22, 2022, https://www.forbes.com/sites/avivahwittenbergcox/2022/10/22/a-designed-death--where--when-the-world-allows-it/.

heartbeat has been changed today to the cessation of brain activity. When it is established that the brain has ceased to function, and that the state is irreversible, the person is considered dead. While this definition has proven medically useful, is it adequate theologically?

There is a strong case for thinking it is. As we noted above, physical death, in Scripture, seems to be regarded as the separation of the material element (the body) from the immaterial element (the soul or spirit). Verses such as Eccl 12:7, Luke 23:46, and 2 Cor 5:8 imply as much. An immaterial element, by its nature, cannot be materially perceived, but since our immaterial nature acts in this world by means of the material element (the body), and the actions of the body are dependent on the brain, the absence of brain activity seems to be the clearest evidence of the separation of soul and body that we can find. This conclusion is important, for it gives us the basis for answering some tough ethical questions.

1. If a person's body is being sustained by machines only, and there has been the irreversible cessation of brain activity, the person is dead. Turning off the machines is simply recognizing that fact, and thus, morally justifiable. This is not somehow evidence of a lack of faith in God's power to miraculously heal, for if God wants to heal someone, he certainly is not dependent on mechanical assistance.

2. Furthermore, if someone has a terminal illness, she is not morally obligated to undergo every surgery, or take every form of chemotherapy or radiation therapy simply to lengthen her life for a short time. Death, while unnatural and an enemy, is inevitable, and we may allow it to come, especially when the choice is between a few weeks or months of relative health and the ability to be with those we love and a few additional weeks or months in a hospital, undergoing the pain of surgery or the debilitating effects of radiation or chemotherapy.

3. Euthanasia and physician-assisted suicide cross an important ethical line. Recognizing that death has come, or allowing an inevitable death to come, is morally and ethically justifiable. Causing a death, or taking a life, is not. The desire to ease suffering can be accomplished in other ways. The goal must be to ease suffering without taking the decision of death into our

own hands. Exactly how much we may do to ease suffering without causing death may be difficult to determine in some exceptional cases, but such cases are not the norm, even among the cases where euthanasia or physician-assisted suicide is advocated as an acceptable solution.

4. What about withholding artificial nutrition and hydration from those in a persistent vegetative state (PVS)? Evangelicals have differed on this issue, but a recent study argues that if we see artificial nutrition and hydration as medical treatment and acknowledge that we are not obliged to pursue every possible medical treatment, it may be possible to withdraw this medical treatment in recognition that God is drawing the life of such a person to a close and we are not morally obligated to lengthen that process.[37]

In addition to the dilemmas raised by modern medicine, are there other motivations contributing to the growing acceptance of various forms of euthanasia and assisted suicide? Three contributing forces may be involved.

One is the loss of a sanctity of life ethic. It is hard to sanction abortion and maintain an ethic that values all life. We have had abortion now for a generation and it cannot help but erode an ethic that values all life; that is, if we casually take life as it just begins, it will be harder to value life as it ends.

A second factor is the desire for personal autonomy. In contrast to the psalmist, who says, "My times are in your hands" (Ps 31:15 NIV), the desire of many today is to control their own times. And if the future involves suffering and decline, they believe they should be able to choose to end it, to avoid any suffering and indignity. But while we should do what we can to eliminate needless suffering, we cannot say that all suffering is bad or needless. God may be working in someone's life via that suffering, either weaning sufferers from the world and giving them a desire to leave, or God may be using one person's suffering in the life of another, perhaps the one caring for her. Indeed, could it be that one of God's purposes in leaving older persons

[37] Erik M. Clary, "On the Ethics of Withdrawing Artificial Nutrition and Hydration from Patients Diagnosed as Being in a Persistent Vegetative State: An Analysis of Prior Evangelical Treatments and a Proposal" (PhD diss., Southeastern Baptist Theological Seminary, 2015).

alive when their mind and memory are gone is to teach us genuine unconditional love? When we bathe and diaper and care for babies, there is the hoped-for reward of seeing them grow and return our love. When we care for older senile or demented persons, there is no chance of their returning our love in this life. Any thanks we receive is dependent on life beyond the grave. So we learn genuine faith and unconditional love. We short-circuit what God may desire to accomplish when we take our times into our hands.

But a third and largely unacknowledged factor driving euthanasia and assisted suicide is financial. Caring for the last months of a terminal illness or providing long-term care for Alzheimer's patients is very costly.[38] With the advent of managed care, minimizing the costs of health care will override caring well for the patient as the ultimate goal. Putting it as simply as possible, euthanasia or assisted suicide is a lot more cost-effective than long-term care through a terminal illness. Though this factor will not be mentioned in the debate, it is likely to be powerfully at work behind the scenes. And while we may understand the desire of some not to be a burden on their family or even the state, or the desire not to have what they wanted to leave to their children eaten up by medical bills, we need to remember what is precious and sacred (life) and what is not (earthly treasures).

Transhumanism[39]

The most recent contemporary development concerning death is the little-known movement called transhumanism, which some see as something like

---

[38] Even for those without terminal illnesses, care over the last twelve months of a person's life in the United States costs an average $80,000. See Eric B. French *et al.*, "End-of-Life Medical Spending in the Last Twelve Months of Life Is Lower Than Previously Reported," *Health Affairs* 36, no. 7 (2017), at https://www.healthaffairs.org/doi/10.1377/hlthaff.2017.0174.

[39] Some of the material in this section previously appeared in John S. Hammett, "Between Radical Freedom and Total Determinism: A Christian View of Human Nature," *Christian Research Journal* 34, no. 2 (2011): 34–42, https://www.equip.org/articles/between-radical-freedom-and-total-determinism-2/. Used with permission of *Christian Research Journal* (https://www.equip.org/).

a secular eschatology. Nick Bostrom, member of the philosophy faculty at Oxford University and one of the founders of the World Transhumanist Association, describes it as an "intellectual and cultural movement that affirms the possibility and desirability of fundamentally improving the human condition," especially by the careful study and use of technology "that will enable us to overcome fundamental human limitations."[40] Some of the limitations they seek to overcome are death, decline of bodily functioning and intellectual capacity, even mood, energy, and self-control.

Two statements illustrate their perspective. From the website of the World Transhumanist Association, we read a statement of transhumanist values: "Transhumanists view human nature as a work-in-progress, a half-baked beginning we can learn to remold in desirable ways."[41] A more explicit statement still is, "Transhumanists place a high value on autonomy—the ability and right of people to plan and choose their own lives," including "the right to choose when and how to die—or not to die."[42] The goal of transhumanists is posthumanism, which they see as the next step in human evolution, indeed "an exponentially greater step in evolutionary development."[43] As Jacob Shatzer succinctly puts it, "Transhumanism is the process, posthumanism the goal."[44]

Technology is the tool transhumanists believe will help them achieve their goals. Kevin Warwick writes words that sound like science fiction, but they are spoken seriously from a leading researcher in cybernetics: "I was born human. . . . But while fate made me human, it also gave me the power to do something about it. The ability to change myself, to upgrade my

---

[40] Nick Bostrom, "The Transhumanist FAQ: A General Introduction," Version 2.1 (World Transhumanist Association, 2003), 4, https://nickbostrom.com/views/transhumanist.pdf.

[41] Nick Bostrom, "Transhumanist Values," https://nickbostrom.com/ethics/values.

[42] Bostrom, "Transhumanist FAQ," 4, 34.

[43] Fazale Rana with Kenneth R. Samples, *Humans 2.0: Scientific, Philosophical and Theological Perspectives on Transhumanism* (Covina, CA: RTB Press, 2019), 18.

[44] Jacob Shatzer, *Transhumanism and the Image of God* (Downers Grove: IVP Academic, 2019), 16.

human form, with the aid of technology. To become cyborg—part human, part machine."[45] In recent years, with the explosion of biotechnology and what are called GRIN technologies (Genetic, Robotic, Information, and Nano), some transhumanists believe they are well on the way to reaching their goal.

While there is some variety among transhumanists (including some Christian transhumanists), one spokesperson sees seven themes as common to all transhumanists: continual progress, self-improvement, an optimistic attitude, the use of technology to overcome limitations, a society with open communication and innovation, self-direction, and reason.[46] But the assertion that all seven of these themes are affirmed by all transhumanists may be open to question. The Christian Transhumanist Association, founded in 2013 by Micah Redding, sees transhumanism simply as "a philosophy which states that we should use science and technology to make the world (including humanity) better."[47] Presumably, as Christians they would not use reason to the exclusion of faith and would qualify self-direction to understand such self-direction as occurring under the lordship of Christ. But there are definitely some similarities among all who call themselves transhumanists.

They are not unaware of potential dangers. They acknowledge that "some of these coming technologies could potentially cause great harm to human life; even the survival of our species could be at risk."[48] They realize the need to address ethical concerns, and the first descriptive phrase of the World Transhumanist Association on their website is "for the *ethical* use of technology to extend human capabilities." Their ethics include advocacy for

---

[45] Kevin Warwick, *I, Cyborg* (London: Century, 2002), 1.

[46] Max More, "Philosophy of Transhumanism," in *The Transhumanist Reader: Classical and Contemporary Essays on the Science, Technology, and Philosophy of the Human Future* (Malden, MA: Wiley-Blackwell, 2013), 4–5. See the discussion in Shatzer, *Transhumanism and the Image of God*, 43–44.

[47] See the website of the Christian Humanist Association (https://www.christiantranshumanism.org/about). For more, see Liuan Huska, "Engineering Abundant Life," *Christianity Today* 63, no. 2 (March 2019): 48–53.

[48] Bostrom, "Transhumanist FAQ," 5.

"the well-being of all sentience," and rejection of racism, sexism, speciesism, nationalism, and religious intolerance. They stress "the moral urgency of saving lives, or, more precisely, of preventing involuntary deaths among people whose lives are worth living,"[49] although this last phrase raises an ethical concern. Are there people whose lives are not worth living, people whose involuntary deaths should not be prevented? But, on balance, transhumanists think the risks associated with exploring the posthuman realm are well worth taking.

By way of evaluation, Christians have always applauded efforts to heal and eliminate disease. We, like transhumanists, recognize death as an enemy (see 1 Cor 15:26). Maxwell Mehlman sees other points of agreement: "What is striking, however, is how closely the transhumanist vision resembles the images of heaven at the heart of most of the world's religions."[50] But most Christian observers of transhumanism find the transhumanist vision of human transformation to be at odds with Christian versions. For example, Christians also recognize the fallenness and transitional nature of this body, but our vision of the posthuman looks to divine resurrection of the body rather than human technology.[51] Christopher Hook, in a perceptive article, reviews some of these developments and asks questions that should make us appropriately skeptical of the goals of transhumanism: "What does it mean that our Lord healed and restored in his ministry—never enhanced? Is it significant that the gifts of the Holy Spirit—wisdom, love, patience,

---

[49] For example, they think cryonic suspension should be available for those who desire it, saying, "While cryonics might be a long shot, it definitely carries better odds than cremation or burial." Bostrom, "Transhumanist Values."

[50] Maxwell Mehlman, *Transhumanist Dreams and Dystopian Nightmares: The Promise and Peril of Genetic Engineering* (Baltimore: Johns Hopkins University Press, 2012), 23, as quoted in Patrick T. Smith, "The Privilege of Being Human," in *Why People Matter: A Christian Engagement with Rival Views of Human Significance*, ed. John Kilner (Grand Rapids: Baker Academic, 2017), 130.

[51] See the helpful analysis by Matthew Eppinette, "Humanism 2.0: Transhumanism as a Cultural Trend," in *Everyday Theology: How to Read Cultural Texts and Interpret Trends*, ed. Kevin J. Vanhoozer, Charles A. Anderson, and Michael J. Sleasman (Grand Rapids: Baker Academic, 2007), 190–207, esp. 204.

kindness—cannot be manufactured by technology? How would the transformation from *homo sapiens* to *techno sapiens* affect our identity as bearers of the image of God?"[52]

Moreover, while genuinely mindful of ethical concerns, transhumanism has no basis for adjudicating issues of good and evil. The mindset that focuses on enhancements and upgrades and sees human nature "as a work-in-progress, a half-baked beginning," would seem inconsistent with any high view of intrinsic human dignity. Jacob Shatzer sees a failure among some transhumanists to "lay out any standard by which their value statements can be judged." Even the central theme of the call to progress and human improvement is problematic. In the end, "transhumanism struggles to build progress on anything solid; the 'better' cannot be defined in their project."[53] Indeed, transhumanism seems to locate human value in what they may become, as opposed to views that ascribe value and dignity to people as they are now.[54]

But the most serious question with transhumanism is the compatibility of its goals with the Christian vision of humanity.[55] With the exception of the much milder form of transhumanism in the Christian Transhumanist Association, transhumanism overall is limited to a this-world perspective on human life. Without any God or the prospect of life beyond the grave, they tend to see death as a violation of an individual's right to life. But who gives any individual a right to life? Moreover, may not the end of life in this world be a severe mercy from God? True, death entered the world as the punishment for sin, but a punishment that opened the door to mercy. For once the man and woman had fallen and become like God in knowing, not just

---

[52] Christopher Hook, "The Techno Sapiens Are Coming," *Christianity Today* 48, no. 1 (January 2004): 35–40, https://www.christianitytoday.com/2004/01/techno-sapiens-are-coming/.

[53] Shatzer, *Transhumanism and the Image of God*, 50, 52.

[54] For a discussion of the meaning of dignity, the reasons for ascribing it to people as they are, and consideration of "objections to the inherent worth of people as they are," see Smith, "The Privilege of Being Human," 118–24.

[55] For an analysis of the naturalism embedded in the transhumanist worldview, see Rana, *Humans 2.0*, 200–201.

good, but now evil, God intervened: "He must not reach out, take from the tree of life, eat, and live forever" (Gen 3:22). It was the mercy of God that established the limitation of life for humans in their fallen state; as redeemed persons, we are welcomed to the tree of life (Rev 22:2–3). Unending life as a fallen human would not at all be an unmixed blessing, and in seeking to overcome that limitation, transhumans are showing a limited, this-worldly vision. Could it be that "the limitations that come with human finitude are themselves valuable; to lose them is to lose the very fulfillment we seek to gain?"[56] Perhaps transhumanists can make life longer but will that make it better? Humanity may be able to alleviate physical suffering, but technological advances will not cure the human propensity for exploitation and the abuse of power.

Finally, in thinking technology can overcome the power of death, transhumans are in danger of being blinded by idolatrous pride. The account of the Tower of Babel in Genesis provides a warning for people today that self ascendancy and any attempt to "play" God will end in disaster. Transhumanism identifies the human problem as a need for greater technological development and human enhancement. Here too, humanity provides its own redemption but through technological means. God established death as the wages of sin; only by dealing with sin can death be dealt with, and only God can deal with sin. He has done so in Christ, and so can give life that is truly abundant and eternal. What transhumanists seek, God offers, but it comes by grace through faith, not by upgrading through technology. Apart from the gift of eternal life, transhumanists will, sooner or later, bump up against the hard limit of death as the destiny now assigned to fallen humans, established by God in mercy and justice.

Personal Application

Since death is universal and the certain end for all, it is an issue for personal application for all, and especially for Christian leaders. There are several

[56] Smith, "The Privilege of Being Human," 129.

practical ways pastors and Christian leaders can help people prepare for death. One way pastors can serve their congregants is to provide access to people and resources who will help them understand matters pertaining to death, such as wills and funeral arrangements. Family lawyers or funeral home directors in one's congregation could offer a church-sponsored workshop to guide people on how to think through these practical issues rather than leaving them to grieving family members to decide after the death of a loved one. For example, will one choose cremation or burial?[57] If cremation, what will be done with the ashes? If burial, has a burial plot been purchased? How much should one spend on a casket? What information should be included on a grave marker? These are questions better asked before the need for an immediate decision, and some today are pre-planning and pre-paying their funeral expenses to spare their family from having to make such decisions in a time of grieving.[58]

Of course, thinking about such practical issues can also open doors for talking about the ultimate issue of one's eternal destination and helping people make sure that they are ready spiritually. Pastors and counselors can point to the numerous verses in hymns that speak of death and our victory over it; they can use illustrations from the famous homegoings of saints of old or illustrations from literature, such as Christian crossing the river in *The Pilgrim's Progress*. In all these ways, pastors and counselors can help people face death and allow its reality to prod all of us into making sure of our preparation.[59]

After death, the goal is to minister to the grieving. Scripture does not say we should not grieve, but that we should not grieve like those who have no hope (1 Thess 4:13). Sometimes we may need to gently help people to

---

[57] For any who have theological or ethical questions about cremation, see David W. Jones, "To Bury or Burn? Toward an Ethic of Cremation," *JETS* 53, no. 2 (2010): 335–47.

[58] My wife and I recently pre-planned and pre-paid for our funerals, in consultation with our children.

[59] Keller's *On Death* is a useful book, containing material Keller and his wife have used in counseling people facing impending death. See Keller, *On Death*, xv.

grieve, by reminding them of special occasions or endearing qualities of those who have died. Mentioning such things may bring tears, but grieving is necessary and not incompatible with the reality of our hope and comfort in Christ.

The more difficult case is, of course, with those who die without making a profession of faith in Christ. There are two dangers to avoid here. One is to give false hope, especially in an age where creeping universalism abounds in the culture. The other is to be insensitive, and so close off any possibility for ministry to those still living. In a funeral sermon, a pastor should explain the gospel and point to Christ's willingness to accept all who come to him. If a grieving friend or family member asks, "Where is my loved one now?" the pastor may turn the question back on the one asking: "You know your loved one better than I do; what do you think?" Make sure they know what the Bible says is required for entrance into heaven, but let them draw their own conclusions about the destiny of their departed loved one. That allows you to be honest and still maintain the ability to minister to those still living. So pastors should present the gospel in funeral messages but do so with sensitivity to those grieving.

But to minister in death situations most effectively, each individual needs to confront their own personal mortality. It may be frightening, but it is spiritually healthy to ponder the questions death raises. In the end, part of every Christian's birthright is liberty from the fear of death (Heb 2:15). Ask yourself questions like, How old do I want to be when I die? Of what do I want to die? Take care of practical necessities like your own will (for parents, name who you would want to raise your children should you die). Consider having clear power of attorney provisions should you become disabled and instructions in a living will concerning medical treatment you do or do not want, which can be of great help to your family should they face such difficult situations. We can face death without fear because we know the Lord of life and death. We may love life and want to live a long time, but we need not fear death. For the believer, this enemy will simply be the door into real life. What that life beyond death's door will be like is the topic of our next chapter.

CHAPTER 3

Between Grave and Final Glory: The Intermediate State

Introduction

The reality of death confronts us every day. Even in our modern society, where death most often takes place in a hospital rather than in homes, as was the case for most of human history, we cannot escape the reality of death; our loved ones are no longer here. The question that presses in on us is inescapable: Where are they? What lies for them—what lies for me—beyond death? It is a question which demands an answer. Our purpose in this chapter is to present the Bible's answer to this question, which is more complex than many realize. In addition to a survey of biblical teaching, we will also consider some related historical developments and theological considerations, as well as concluding with some practical applications.

We will argue below that the belief in an afterlife was present but dim in the Old Testament; it became clear in the New Testament.[1] As Paul says, it was left to Christ to bring "life and immortality to light through the gospel" (2 Tim 1:10). Before Christ, the idea of an afterlife was present but in the shadows; Jesus brought it to light. After Christ, a very positive belief in an afterlife became and has remained a consensual item of Christian faith.[2] But before we examine the biblical evidence for this belief, we should note that it has become much less the norm among people, at least people in the United States, today. According to a 2011 Global Poll, only 51 percent of those surveyed affirmed their belief in an afterlife, 23 percent said they believe we simply cease to exist, and 26 percent remain agnostic on the question; they simply do not know what happens to us after death.[3] Clearly, some assumptions that once supported the widespread Christian belief in an afterlife are no longer as widely shared as they once were. We need to remind ourselves of the evidence for this belief in Scripture.

Biblical Teaching

The Promise of Eternal Life

The promise of life beyond the grave is embedded in what may be the most well-known verse of the Bible, John 3:16. The purpose of the Father in sending and giving his Son was that those who believe in him might have "eternal life." That promise is reiterated as the destiny of the righteous following the day of judgment (Matt 25:46) and the gift of God to all those in Christ (1 John 5:11).

---

[1] For a similar assessment of the biblical teaching, see Paul R. Williamson, *Death and the Afterlife: Biblical Perspectives on Ultimate Questions*, New Studies in Biblical Theology 44 (London: Apollos, 2018), 22.

[2] John W. Cooper, *Body, Soul & Life Everlasting: Biblical Anthropology and the Monism-Dualism Debate* (Grand Rapids: Eerdmans, 2000), 7. Cooper states, "From earliest times Christians have affirmed continuing personal existence after biological death."

[3] Williamson, *Death and the Afterlife*, 5n1.

It is linked to the resurrection power of Christ, promised to Martha and all who believe in the one who is the resurrection and the life (John 11:25–26), and demonstrated in the resurrection of Christ himself. Because he conquered death, we have the hope of sharing in his resurrection power. But the resurrection of the body is associated with the return of Christ (1 Cor 15:51–53), for which we have been waiting nearly two thousand years. Is there life beyond the grave now for those who die before Christ's return? Does eternal life begin only with the resurrection of the body, or is it our present possession? Moreover, what is the state of those who die without Christ? Eternal life is promised only to those united to Christ by faith. Is physical death the end of existence for nonbelievers? What does the Bible say about these questions?

Eternal Life Now: The Intermediate State

The traditional Christian term for the life we experience beyond death now is the "intermediate state." The final and eternal state which we await will be our life in resurrected bodies, in the new creation, following the return of Christ. Three texts speak clearly of life immediately upon the death of the body. In Luke 23:43, Jesus promises the thief on the cross that death will not be the end for him. By the end of that day, his body, like that of Jesus, would be in a grave, but Jesus promises this thief he would be with him "in paradise." Paul, in reflecting on what lies beyond death, says to be "away from the body" is to be "at home with the Lord" (2 Cor 5:8). In Phil 1:23, Paul longs for death because it would mean "to depart and be with Christ." Continued existence beyond the grave is promised for those in Christ. Even for those not in Christ, one of Christ's parables about life above the grave (Luke 16:19–31) includes both a righteous and an unrighteous man. Both experience an existence beyond the grave, but for the wicked man this existence is so miserable that it is better described as "eternal destruction" (2 Thess 1:9) rather than eternal life.[4]

[4] The claim of some that nonbelievers will eventually be annihilated and cease to exist will be considered at greater length in a later chapter addressing the issues of hell and eternal destinies.

One area of controversy has been the nature of this intermediate life. We know the state of our bodies before the resurrection; they return to dust (Gen 3:19; Eccl 12:7). If we continue to exist after death, it must be apart from those bodies, in a temporarily disembodied form. Stephen Davis gives this description of the intermediate state:

> Its basic claim is that when I die, my body disintegrates, but my soul continues to exist; for an interim period of time, I exist in the presence of God as a mere disembodied soul. Then, on one future day, God will raise my body, reunite it with my soul, and constitute me as a whole and complete person again.[5]

While this description is for the most part accurate, two qualifications are in order. First, the nonmaterial element of our human constitution that survives the death of the body is sometimes called the "soul" in Scripture (Gen 35:18; 1 Kgs 17:21–22; Rev 6:9) but is also sometimes called the "spirit" (Eccl 12:7; Luke 8:55; Heb 12:23). Thus, the state in which we exist after death in the intermediate state is as a disembodied soul or spirit. Second and more significantly, Davis seems to look down on this form of existence as "a mere disembodied soul," less than a "whole and complete person." But perhaps we should emphasize that this disembodied soul exists **in the presence of God**. Indeed, it exists with Christ in the paradise of God (Luke 23:43) and not as a "*mere* disembodied soul" but as a *perfected* spirit (Heb 12:23). The resurrection of the body may be our final and most desired state, but because the intermediate state puts us with Christ, Paul sees it as "far better" (Phil 1:23) than life on earth in our present state.

The intermediate state has been the consensus Christian view of the afterlife "from the second century onward,"[6] but has come under criticism since the middle of the twentieth century. Some have charged the intermediate state as teaching the immortality of the soul, which they see as an

[5] Stephen T. Davis, "Eschatology and Resurrection," in *The Oxford Handbook of Eschatology*, ed. Jerry L. Walls (Oxford: Oxford University Press, 2008), 387.

[6] Davis, 387.

alien concept, brought in from Greek philosophy.[7] But Anthony Hoekema and Stephen Davis both show that a careful formulation of the intermediate state need not invoke traditional understandings of the immortality of the soul,[8] a point we will discuss further later in this chapter. However, any formulation of the intermediate state does require some degree of dualism in the human constitution; that is, that humans are composed of more than just the body. Dualism affirms a nonmaterial element or aspect of the human constitution, called the soul or spirit, and dualism has been attacked since the mid-twentieth century from a multiplicity of perspectives.[9]

Many philosophers have adopted materialistic views of human nature which leave no room for a nonmaterial soul or spirit. Neuroscientists have challenged the traditional dualism between the brain and the mind with evidence that mental activity is dependent on brain activity. Some biblical scholars claim that there is a consensus in their field "that both Old and New Testaments assume or testify to an anthropological monism."[10]

It is beyond the scope of this volume to fully address the debate over dualism within theological anthropology, but there is good evidence to suggest that the supposed consensus on monism among philosophers, scientists, and biblical scholars has been seriously overstated. There are lively debates concerning dualism going on within all these disciplines, and the objections

---

[7] This idea of the immortality of the soul figures in the objections to the intermediate state cited by G. C. Berkouwer, *The Return of Christ*, trans. James Van Oosterom, ed. Marlin J. Van Elderen (Grand Rapids: Eerdmans, 1972), 38–40; and in Davis, "Eschatology and Resurrection," 388–89.

[8] Anthony A. Hoekema, *The Bible and the Future* (Grand Rapids: Eerdmans, 1979), 86–91; Davis, "Eschatology and Resurrection," 389.

[9] For a presentation of and response to challenges from philosophy, neuroscience, and biblical scholarship, see Cooper, *Body, Soul & Life Everlasting*, 204–32; for further discussion of objections to and defenses of dualism, see Thomas M. Crisp, Steven L. Porter, and Gregg A. Ten Elshof, eds., *Neuroscience and the Soul: The Human Person in Philosophy, Science, and Theology* (Grand Rapids: Eerdmans, 2016).

[10] Joel B. Green, "Body and Soul, Mind and Brain," in *In Search of the Soul: Four Views of the Mind-Body Problem*, ed. Joel B. Green and Stuart L. Palmer (Downers Grove: InterVarsity, 2005), 18.

to dualism have themselves been subjected to critique and qualification.[11] In what many consider to be the most important study of this topic, John Cooper in his book *Body, Soul & Life Everlasting* observes that the traditional Christian belief in some type of ontological distinction between body and soul has been primarily grounded in the doctrine of the intermediate state, a doctrine seen by most of Christian history to be the unmistakable teaching of Scripture.[12] We turn then to an examination of biblical teaching on the doctrine of the intermediate state, first in the Old Testament.

The Intermediate State in the Old Testament

The most important word for the intermediate state in the Old Testament is "Sheol." It is found 65 times—46 of those times in poetic literature and always without an article, somewhat like a proper noun. While 65 occurrences may seem to be a considerable number, Philip Johnston argues that in view of the exactly 1,000 uses of the terms for "die/death" in the Old Testament, Sheol is mentioned a relatively small number of times, showing that it is "a minor Old Testament theme."[13] Minor though it may be, Sheol is important as "the Old Testament manner of asserting that death does not terminate human existence."[14]

While it is variously translated as "grave" and "realm of the dead,"[15] and while there are various nuances of meaning, Johnston asserts, "By far its

---

[11] See the discussion in John S. Hammett and Katie J. McCoy, *Humanity*, Theology for the People of God, ed. David S. Dockery, Nathan A. Finn, and Christopher W. Morgan (Brentwood, TN: B&H Academic, 2023), 291–308.

[12] Cooper, *Body, Soul & Life Everlasting*, 32.

[13] Philip S. Johnston, *Shades of Sheol: Death and Afterlife in the Old Testament* (Leicester, UK: Apollos, 2002), 72–73.

[14] G. E. Ladd, *A Theology of the New Testament* (Grand Rapids: Eerdmans, 1974), 194.

[15] The 2011 NIV translates *Sheol* as "grave" 28 times, and "realm of the dead" 24 times. The CSB and ESV leave *Sheol* untranslated, as if a proper noun, though ESV makes one exception, translating *Sheol* as "grave" in Song of Songs 8:6.

most frequent use is to indicate human destiny."[16] This is seen for example in Prov 9:18, where Sheol is parallel to "the departed spirits," or Isa 14:9, where Sheol is parallel to "the spirits of the departed." In Isa 38:18–19, King Hezekiah contrasts those in Sheol with "the living."

There is no problem with seeing Sheol as the destiny of the ungodly spirits, for Sheol is viewed as "the opposite theological extreme to Yahweh, and the dominant feature for its inhabitants is their separation from him."[17] It is described as a dark place, where there is no memory, no knowledge, no praise of God, and only a very shadowy existence (Ps 88:10–12; Isa 38:18–19). This seems fitting as the destiny of the wicked, but some feel a theological difficulty in seeing Sheol as the destination of the spirits of the righteous. Does not Scripture see as axiomatic the fact that God makes a distinction between the destination of the righteous and the wicked (Ps 1:6; Mal 3:18)?

Johnston acknowledges that most scholars view Sheol as the destiny of all and that certain righteous individuals in the Old Testament seem to see Sheol as their destination (Jacob in Gen 37:35; Hezekiah in Isa 38:10; and Job in Job 17:13–16). He carefully examines the context of these cases, and two other texts where he says Sheol is "apparently presented as the destiny for all," but concludes that "Sheol cannot be identified simply as the Hebrew term for the underworld which awaits all." He explains, "It is almost exclusively reserved for those under divine judgment," and "arguably, the righteous only envisage Sheol when they face unhappy and untimely death, which they interpret as divine punishment. By contrast, when they face a contented death at the end of a full and happy life . . . there is no mention of Sheol."[18]

In terms then of the destiny of the righteous, Johnston is somewhat ambivalent. He says, "There is no clearly articulated alternative to Sheol, no other destiny whose location is named, no other fate whose situation is

---

[16] Johnston, *Shades of Sheol*, 80.

[17] Johnston, 75.

[18] Johnston, 81–83.

described, however briefly." And yet he does note a few texts which indicate that this is an open-ended question: "There seem to be some exceptions, a few texts which hint at or hope for some sort of continued communion with God beyond death."[19]

Matthew Emerson offers a more positive assessment of the data, bringing in developments of Old Testament thought in Second Temple Judaism. He agrees that "Sheol in the Old Testament and *Hades* in the LXX and in Greco-Roman thought can be used to refer to a general place for all the dead," but adds, "over time, and especially during Second Temple Judaism, this general place of the dead was increasingly discussed in terms of its compartments, namely one for the righteous and another for the unrighteous," with the former called "paradise" or "Abraham's bosom" and the latter called *Hades* and *Gehenna*.[20] This avoids the problematic idea that the same destiny, Sheol, awaits the righteous and the wicked, but the notion of differing compartments in Sheol for the righteous and the wicked is something not seen in the Old Testament itself, but only as a post-Old Testament development.

There is one final alternative to Sheol as a destination for the righteous found in the Old Testament. It is not brought to full light but is developing in the shadows. It is the promise of divine deliverance from Sheol. Psalm 16:10–11 posits such deliverance from Sheol for God's "faithful one." Rather than being abandoned to Sheol, the psalmist anticipates life in God's presence, with "eternal pleasures." Yet, Johnston says, this description of "continued communion remains tantalizingly vague." He adds, "By affirming something which partly fitted received views on human destiny but also partly transcended them, the psalm sets up a tension which awaits resolution. This resolution is sketched at the margins of the Old Testament, in resurrection and post-mortem distinction between righteous and wicked."[21]

---

[19] Johnston, *Shades of Sheol*, 199.

[20] Matthew Y. Emerson, *"He Descended to the Dead": An Evangelical Theology of Holy Saturday* (Downers Grove: IVP Academic, 2019), 31.

[21] Johnston, 202.

An even stronger affirmation is found in Ps 49:15: "Here, more explicitly than anywhere else in the Hebrew Bible, the consignment of the ungodly to Sheol is contrasted with the ransom of the godly from Sheol."[22] And while not as explicit, Ps 73:23–24 can be cogently interpreted as reflecting a post-mortem hope for life in God's presence.[23] To these can be added the language of Pss 17:15 and 139:18, which mention awakening in God's presence, the awakening seen as awakening from death, and again reflecting the hope of post-mortem life in God's presence.[24] Finally, Johnston includes a few proverbs which "suggest that Sheol is not for the wise and disciplined."[25] Proverbs 15:24 says the prudent can live in a way that avoids "going down to Sheol," and Prov 23:14 encourages discipline of a youth to "rescue his life from Sheol." While these texts do not mention an alternative destination in the presence of God, they suggest that Sheol may not be the destination for all.

The claim that there was, in the Old Testament, a real but dim hope for an afterlife in the presence of God for the righteous, a hope that awaited the fuller illumination provided by Christ, seems strengthened by the progression of Israel's thought concerning the afterlife in Second Temple Judaism and the intertestamental period. In assessing this progression of thought, Matt Emerson insists that "it is a *coherent* progression. That is, Israel's later thought does not contradict her earlier thought and vice versa, but rather they are both pieces of a whole cloth (along with the New Testament) that together provide a full and coherent picture."[26] What is initially present in the shadows eventually emerges into light. For that greater clarity, we turn to the New Testament.

---

[22] Johnston, *Shades of Sheol*, 203.

[23] Both Johnston, *Shades of Sheol*, 205, and Williamson, *Death and the Afterlife*, 168, allow for this interpretation, but both also find verse 24 "ambiguous."

[24] Johnston mentions these two verses. He himself thinks this idea of post-mortem hope "is unlikely to have been the original focus of these psalms," but acknowledges that "traditional Christian interpretation has taken Psalm 17:15b as an expectation of seeing God after death." Johnston, *Shades of Sheol*, 206–7.

[25] Johnston, 207.

[26] Emerson, *"He Descended to the Dead,"* 28n21.

The Intermediate State in the New Testament

The New Testament confirms the idea that the souls of the just and unjust do not go to the same place after death, for the closest New Testament equivalent to Sheol, Hades, is never used for the destination of the just after death but only the unjust. Dale Moody sees the New Testament as fulfilling the hope of the Old Testament: "The Old Testament belief that the saint (*chasid*) would not be abandoned to *Sheol* has borne fruit, and *Hades* is left only to the wicked."[27]

Hades is the word used to describe the destiny of the rich man in Luke 16:19–31. We should note that it is a description of the intermediate state and not hell, which is used for the final state of the wicked.[28] The principal theme is the reality of judgment in the world to come and the need to prepare for it now by believing God's Word. The difficulty comes in understanding some of the details.

For example, what is the "side" of Abraham, and where is it? We find this phrase only in this passage. It appears to be a place of honor and happiness,[29] but we have little to go on. Even more difficult are the references to fingers, eyes, and tongue in verses 23–24. On the basis of these references, Joel Green argues that "the notion of the disembodied existence of a soul must be read back into the story since the characters in Hades act as human agents with a corporeal existence."[30] But such a conclusion overlooks the fact that all those reading the parable know the location of the bodies of dead people—they are decaying in the grave. Where then do

---

[27] Dale Moody, *The Hope of Glory* (Grand Rapids: Eerdmans, 1964), 58.

[28] While there is not unanimity among commentators, I. H. Marshall judges the intermediate state as the "most likely" interpretation, see I. H. Marshall, *The Gospel of Luke*, NIGTC (Grand Rapids: Eerdmans, 1978), 636.

[29] Joel B. Green calls it "a position of intimacy and honor," even "paradisical bliss." Joel B. Green, *The Gospel of Luke*, NICNT (Grand Rapids: Eerdmans, 1997), 607. Darrell L. Bock says Abraham's bosom "represents the patriarch's reception of the faithful into heaven;" it is "a place of blessing." Darrell L. Bock, *Luke 9:51–24:53*, BECNT (Grand Rapids: Baker, 1996), 1368.

[30] Green, *The Gospel of Luke*, 607–8, n. 343.

these body parts come from? Possibly Jesus is using figurative language (it is, after all, a parable); possibly the only way to communicate the story is to use material images. I. H. Marshall says, "The dead are visualized in bodily terms, since there is no other way they can be visualized," but he adds that it is "manifest . . . that the details are not to be taken literally."[31] Either way, support for the traditional view of the intermediate state as existence as unembodied spirits is found elsewhere, for the Bible refers to humans after death as "souls" (Rev 6:9) or "spirits" (Eccl 12:7; Heb 12:23). Despite the corporeal language of Luke 16, there is little basis for the idea of an intermediate body, though it has been occasionally suggested.[32] Either way, the main point concerning our destiny beyond death is clear: the intermediate state involves happiness for the just, punishment for the unjust, and the two are permanently separated.

Another important New Testament term for the destination of the righteous after death is "paradise." This is the word used in Jesus's promise to the thief on the cross (Luke 23:43), and it is where Jesus is after his bodily death. Paradise as the location of the Son of God would seem to be, in some sense, heaven, since that word is most often used to refer to the dwelling place of God.[33] But God's present dwelling place is not yet his eternal dwelling place; that awaits the coming of the new creation (Rev 21:3). Thus the paradise to which the thief went is an intermediate destination, what could also be called intermediate heaven, a fitting place for those in the intermediate state, which is the state of the thief.[34] Paradise is also associated with the tree of life in Rev 2:7, which in turn is associated with the garden of Eden in Gen 2:8–9 and with the new heavens and new earth

---

[31] Marshall, *Luke*, 637.

[32] Randy Alcorn suggests intermediate bodies as a possibility, though he acknowledges that "this is certainly debatable." Randy Alcorn, *Heaven* (Carol Stream, IL: Tyndale, 2004), 57.

[33] "Heaven is . . . the abode of God." Herman Austel, "*shāmayim*," in TWOT, 2:935.

[34] As Marshall, *The Gospel of Luke*, 873, and Bock, *Luke 9:51–24:53*, 1857, affirm.

in Rev 22:1–2. Thus, paradise might be an accurate term to describe our original state in Eden ("Paradise Lost"), our eternal state in the new creation ("Paradise Perfected"), and our intermediate state in Christ's presence now ("Paradise Present").

Aside from the terms "Abraham's side" and "paradise," there are three key texts that give the clearest basis for the intermediate state of believers. We mentioned them earlier, but now we want to look at them more closely for further details on the life that awaits believers in the intermediate state. The first of these three key texts is Luke 23:43. Here, the thief's faith is demonstrated in his regarding Jesus as a king, though he was hanging on a cross. The thief clearly claimed nothing of merit, but simply asked for mercy, as one would ask of a king. Jesus's promise emphasizes that the favor sought would be granted, not at some distant future date, but that very day, and that the favor would be to enjoy Jesus's presence in paradise. This would seem to exclude any idea of "soul sleep"—the idea that the soul sleeps in the time between death and the resurrection of the body—for the thief would have to be conscious to be comforted by being in Christ's presence. Thus, one detail we have about the intermediate state of believers is that immediately after death they are consciously enjoying being with Christ, in his presence.

The second key text is Phil 1:21–23. Here Paul links departing (death) and being with Christ with a single article, indicating that he regards them as one experience (*to analysai kai sun Christo einai*). He sees such a prospect as far better than the continuation of earthly life. Contrary to some who deprecate the intermediate state as "a highly attenuated and limited type of existence,"[35] Paul sees the prospect of being with Christ as making even a limited type of existence so desirable that he places it above continuation of his embodied life on earth apart from Christ.

Yet, the intermediate state is still just that, intermediate, and it should not be surprising if there is a stronger desire for our final state, with resurrected and glorified bodies as well as perfected spirits. This desire may

---

[35] Davis, "Eschatology and Resurrection," 387.

explain some of Paul's comments in the third key text on the intermediate state, 2 Cor 5:1–10. The key phrase for the doctrine of the intermediate state in this text is from verse 8: "away from the body and at home with the Lord." The preceding phrase of verse 7 gives another blessing of the intermediate state: we will no longer "walk by faith," but then by sight. However, much scholarly discussion has been concerned with the reference to "an eternal dwelling in the heavens" in verse 1.[36] Paul contrasts this eternal house with the earthly tent we live in now (our present body) which is destroyed in death. Paul speaks of the longing to be clothed with this "heavenly dwelling," and thus not to be found "naked" (vv. 2–3).

There are several understandings of what Paul is longing for here. Some see Paul expressing such repugnance for the nakedness of disembodied existence that he longs for and expects that immediately at death he will receive a "heavenly dwelling" (v. 2), an intermediate form in which he will live until the resurrection. [37] But the "heavenly dwelling" of verse 2 is more likely to be identified with the "eternal dwelling in the heavens," which is eternal, not intermediate. This notion of an intermediate body is thus not a very widely held opinion.

Some appeal to this text as support for the idea of immediate resurrection, that "at the moment of death, God raises the body and reconstitutes the person."[38] This would allow the heavenly dwelling which Paul desires to be the eternal dwelling of his resurrected body, but this theory faces the strong New Testament evidence that the resurrection of the body awaits the return of Christ and the eschaton, not the moment of each person's death. Moreover, we can see that, rather than immediately being resurrected, bodies remain in the grave after death.

Murray Harris suggests that Paul is responding to opponents of the bodily resurrection at Corinth, those he called "proto-Gnostics," who

---

[36] Hoekema, gives a good discussion of the issues and lists numerous defenders of the differing positions, see Hoekema, *The Bible and the Future*, 104–8.

[37] Alcorn, *Heaven*, 58.

[38] Davis, "Eschatology and Resurrection," 388.

"denied any future, bodily resurrection but envisaged a disembodied immortality."[39] This may be a part of Paul's purpose, but it may also be that he is simply expressing his longing to still be alive when Christ returns. Then he could put on his "eternal dwelling," his resurrected and glorified body, without first experiencing the nakedness of the disembodied experience of the intermediate state. On this view, the intermediate state, while a gain because it means being with Christ in a state of "peace and bliss," it is not the consummation of our hope, which is to exist as God created and intended, as embodied spirits with resurrected bodies and perfected spirits.[40]

Historical Developments

Purgatory

One of the most important developments in Christian thinking about the afterlife was what we see as a deviation: the development of the idea of purgatory. To grasp purgatory, one must understand its background in the Catholic understanding of sin and its consequences and how we are purified from sin. Sin leaves us in need of forgiveness. The way forgiveness came to be dispensed in Catholicism was through the sacrament of penance. The sinner is called to contrition of heart, confession with the mouth, and satisfaction of works; the Church is then authorized to pronounce God's forgiveness. This sacramental forgiveness brings "remission of the eternal punishment of sin, but temporal punishment of sin remains."[41] As one Catholic theologian puts it, the Church could administer the forgiveness

[39] Murray J. Harris, "2 Corinthians," in *EBC*, vol. 10 (Grand Rapids: Zondervan, 1976), 347.

[40] See P. E. Hughes, *Paul's Second Epistle to the Corinthians*, NICNT (Grand Rapids: Eerdmans, 1962), 170–71.

[41] *Catechism of the Catholic Church* (Rome: Urbi et Orbi, 1994), 370 (par. 1472, 1473).

that removes the *guilt* of sin, but the individual was still responsible to pay "the *penalty* of sin."[42]

In the eleventh century and following, paying the penalty of sin was seen as involving the purging of the remnants of sin from one's being.[43] The possibility of doing this during one's life was doubtful, and thus the idea of purgatory grew up as the place where one went in the afterlife to complete the process of paying the penalty, which was often seen in terms of flames and punishment. The horrifying nature of purgatory, coupled with the idea that the living may do things to affect those in the afterlife, sparked the selling of indulgences in the period preceding the Reformation. An indulgence was seen as an act of the Church to cancel the penalty or temporal punishment one had to pay for their sins. Initially they were awarded by the Church in recognition of those who had done something noteworthy in service to the Church (such as serving in the Crusades), but in the years preceding the Reformation, they became "a convenient source of income for the Church" and were crassly sold to release a person, living or dead, from purgatory.[44] Luther was particularly incensed by the jingle of one indulgence-seller in his area, named Johann Tetzel: "When the coin in the coffer clings, the soul from purgatory springs."[45]

Even the Council of Trent recognized these problems and condemned the abuses involved with indulgences, but not the idea itself. More recently, the traditional idea of purgatory as a place of punishment, while still affirmed, has been largely replaced by the idea of purgatory as purification and preparation for entering the presence of God. Richard McBrien defines purgatory as "a process by which we are purged of our residual selfishness."[46]

---

[42] Richard P. McBrien, *Catholicism*, new ed. (New York: HarperSanFrancisco, 1994), 1169. Emphasis in original.

[43] McBrien, 1167. He adds, "It was not until the twelfth century, however, that the existence of purgatory as a place came into prominence."

[44] McBrien, 1170.

[45] See the fuller description of Tetzel's sales pitch in Roland H. Bainton, *Here I Stand: A Life of Martin Luther* (Nashville: Abingdon, 1950), 59–60.

[46] McBrien, *Catholicism*, 1168.

The *Catechism of the Catholic Church* says the punishment of purgatory is not something imposed from the outside but that it follows "from the very nature of sin," and that the pain involved is that of purifying oneself from sin.[47] This is the sense in which C. S. Lewis affirmed purgatory. He says,

> Our souls *demand* Purgatory, don't they? Would it not break the heart if God said to us, "It is true, my son, that your breath smells and your rags drip with mud and slime, but we are charitable here and no one will upbraid you for these things, nor draw away from you. Enter into joy"? Should we not reply, "With submission, sir, and if there is no objection, I'd *rather* be cleansed first." "It may hurt, you know"—"Even so, sir."[48]

There are numerous problems with the idea of purgatory. Some modern Catholics such as McBrien acknowledge that "there is, for all practical purposes, no biblical basis for the doctrine of purgatory."[49] Official Catholic teaching continues to affirm purgatory, more on the basis of tradition than biblical teaching, though the *Catholic Catechism* makes a brief reference to "certain texts of Scripture."[50] Purgatory is also claimed to be based on "the practice of prayer for the dead," which the *Catechism* claims is supported by 2 Macc 12:38–46.[51] In that text Judas Maccabeus takes up a collection to make a sin offering for comrades who had died in battle because they had not been loyal to the Lord, and he offers prayer for the dead. Yet even prayer for the dead gives no explicit basis for purgatory, not to mention that

---

[47] *Catechism of the Catholic Church*, 370 (par. 1472).

[48] C. S. Lewis, *Letters to Malcolm: Chiefly on Prayer* (London: Geoffrey Bles, 1963), 140.

[49] McBrien, *Catholicism*, 1166.

[50] *Catechism*, 268–69 (par. 1031), describes this doctrine as formulated at the Councils of Florence and Trent and thus established as a part of authoritative church tradition. The "certain texts of Scripture" are only identified in a footnote (1 Cor 3:15 and 1 Pet 1:7). Nowhere is exegetical evidence provided which shows that these texts do indeed support purgatory.

[51] *Catechism*, 269 (par. 1032).

2 Maccabees is not part of the canon that seems to have been recognized by Jesus, the apostles, and Protestant churches.[52]

Conversely, there are numerous texts that conflict with the idea of purgatory. How could the thief on the cross be promised to be with Christ in paradise the day of his death (Luke 23:43) if time in purgatory awaited him? Paul's expectation that death would result in being present with the Lord (Phil 1:21–23; 2 Cor 5:8) lacks the reservation of Lewis that cleansing would be needed first. The problem of cleansing that troubled Lewis reflects a deficient doctrine of glorification, traditionally understood by evangelicals as involving a completion of the process of sanctification, such that at death the spirits of the righteous are "made perfect," as those described in Heb 12:23.[53]

Jerry Walls understands this Protestant response to the doctrine of purgatory. Regarding the problem of how we become completely cleansed he says, "The common Protestant answer is that we get this character at the moment of death when God zaps us and instantly perfects us."[54] Walls, though himself a Protestant, disagrees with this view and argues that there is no reason why the sanctification process should not continue in the intermediate state, as we continue to cooperate with God. Of the texts cited above as contrary to purgatory, he says, "I do not see that these texts rule out purgatory."[55]

But Walls is mistaken to think that a person could be brought into God's presence with the sanctification process still incomplete. The prophet Habakkuk tells us that God's eyes "are too pure to look on evil" (Hab 1:13). He is also mistaken to think that by receiving punishment or doing anything

---

[52] On the issue of the canon, see Roger T. Beckwith, *The Old Testament Canon of the New Testament Church and Its Background in Early Judaism* (London: SPCK, 1985).

[53] Bruce A. Demarest calls this the "first phase" of glorification and cites the Westminster Shorter Catechism's description of this phase: "The souls of believers are at death made perfect in holiness, and do immediately pass into glory." Bruce A. Demarest, *The Cross and Salvation: The Doctrine of Salvation* (Wheaton, IL: Crossway, 1997), 469–70.

[54] Jerry L. Walls, *Heaven, Hell, and Purgatory: Rethinking the Things That Matter Most* (Grand Rapids: Brazos, 2015), 112.

[55] Walls, 114.

else that we can purge our sins. This is to call into question the finality and sufficiency of Christ's atonement and the centrality of grace in all of salvation. It is Christ who "gave himself for us to redeem us from all lawlessness" (Titus 2:14); it is God who cleanses us "from all unrighteousness" (1 John 1:9). We can do nothing to atone or purge or complete this process. We make no contribution to being predestined, to being called, to being justified, or to being glorified (Rom 8:30). God is the actor in all these phases of salvation. When we sing "Jesus paid it all," we deny the idea that there is a temporal punishment for sin, which believers work off in the afterlife. Sin may have temporal *consequences*, but we believe Jesus paid the penalty of sin and there is no temporal *punishment*. There is nothing we can or must do to add to or complete his punishment-bearing work. Jesus truly paid it all. And while it may seem inappropriate to just move from our present sinful existence straight into God's presence without being purged of our remaining sinfulness, that is what the purifying grace of glorification is all about. This grace is not so much a zap as it is bringing us to the end of the road we have chosen and been walking upon. Purgatory, even in its modern, milder, less fiery versions, contains some serious distortions of biblical truth.

Soul Sleep

Another historical development on what happens after death has been much less widely held than purgatory but perhaps also deserves brief mention. This is the idea called "soul sleep," or more technically, psychopanny. It attracted enough of a following around the Reformation among some Anabaptists, and even enough consideration from Martin Luther,[56] that

[56] There are varying opinions as to whether Luther believed in soul sleep or not. Bernhard Lohse, *Martin Luther's Theology: Its Historical and Systematic Development*, trans. and ed. Roy A. Harrisville (Minneapolis: Fortress, 1990), 326–28, cites statements from Luther on both sides of the issue and concludes that neither position can be claimed as Luther's true opinion. Rather, he says, "Luther could express himself in various ways" (328).

it drew forth from John Calvin his first theological treatise.[57] The lengthy subtitle to this tract explains the essential idea Calvin was attacking: "A refutation of the error entertained by some unskillful persons, who ignorantly imagine that in the interval between death and the judgment the soul sleeps, together with an explanation of the condition and life of the soul after this present life." This idea also attracted some interest in the late nineteenth century, becoming a doctrine of the Seventh-Day Adventists and Jehovah's Witnesses.[58]

The case for soul sleep rests on two points. First is the claim, "Human existence demands the unity of soul and body. If the body ceases to function, so must the soul." Second, "The use of 'sleep' in Scripture for death allegedly points to the cessation of consciousness."[59] But the first claim ignores the verses considered earlier that speak of the soul existing in God's presence after the death of the body, as well as the claims of many, including Paul, to have had out-of-body experiences.[60] The second claim is weakened by the agreement of most exegetes that sleep is a metaphor for death rather

---

[57] John Calvin, "Psychopannychia," in *John Calvin: Tracts and Treatises*, trans. and ed. Henry Beveridge, vol. 3: Tracts, Part 3 (Carlisle, PA: Banner of Truth, 2009), 413–90. It was originally published in 1534, when Calvin was only twenty-five, two years before the first edition of the *Institutes*.

[58] The website for Seventh-Day Adventists lists as Belief 26 the affirmation that before Christ's return and the resurrection, "death is an unconscious state for all people." They explain: "Death is like a deep sleep. Your body and spirit rests [sic] as the breath of life—which makes body and soul one and alive—has returned to God until the resurrection." "Death, the State of the Dead, and Resurrection," Seventh-day Adventist Church, accessed April 3, 2023, https://www.adventist.org/death-and-resurrection/. For Jehovah's Witnesses' advocacy of soul sleep, see *Knowledge that Leads to Everlasting Life* (Brooklyn: Watch Tower Bible and Tract Society of Pennsylvania, 1995), 82–83.

[59] E. F. Harrison, "Soul Sleep," in *Evangelical Dictionary of Theology*, 3rd ed., ed. Daniel J. Treier and Walter A. Elwell (Grand Rapids: Baker Academic, 2017), 829.

[60] For Paul, see 2 Cor 12:2–4; for others, see the discussion of near-death experiences in chapter 1 and Carol Zaleski, "Near-Death Experiences," in *The Oxford Handbook of Eschatology*, ed. Jerry L. Walls (Oxford: Oxford University Press, 2008), 614–17.

than the state of the soul after death.[61] Thus soul sleep has remained very much a minority view among Christians.

Theological Considerations

The Immortality of the Soul

An issue that warrants not only historical interest but also theological evaluation is one we mentioned briefly above, the immortality of the soul. Our question is, Does the Christian doctrine of the afterlife include the idea of the immortality of the soul? The immortality of the soul is a widespread belief found in many cultures, from the early Greek philosophers (particularly Plato), to Enlightenment thinkers like Kant, and continuing to be defended into recent times.[62] Perhaps due to the influence of Greek philosophy on early Christian theologians, the idea of the immortality of the soul came into Christian theology in the patristic era and is still explicitly affirmed today in the *Catholic Catechism*: "The Church teaches that every spiritual soul is created immediately by God . . . and also that it is immortal; it does not perish when it separates from the body at death, and it will be reunited with the body at the final resurrection."[63] Among Protestants, Calvin affirmed the idea but with some caution. In view of the statement in 1 Tim 6:16 that God alone possesses immortality, the soul cannot have immortality as part of its intrinsic nature, but only derivatively, as the gift of God.[64] Nevertheless, support among Protestants continued through the middle of the twentieth century until prominent New Testament scholar

---

[61] See the discussion of sleep as a metaphor for death rather than literal sleep in Leon Morris, *The Gospel According to John*, NICNT (Grand Rapids: Eerdmans, 1971), 542–43, n. 23.

[62] Davis, "Eschatology and Resurrection," 386, lists Plato, Kant, and many nineteenth and twentieth-century philosophers and thinkers among its defenders.

[63] *Catechism of the Catholic Church*, 93 (par. 366).

[64] See the discussion of Calvin's view and relevant citations from Calvin's works in Hoekema, *The Bible and the Future*, 88.

Oscar Cullmann issued a strong challenge to the idea of the immortality of the soul.[65] He attacked it as an "alien concept," arguing that "only resurrection is a genuinely Christian notion."[66] Since this time, most support for the immortality of the soul has been guarded and cautious. A good example of this is the discussion by Anthony Hoekema.[67]

He begins by surveying the relatively rare occurrences of the two Greek words often translated as "immortality" in English translations of the Bible, *athanasia* and *aphtharsia*. The first is found only three times, once to describe something true only of God (1 Tim 6:16) and twice to describe something that will be true of believers upon their resurrection (1 Cor 15:53–54). The second is used slightly more often, with the noun form appearing seven times, as does the corresponding adjective (*aphthartos*). The primary meaning and most common English translation of the noun form is incorruptibility, and for the adjective, imperishable,[68] though the adjective is used twice to call God "immortal" (Rom 1:23; 1 Tim 1:17). The strongest cluster of occurrences is in 1 Cor 15, where *athanasia* appears twice, *aphtharsia* four times, and *aphthartos* once, all in reference to what happens to humans in the final resurrection. Of this cluster of references, Hoekema says the immortality spoken of in these verses is of believers only, it is described as future, not a present possession, and it is of the person, not the soul. In fact,

---

[65] Hoekema lists A. A. Hodge, W. G. T. Shedd, and Louis Berkhof among Reformed theologians advocating the immortality of the soul in the nineteenth and twentieth centuries, see Hoekema, *The Bible and the Future*, 89.

[66] Davis, "Eschatology and Resurrection," 389. He adds that the challenge was first issued in 1956, but Cullmann's central work on the topic only appeared in English in 1964; Oscar Cullmann, *Immortality of the Soul or Resurrection of the Dead?* (New York: Macmillan, 1964).

[67] The following paragraph draws heavily from Hoekema, *The Bible and the Future*, 87–91.

[68] The BDAG lexicon lists "incorruptibility" as the first translation for *aphtharsia*, and that is the most common English translation in the CSB; it lists "imperishable" as the first translation for *aphthartos*, and that is the most common English translation in the CSB. Walter Bauer et al., eds., *A Greek-English Lexicon of the New Testament and Other Early Christian Literature*, 3rd ed. (Chicago: University of Chicago Press, 2000), 155.

he says categorically, "The Scriptures do not use the expression, 'the immortality of the soul.'"[69]

At the same time, the Scriptures do not explicitly deny the immortality of the soul. What the Scriptures do seem to rule out is immortality as "a natural property of souls,"[70] or the "inherent indestructibility" of souls.[71] This is a common philosophical understanding but is contrary to the biblical understanding. As we argued, the Bible does affirm the continuing existence of souls in the intermediate state, but whether that continuing existence is included in the Son's "sustaining all things by his powerful word" (Heb 1:3), is due to some unexplained "gracious and miraculous act of God,"[72] or is due to God granting the soul a derived immortality is not made clear. All these are possibilities.

The Intermediate State and Glorification

A second theological issue related to life in the intermediate state is the idea of glorification. Calling our present life beyond the grave "intermediate" could seem to separate it from glorification as it is usually related to our final state, but this distinction between what is intermediate and what is final may be important and is often overlooked. It reminds us that salvation is more than just the event of conversion. Paul mentions the sequence of predestined, called, justified, and glorified (Rom 8:30); some include sanctification and see a sequence of justification as the past tense of salvation, sanctification as the continuing or present tense of salvation, and glorification as the future and "final stage of the process of salvation."[73] Contrary to what many assume, salvation is not completed at the moment of conversion

---

[69] Hoekema, *The Bible and the Future*, 88.

[70] Davis, "Eschatology and Resurrection," 389.

[71] Hoekema, *The Bible and the Future*, 90.

[72] Davis, "Eschatology and Resurrection," 389.

[73] Millard F. Erickson, *Christian Theology*, 3rd ed. (Grand Rapids: Baker Academic, 2013), 924.

and not even at death. We do not take on our final and eternal state or go to our final or eternal home at death.[74]

So, if at death we enter the intermediate state, is glorification still a future hope for believers? Millard Erickson says it depends on how one defines glorification.[75] Some restrict glorification to what will happen to the bodies of believers at Christ's return, and the transformation described in 1 Cor 15:51–53 certainly merits the description of glorification and is a future event.[76] Others think the transformation of the spirit that will occur when we see Christ as he is (1 John 3:2) qualifies as the first phase of glorification.[77]

John Murray insists on the importance of limiting glorification to the future transformation of the body: "It is to dishonour Christ and to undermine the nature of the Christian hope to substitute the blessedness upon which believers enter at death for the glory that will be revealed when 'this mortal will put on immortality' (1 Cor. 15:54)."[78] But to argue that "the perfecting of the spiritual nature of the individual believer . . . at death" is the first phase of glorification is not a substitution for the glorification that all will experience at Christ's return but a complementary addition to it, recognizing glorification as "multidimensional,"[79] extending to spirit and body.

Murray further argues for limiting glorification to the resurrection of the body on the grounds that "glorification is something upon which all

---

[74] Alcorn, *Heaven*, 44. Alcorn thinks distinguishing where believers go after death, "the present Heaven or intermediate Heaven," from their final destination and true home, "the eternal Heaven or the New Earth" is an "important distinction."

[75] Erickson, *Christian Theology*, 924, n. 19.

[76] This is the position of John Murray, *Redemption Accomplished and Applied* (Grand Rapids: Eerdmans, 1955), 174–75; Wayne Grudem, *Systematic Theology: An Introduction to Biblical Doctrine* (Leicester, UK: InterVarsity, 1994), 828.

[77] Bernard Ramm, *Them He Glorified: A Systematic Study of the Doctrine of Glorification* (Grand Rapids: Eerdmans, 1963), 65; Erickson, *Christian Theology*, 924; Demarest, *The Cross and Salvation* (Wheaton: Crossway, 1997), 469–70. Demarest calls the glorification of the soul or spirit the "first phase" of glorification, but terms the glorification of the body as "glorification proper."

[78] Murray, *Redemption Accomplished and Applied*, 175.

[79] Erickson, *Christian Theology*, 924.

the people of God will enter *together* at the same identical point in time."[80] Receiving our resurrected and glorified bodies at the same time is certainly a wonderful way of manifesting the unity of all the members of Christ's body, but does it require restricting the use of the term "glorification" to refer to that event? We are called and justified at different moments in time. More important is the description of the spirits of the righteous who are now in "the heavenly Jerusalem" as already "made perfect" (Heb 12:22–23). If they are already "made perfect," should we not see them as glorified?

The stronger case seems to lie with those who argue for seeing glorification as "multidimensional," or as occurring in multiple phases,[81] with the glorification of the spirit being the first stage. Thus, at death the intermediate state begins to overlap with the final state, with the state of the spirit partaking of some of the blessedness of the final state, though that final state is still incomplete until the body is glorified as well.

Practical Applications

Contact with the Departed

If we continue to exist beyond death, it raises the question of the possibility of contact between those in the afterlife and those in this life. For example, there is the widespread assumption that after death, our departed loved ones are looking over our lives. We speak of them watching over us, perhaps being proud of what we are doing. There is one verse, Heb 12:1, that speaks of us as being surrounded by a "large cloud of witnesses," referring to those who have gone before us. The imagery may suggest that they are cheering us on, but if so, it is by their example of faith, not by their personal presence. It may be difficult for us to understand how painful it might be for a fully glorified spirit to behold all the sinfulness of this earth when they have the

---

[80] Murray, *Redemption Accomplished and Applied*, 175. Emphasis in original.

[81] "Multidimensional" is Erickson's word, see Erickson, *Christian Theology*, 924; Demarest speaks of "several phases," see Demarest, *The Cross and Salvation*, 469.

beauty of paradise and the presence of Jesus to hold their attention. It may be suggestive that one of the blessings promised to righteous King Josiah was the privilege of dying and not having to see the judgment that was about to fall on Jerusalem (2 Chr 34:28).

But what of the possibility of departed spirits actually appearing to those on earth? The Bible clearly commands people not to contact the departed, not to "consult a medium or spiritist, or inquire of the dead" (Deut 18:11). Isaiah commands the people rather to inquire of their God: "Should they inquire of the dead on behalf of the living? Go to God's instruction and testimony! If they do not speak according to this word, there will be no dawn for them" (Isa 8:19–20). Peter Kreeft suggests that the reason for this prohibition is our need for "protection against the danger of deception by evil spirits."[82] But as to the reality of the possibility of contact with the departed, Kreeft is emphatic: "Without our action or invitation, the dead often *do* appear to the living. There is enormous evidence of 'ghosts' in all cultures." He cites the "many trustworthy accounts" of appearances of three types of ghosts,[83] and states that "only a dogmatic *a priori* prejudice against them could prevent us from believing they exist."[84]

Kreeft himself may be too dogmatic on this point. There is only one text in Scripture that deals explicitly with the issue, Saul's attempt to communicate with Samuel after Samuel's death through a woman recognized as a medium (1 Sam 28:3–20).[85] Ronald Youngblood comments that this

---

[82] Peter Kreeft, *Everything You Ever Wanted to Know about Heaven: But Never Dreamed of Asking* (San Francisco: Ignatius, 1990), 33.

[83] Kreeft, 33–34, emphasis in original. He believes we can distinguish one type of ghosts who are "working out some unfinished earthly business or suffering some purgatorial purification," a second type who are "malicious and deceptive spirits," and a final type, "bright, happy spirits . . . who appear unbidden, at God's will, not ours, with messages of hope and love. They seem to come from heaven" (34).

[84] Kreeft, 34–35.

[85] It may be possible to argue that Moses and Elijah came in ghost form to appear with Jesus on the Mount of Transfiguration (Matt 17:3), but I have not found any commentator who makes that argument.

incident "has been the subject of intense debate since the earliest time," with some arguing that the woman had no real power over departed spirits and thus what really appeared was a demon masquerading as Samuel or that it was not the woman but God himself who sent Samuel to pronounce Saul's doom.[86] In any case, the text itself evidences the woman's shock when she sees Samuel (1 Sam 28:12), leaving the implication that it is God, and not her, who is in control of the situation. Moreover, since Saul does not see Samuel (v. 14), we are left to wonder if the woman saw a vision of Samuel or if his spirit truly appeared. Youngblood wisely comments, "An element of mystery suffuses 1 Samuel 28,"[87] and to claim this as a proof text for ghosts claims too much.

While the biblical evidence for ghosts and contact between the living and the dead is very sparse, with the emphasis on not seeking such contact, Kreeft is right that there is considerable extra-biblical evidence in the form of testimonies from individuals many would regard as reliable,[88] and to rule out the possibility of contact with the departed may be to go further than Scripture. It seems best to leave it as a possibility, but one we are encouraged not to explore.

Understanding Human Nature

We mentioned earlier the heated debate going on in theological anthropology concerning the human constitution: Are humans composed of only one substance (the body), or is there a dualism to the human constitution, even if we function holistically? The continued existence of persons, after and apart from their bodies, in what is commonly called the intermediate state, is the

---

[86] Ronald F. Youngblood, "1, 2 Samuel," in *EBC*, vol. 3 (Grand Rapids: Zondervan, 1992), 779.

[87] Youngblood, 780.

[88] Kreeft mentions the testimony of C. S. Lewis and Sheldon Vanauken of receiving visits from their departed spouses, see Kreeft, *Everything You Ever Wanted to Know about Heaven*, 33.

strongest evidence for some type of dualism.[89] The practical application of this understanding of our human nature is the need to care for both aspects of our nature, the physical and the spiritual. Some, indeed many Christians, care for their spirit but fail to care for their body, because they do not consider it a spiritual issue.[90] As we mentioned at the beginning of this chapter, nearly half of all those in a 2011 global survey stated they are unsure if there is anything that survives the death of the body.[91] Such people would probably not even be aware of the need to care for their spirit. Interestingly, God seems to recognize that these two aspects of our nature can affect each other and thus addresses the prophet Elijah's physical needs for food and rest before addressing his spiritual needs for encouragement and re-commissioning to ministry (see 1 Kings 19). We need to live with a similar recognition that we are more than just bodies (there is a dualism in our constitution) and that the body and spirit can each affect the other (we function holistically).

An Answer to the Most Important Question

The answer to the question of this chapter, What lies beyond death?, is of eternal importance and thus incredible practical relevance. Biblical teaching on the intermediate state assures believers that the road they are on, though it may be "narrow" and "difficult" (Matt 7:14), leads to life. We know that what awaits us immediately after death is more than sleep, and certainly

---

[89] This is the principal argument of Cooper in *Body, Soul & Life Everlasting*: "Some sort of 'dualistic' anthropology is entailed by the biblical teaching on the intermediate state, a doctrine that is affirmed by the vast majority in historic Christianity." Copper, *Body, Soul & Life Everlasting*, xv.

[90] For example, on the simple issue of caring for one's weight, there is evidence that Christians are worse than most Americans. See Wendy Ashley, "Obesity in the Body of Christ," Baptist Press, January 1, 2007, https://www.baptistpress.com/resource-library/sbc-life-articles/obesity-in-the-body-of-Christ/.

[91] Williamson reports on a 2011 Global poll which found that 23 percent of those surveyed believed that at death we cease to exist, while 26 percent are agnostic on the question, acknowledging that they did not know what will happen to them after death, see Williamson, *Death and the Afterlife*, 5n1.

does not involve self-purging. It is life in the presence of Jesus. This doctrine is also a practical necessity in ministering to the grieving. What do we say to those who have lost a loved one and ask where is he or she now? We tell them that believers are rejoicing in the presence of Jesus, in peace and happiness. If asked about the destination of those who were not believers, we could respond to their loved ones, "You know him better than I do. What do you think?" Such a response avoids misrepresenting the situation but shows tact and sensitivity that can maintain open lines of communication for a gracious proclamation of the gospel.

CHAPTER 4

The Rapture and Tribulation

Introduction

Discussions of eschatology often utilize timelines in which the eschatological events to come are set in order. We have followed that example to some extent in the previous chapters. The first of the last things that happens to everyone is death. Though it comes at different times for different individuals, it is an important transition point for everyone. We next asked, What lies beyond death? That led us into last chapter's study of the intermediate state. The next event on the eschatology timeline is a matter of some debate and discussion.

Some look at the intense sense of expectation for the return of Jesus in the New Testament and think the next eschatological event is the return of Jesus for the church, or what some call the rapture. Daniel Akin champions this view and believes "the doctrine of *imminency* is a crucial and decisive argument" for the rapture as the next event.[1] Akin and those who

[1] Daniel Akin, "A Rapture You Can't Miss (1 Thess. 4:13–18); A Judgment You Must Face (2 Cor. 5:10); A Supper You Will Want to Attend (Rev. 19:1–10),"

share his view see imminent as meaning something that could happen at any moment. They argue the rapture will occur before the beginning of another major debated event within eschatology—a seven-year tribulation. This relationship of rapture to the tribulation is the dividing line between major camps within evangelical theology, from Akin's pretribulational rapture position to another major view, that of a posttribulational rapture, with several less popular mediating positions (midtribulational, prewrath, and partial rapture).[2]

A discussion of these positions on the relationship of the rapture to the tribulation is the main topic of this chapter, but there are two preliminary issues we will address first: the signs of the times in general and the sign of the great tribulation. Are there any signs that must precede the coming of Jesus?

Signs of the Time

Throughout church history, there have been many who have seen different events on earth as signs that the time for the return of Christ was nearing.[3]

---

in *The Return of Christ: A Premillennial Perspective*, ed. David L. Allen and Steve W. Lemke (Nashville: B&H Academic, 2011), 54. Akin provides a timeline which actually puts Israel being reestablished in the land before the rapture, but while Akin sees this as heightening expectation for the imminent rapture, he adds that "the rapture could have happened anytime following Jesus' ascension and before Israel was reestablished in the land" (50).

[2] See Akin, 53, and J. Daniel Hays, J. Scott Duvall, and C. Marvin Pate, *Dictionary of Biblical Prophecy and End Times* (Grand Rapids: Zondervan, 2007) for brief descriptions of these positions.

[3] The coronavirus pandemic of 2020 and following seems to have heightened this sense of the nearness of Christ's return. A 2006 Pew Research Center survey found 20 percent of Christians believed that Christ would return in their lifetime. A 2022 survey asked a slightly different but closely related question (Do you believe we're living in the end times?) and found 39 percent of all Americans answered yes; the percentage rose to 47 percent for Christians, 63 percent for evangelical Christians, and 76 percent of those in historically black churches. For the 2006 survey, see Russell Heimlich, "Christians Views on the Return of Christ," Pew Research,

Jesus himself is the source for many of these signs, particularly in what is called the Olivet Discourse (Matthew 24, with parallels in Mark 13 and Luke 21). To some, Paul contributes to the list of signs in his discussion of Israel's future in Rom 11:25–26 and his prophecy of a coming "man of lawlessness" in 2 Thess 2:1–12. Others connect this "man of lawlessness" with the figure that appears in Revelation 13, the beast or Antichrist.[4] Indeed, one major approach to the book of Revelation, the "futurist," interprets "everything from Revelation 4:1 [to the end of the book] as belonging to a period of time yet future,"[5] a period many associate with the return of Christ.

Some of the signs, like wars, earthquakes, and famines (Matt 24:6–7), seem to be characteristic of human history, and some have understood all the signs in this sense. Anthony Hoekema claims that "all the signs described in the New Testament characterize the entire period between Christ's first and second comings, and every decade of that period."[6] Others see a number of the signs as future. Since this means that certain events must happen before the return of Christ, can such people still use the word "imminent" to describe the Second Coming? Daniel Akin does not think so, assuming an "any moment" definition of imminent. Dictionaries differ in their definitions of "imminent," with some using the language of "likely to happen very soon," and others likely to happen "at any moment,"[7] and so some who

---

April 9, 2009, https://www.pewresearch.org/religion/2009/04/09/Christians-views-on-the-return-of-Christ/; for the 2022 survey, see Jeff Diamant, "About four-in-ten U.S. Adults believe humanity is 'living in the end times,'" Pew Research, December 8, 2022, https://www.pewresearch.org/short-reads/2022/12/08/about-four-in-ten-u-s-adults-believe-humanity-is-living-in-the-end-times/.

[4] Douglas Moo, "A Case for the Posttribulation Rapture" in *Three Views on the Rapture: Pretribulation, Prewrath, or Posttribulation*, 2nd ed., ed. Alan Hultberg (Grand Rapids: Zondervan, 2010), 209.

[5] Robert Mounce, *The Book of Revelation*, NICNT (Grand Rapids: Eerdmans, 1977), 42.

[6] Anthony A. Hoekema, *The Bible and the Future* (Grand Rapids: Eerdmans, 1979), 130.

[7] The Cambridge Dictionary and Collins Dictionary use the language of "very soon"; Dictionary.com uses "any moment." See *The Cambridge Dictionary*, "imminent," accessed May 7, 2023, https://dictionary.cambridge.org/dictionary/english/imminent;

see certain events as necessarily happening before the Second Coming see themselves as free to use the term "imminent" to describe their expectation of the Second Coming.[8]

However, dispensationalists affirm that while numerous signs will precede the Second Coming, there are none that must precede the rapture, which they differentiate from the Second Coming. Thus, they can affirm future signs to be fulfilled before the Second Coming and still maintain that the rapture is imminent, in their sense of "any moment." The signs to precede the Second Coming happen in the seven years following the rapture, a period they call the "great tribulation."[9]

The signs viewed by many as future events preceding the Second Coming are the preaching of the gospel to all nations (Matt 24:14), the saving of "all Israel" (Rom 11:26), the great tribulation and apostasy (Matt 24:21–24; 2 Thess 2:3), and the associated coming of the man of lawlessness (2 Thess 2:3), which is identified by many with the Antichrist (Revelation 13).[10] Ben Merkle is concerned that an overemphasis on the need for future signs to be fulfilled can dull the expectancy for the Second Coming and the call to watchfulness he sees in the New Testament. He argues that while there may be elements of these four signs that are still in the future, when and how those future elements are fulfilled may be "ambiguous to us," an ambiguity that he thinks is by "God's design." Since we cannot know when Jesus will return, Merkle argues, to say that he cannot return now is "presumptuous."[11] If Jesus can return now (or at least very soon), we must be constantly watchful and live in eager expectation.

Collins Dictionary, "imminent," accessed May 7, 2023, https://www.collinsdictionary.com/us/dictionary/english-word/imminent; Dictionary.com, "imminent," accessed May 7, 2023, https://www.dictionary.com/browse/imminent.

[8] See the discussion of different views of imminence in Hays, Duvall, and Pate, *Dictionary of Biblical Prophecy*, 208–9.

[9] Akin, "A Rapture You Can't Miss," 56.

[10] This list is from Benjamin L. Merkle, "Could Jesus Return at Any Moment? Rethinking the Imminence of the Second Coming," *Trinity Journal* 26, no. 2 (Fall 2005): 280.

[11] Merkle, 291–92.

In the opinion of this author, there is good reason to think that Rom 11:25–26 is not referring to a future event. The key phrase in verse 26 is "in this way all Israel will be saved," not "at this time all Israel will be saved." Merkle says, "Paul is not thinking temporally ('and then'), but modally ('and in this manner')."[12] But the case for a future fulfillment regarding the preaching of the gospel to all the nations and the coming of a great tribulation, apostasy, and a future man of lawlessness before Christ's return seems much stronger. At the very least, these signs will intensify and become clearer in the future as they reach their climax. As we mentioned earlier, one of these future signs, that of a great tribulation, is the dividing line concerning the relationship of the rapture and the tribulation. We turn now to the issue of this great tribulation and its relationship to the timing of the rapture.

Tribulation and the Great Tribulation

The normal New Testament word for "tribulation" is *thlipsis*, though it is also translated as "distress, persecution, and affliction." Robert Gundry, in his book *The Church and the Tribulation*, notes that it is overwhelmingly used (47 times out of 55) for the difficulties endured by God's people.[13] These difficulties include persecution (Acts 14:22; 1 Thess 1:6), imprisonment (Acts 20:23), and emotional distress (2 Cor 2:4). Though it may be sent from Satan to destroy us, tribulation is allowed by God to develop perseverance, character, and hope; thus, it is not to be viewed with horror but endured with faith. Paul says we are to rejoice in it (Rom 5:3–5), and Christ says tribulation is to be expected as characteristic of our life in this world (John 16:33). But the coming great tribulation is seen by many, especially by dispensationalists, to be radically different from the tribulation common to our lives today. They view this future great tribulation as a time of the outpouring of God's wrath on the unbelieving world. What is the biblical basis for this coming great tribulation?

---

[12] Merkle, 282.

[13] Robert H. Gundry, *The Church and the Tribulation* (Grand Rapids: Zondervan, 1973), 49.

There are two explicit references to a time of "great tribulation" in the New Testament,[14] Matt 24:21(ESV) and Rev 7:14 (ESV, NIV). A third verse that may serve as a background for both is Dan 12:1, which speaks of "a time of distress such as never has occurred since nations came into being." In the dispensational view of the great tribulation, these verses refer to an end-time period of seven years. The length of that time is derived from Dan 9:24–27 (the so-called seventieth week of Daniel 9) and from various references in the book of Revelation to "forty-two months" (Rev 11:2; 13:5), to "1,260 days" (11:3; 12:6), and even the phrase "time, times, and half a time" (12:14), interpreted as another reference to three and a half years.[15] While the context of Matt 24:21 and Rev 7:14 is that of *tribulation* due to *persecution of God's people*, the understanding of the great tribulation as a time of the outpouring of *God's wrath* on *the unbelieving world* comes from seeing much of Revelation 4–18 as describing that seven-year period, in which the great day of the wrath of God comes (Rev 6:17). John Walvoord says these chapters of Revelation "describe in the most graphic language possible the great catastrophic time of trouble that is ahead for the world."[16]

Israel also looms large in the dispensational view of the tribulation. The tribulation shows the collapse of Gentile power upon the return of Christ, but even more centrally, it deals with the restoration of Israel as a nation.[17] Dispensationalists affirm the rapture of the church as preceding the resumption of God's dealing with Israel. They anticipate a massive conversion of Israel during the tribulation, even as they undergo severe persecution from the Antichrist.[18]

---

[14] The phrase is found two additional times, in Acts 7:11 and Rev 2:22, but the first refers to a time of famine described in Gen 41:53–57, and the second refers to a specific act of divine judgment.

[15] Alan E. Johnson, "Revelation," in *EBC*, vol. 12 (Grand Rapids: Zondervan, 1981), 503.

[16] John F. Walvoord, *The Rapture Question*, rev. and enl. ed. (Grand Rapids: Zondervan, 1979), 45.

[17] Walvoord, 41–42.

[18] Paige Patterson, "Israel and the Great Tribulation," in Allen and Lemke, *The Return of Christ: A Premillennial Perspective*, 71.

Sam Storms notes the importance of Daniel 9 for this view of the great tribulation.[19] John Walvoord, for example, interprets the first sixty-nine "sevens" of Dan 9:24–26 as sixty-nine "weeks" of seven years each, indicating a total period of 483 years between "a decree to restore and rebuild Jerusalem" and the coming of Christ and his crucifixion ("the Anointed One will be cut off," v. 26). But Walvoord sees no literal fulfillment of verse 27 and the seventieth week in history thus far and thinks we should read this last week of years as a prophecy of a future seven-year end time tribulation, between the rapture and Christ's Second Coming.[20]

Apart from Daniel 9, it is difficult to see a strong basis for the idea of a seven-year tribulation. There are the references mentioned above in Revelation 11 and 12, but they place the emphasis on three and a half years, not seven—and it is far from certain that these numbers should be interpreted as literal units of time as opposed to symbolic.[21] As for Dan 9:24–27, Storms and others argue strongly that the dispensational interpretation of Daniel 9 is unlikely for several reasons, including the difficulty involved in finding a 483-year period which fits from Daniel's time to Christ's crucifixion.[22] A further difficulty is seeing an intended gap between the sixty-ninth

---

[19] "There's simply no way to overemphasize how crucial this paragraph in Daniel 9 is for dispensationalism, as well as the role it plays in the debate over the timing of the rapture." Sam Storms, *Kingdom Come: The Amillennial Alternative* (Ross-shire, Scotland: Christian Focus, 2012), 72.

[20] Walvoord, *The Rapture Question*, 26.

[21] G. K. Beale says the following about seeing the references to 42 months; 1,260 days; or time, times, and half a time as literal: "The futurist literalist perspective is implausible because of its misreading of John's visions, which contain heavenly symbols and not photographic images with a one-to-one identity to earthly realities." G. K. Beale, *The Book of Revelation: A Commentary on the Greek Text*, NIGTC (Grand Rapids: Eerdmans, 1999), 568. See Mounce for another commentator who sees the numbers in Revelation as "a conventional symbol for a limited period of time." Mounce, *The Book of Revelation*, 221.

[22] But see the complex argument offered by Gleason Archer to make a literal 483 years fit Daniel 9:24–26 in Gleason L. Archer Jr., "Daniel," *EBC*, vol. 7 (Grand Rapids: Zondervan, 1985), 111–21. The very complexity of the arguments of Archer and others suggests they may be forcing Daniel to fit a more literal pattern

and seventieth weeks, as there is nothing in the text that leads us to expect such a delay.[23] Storms concludes, "The meaning of the period [the seventy weeks], therefore, is THEOLOGICAL, not calendrical."[24]

This understanding of Daniel 9 leads to a quite different interpretation of the great tribulation. Rather than a future seven-year period in which the wrath of God is poured out on the earth, some view "the great tribulation" or "great distress" of Matt 24:21 as an event in the past, the destruction of Jerusalem in AD 70. D. A. Carson understands the instructions Jesus gives his disciples about what to do when this time falls (Matt 24:15–20) as "so specific that they must be related to the Jewish War," and adds that Jesus's comment that such distress will never be equaled again (Matt 24:21) implies that this time of great distress "cannot refer to the Tribulation at the end of the age," for there will be no distress or tribulation at all after Jesus returns.[25] Charles Quarles responds to the objection that the destruction doesn't qualify as the worst distress in the history of the world by pointing to the description left by the Jewish historian Josephus, which he believes proves that Jesus's statement "was no exaggeration." More than one million died and 97,000 were taken prisoner. From the atrocities cited by Josephus, Quarles says those who died "suffered so horribly that death must have been a relief" and those who survived "would live to regret it."[26]

One view of the great tribulation affirms a future seven-year time of cataclysmic judgments on the earth and intense persecution of those who have come to Christ since the rapture of the church, which happened before the tribulation began. A second view of the great tribulation takes

---

than he intended. For the difficulties with the interpretation of Archer, see Storms, *Kingdom Come*, 76–91.

[23] Walvoord, *The Rapture Question*, 26, acknowledges the criticism over the gap between weeks sixty-nine and seventy; whether his response is adequate or not may be left to the reader. See Storms, *Kingdom Come*, 83–84, for his argument against the idea of a gap between the last two weeks.

[24] Storms, 90. Emphasis in original.

[25] D. A. Carson, "Matthew," *EBC*, vol. 8 (Grand Rapids: Zondervan, 1984), 501.

[26] Charles L. Quarles, *Matthew*, EBTC (Bellingham, WA: Lexham Academic, 2022), 619–20.

it as entirely past. It occurred with "the events surrounding the forty-two-month long Neronic persecution" of the early church (AD 64–68, Rev 13:5) and the "forty-two-month long Jewish War with Rome" (AD 67–70, Rev 11:1–2), which included the destruction of the Jewish temple.[27] But a third view thinks that while the "great distress" of Matt 24:21 may be referring to what happened in AD 70, other passages in Scripture teach that tribulation characterizes the entire period between Christ's resurrection and second coming (John 16:33; Rev 7:14) with an intensification of that tribulation as Christ's return nears (2 Thess 2:1–8).[28] They anticipate a future time of intense tribulation, just not necessarily a literal seven-year period.

For all those who see a future element of eschatological tribulation, we can now return to the question with which we began this chapter: What comes next on the eschatological timeline? Is it the rapture or the tribulation?

The Rapture and the Tribulation

The rapture is the event described in 1 Thess 4:16–17. The Lord descends from heaven, the dead in Christ rise first, and then those still alive will be "caught up together with them in the clouds to meet the Lord in the air." Thus, "the rapture of the church refers to the 'catching up' of believers to

---

[27] Kenneth L. Gentry Jr., "Postmillennialism," in *Three Views on the Millennium and Beyond*, ed. Darrell L. Bock (Grand Rapids: Zondervan, 1999), 21–22. Gentry describes this as the "preterist approach" to the major judgment passages in the New Testament, including the events of Revelation 6–19, and as an approach held by some down through church history, but characteristic of the "theonomic strain of postmillennialism." Gentry lists twenty published advocates of this view, including himself.

[28] This is the view of Hoekema, *The Bible and the Future*, 150–51; Beale, *The Book of Revelation*, 567; Merkle, "Could Jesus Return at Any Moment?", 285; and Kim Riddlebarger, "The Great Tribulation—When and How Long?," *The Riddleblog*, October 6, 2022, https://www.kimriddlebarger.com/the-riddleblog/the-great-tribulation. It seems to be prevalent among contemporary evangelical amillennialists.

be united with Christ at his coming."[29] The event gets its name from the Latin translation (*rapiemur*) of the Greek word *harpagésometha*. The roots of the two words are *rapto* and *harpazō*, with *rapto* giving us "rapture." The Greek term *harpazō* has different shades of meaning, but the meaning here of being carried away by the Spirit is the basic idea of the rapture.[30]

For all those who accept the authority of Scripture, the truth of the rapture should not be a question. Scripture clearly teaches that it will happen.[31] The debate is over when it will happen, in relation to the future tribulation. As we mentioned at the outset of this chapter, the main options are the pretribulational rapture and the posttribulational rapture, with midtribulational, prewrath, and partial rapture as less prominent options. For all these positions with the exception of the first, the next event on the eschatological timeline is the tribulation; for the pretribulationist, the next event is the rapture.

Pretribulationism

The view that the rapture will precede the tribulation is closely associated with dispensational theology and is the most popular option among evangelical senior pastors today, affirmed by 43 percent.[32] While past defenders of this view often offered dozens of arguments, many of those arguments assumed interpretations of key texts that were themselves the subject of

---

[29] Hays, Duvall, and Pate, "Rapture," in Hays, Duvall, and Pate, *Dictionary of Biblical Prophecy*, 363.

[30] See Hays, Duvall, and Pate, 362, for the other shades of meaning of *harpazō* and all fourteen of the verses in which this term is found in the New Testament.

[31] Sadly, however, a 2016 survey of 1,000 Protestant senior pastors found one in four do not believe in a literal rapture. See Bob Smietana, "End times, rapture & Antichrist focus of new study," Baptist Press, April 24, 2016, https://www.baptistpress.com/resource-library/news/end-times-rapture-antichrist-focus-of-new-study/.

[32] Smietana, 3. However, the number supporting the pretribulation rapture drops to 28 percent among pastors under forty-five.

debate or assumed dispensational theology.[33] Recent defenses seem more modest and charitable. We will discuss here the case made for this position by Daniel Akin and Craig Blaising.[34]

Both make much of the relationship of the rapture to the day of the Lord as presented in 1 Thessalonians 4–5. The clearest biblical description of the rapture in Scripture is 1 Thess 4:17; that is followed by teaching on the day of the Lord in 1 Thess 5:2–11. Akin argues that a "natural chronological reading of 1 Thess 4:13–5:11 presents the rapture *before* the Day of the Lord."[35]

Blaising connects this day to the wrath from which believers are saved (1 Thess 5:10) and then gives detailed attention to the question he raises, "Should we understand the day of the Lord here to be coextensive with or identical to the seventieth week of Daniel [Daniel 9:27], which pretribulationists understand by the term *tribulation*?"[36] He believes the evidence from Daniel and the Olivet Discourse (Matthew 24; Mark 13; Luke 21) justify answering that question, yes. When Paul speaks of the day of the Lord in 1 Thessalonians 5, he is speaking of the seventieth week of Daniel, referenced by Jesus in Matt 24:15–21—the final tribulation. Suddenly, just before the onset of that time of tribulation, "without warning, like a thief, . . . those who belong to Christ will be raptured to be forever with the Lord while destruction overtakes the rest."[37]

To summarize, the major argument for the pretribulation rapture begins with the categorical statement that believers are delivered from the wrath of God (1 Thess 5:9); that wrath will be poured out on the day of the

---

[33] See Walvoord, "Fifty Arguments for Pretribulationism," in *The Rapture Question*, 269–76; J. Dwight Pentecost, *Things to Come: A Study in Biblical Eschatology* (Findlay, OH: Dunham, 1958), 193, gives twenty-eight such arguments.

[34] Akin, "A Rapture You Can't Miss," in *The Return of Christ*, 53–55; Craig A. Blaising, "A Case for the Pretribulation Rapture," in Hultberg, *Three Views on the Rapture: Pretribulation, Prewrath, or Posttribulation*, 25–73.

[35] Akin, "A Rapture You Can't Miss," 53.

[36] Blaising, 32. Emphasis in original.

[37] Blaising, 54.

Lord, which is the great tribulation, Daniel's seventieth week;[38] believers are delivered from that day of wrath by the rapture, which precedes that day.

The posttribulation response to this argument has been to claim that the wrath from which believers are saved is not that which happens in the tribulation,[39] but the eternal wrath of God, "the wrath of the final judgment."[40] And the means by which we are saved from that wrath is not the rapture; rather, the promise is that we will "be saved from God's wrath through him" (Rom 5:9 NIV)—"him" referring to Christ and his atoning death. Moreover, while believers are promised exemption from wrath, it is not necessary for God to remove believers from the world via the rapture to protect them. A parallel found in Scripture is the protection of the people of Israel. They were present in Egypt when the plagues fell, but some of those plagues fell selectively, only on the Egyptians (Ex 8:22; 9:6, 26; 10:23).

A second prominent argument offered for the pretribulation position is imminence.[41] Pretribulation advocates note the many passages warning us that the Lord will come at an unexpected time, as a thief in the night (Matt 24:42–44; 1 Thess 5:2). Thus, there can be no necessary "intervening events."[42] If the tribulation had to come first, these warnings would lose their force. If the tribulation had not occurred, they could know that Christ could not come. The only sense of imminence that fits these warnings is one that affirms that Christ could come "at any time."[43]

---

[38] The association of the day of the Lord with the wrath of God being poured out is strengthened, in Blaising's view, by the connection of the day of the Lord with the events of Revelation 6, which concludes with the cry that "the great day of their wrath has come" (Rev 6:17). See Blaising, "A Case for the Pretribulation Rapture," 59–61 for his argument for this connection.

[39] "According to the posttribulation view, there is a fundamental difference between the wrath of God and the Tribulation." Hays, Duvall, and Pate, "Rapture," 338.

[40] Moo, "A Posttribulation Response," in Hultberg, *Three Views on the Rapture*, 172.

[41] Akin, "A Rapture You Can't Miss," 54, regards this argument as "crucial and decisive."

[42] Walvoord, *The Rapture Question*, 73.

[43] Blaising, "A Case for the Pretribulation Rapture," 66.

The posttribulation response is to suggest that imminent may mean "very soon," not necessarily "at any time," and to argue that a sign such as the tribulation would not destroy watchfulness for, even with signs, some will be surprised by his coming (1 Thess 5:3). Moreover, it seems that the first Christians would not have thought Jesus could come at any moment, for Peter had been promised that he would live to see old age (John 21:18); Paul had been promised he would live to bear testimony in Rome (Acts 23:11); the whole church had been promised that they would bear witness "in Jerusalem, in all Judea and Samaria, and to the ends of the earth" (Acts 1:8). Would anyone having such promises think that Christ could rapture them and the whole church at any moment?

Blaising and Akin differ in how they argue for their position from the book of Revelation. Blaising says there is no "*explicit* mention of the rapture in the book of the Revelation," but he sees a possible implicit reference in the promise to the Philadelphian church in Rev 3:10.[44] Yet, when he asks the question of whether or not the promise of Rev 3:10 has "anything to do with the rapture's relationship to the tribulation," his answer is, "Maybe not." He adds that a pretribulation rapture is one possible way for the promise to be fulfilled, while a posttribulational rapture would not.[45] Akin and many other defenders of the pretribulational view are stronger on reading Rev 3:10 as an argument for their position.[46]

One final interesting aspect of Blaising's argument for the pretribulational position is his recognition that in the past, many dispensational defenders of this view have made use of arguments that presuppose classical dispensational theology.[47] He says that he has sought to offer an argument

---

[44] Blaising, 61–62.

[45] Blaising, 64.

[46] Akin, "A Rapture You Can't Miss," 54; Walvoord, *The Rapture Question*, 272.

[47] Akin, 54, does so to an extent in his argument concerning the "restrainer" of 2 Thess 2:6–7 and his argument concerning the prominence of Israel in the end times, but Blaising cites Pentecost, *Things to Come* and Walvoord, *The Rapture Question* as examples of this approach, see Blaising, "A Case for the Pretribulation Rapture", 70, n. 72.

that is textually based and could appeal to dispensationalists and non-dispensationalists alike. He states, "For progressive dispensationalists, the rapture occurs at the beginning of the tribulation because God wills it so, as revealed by Paul in his Thessalonian correspondence, not because it is necessary to separate the program of the church."[48]

Before discussing the other major option—the posttribulational position—we will mention more briefly three less widely affirmed options:[49] the **prewrath rapture** (Christ will rapture the church sometime during the second half of Daniel's seventieth week), the **midtribulational** position (Christ will rapture the church at the midpoint of Daniel's seventieth week, before the outpouring of wrath in the second half of that week), and the **partial rapture** position (Christ will rapture different believers at different times, based on their "spiritual maturity and preparedness"[50]). Of these three, prewrath seems to be growing in popularity, given its inclusion in the place of midtribulationism in a recent multiview book;[51] midtribulationism and partial rapture are less well represented in the literature on this topic.[52] Thus we begin with the prewrath position.

---

[48] Blaising, 71.

[49] According to a survey of 1,000 Protestant senior pastors, about 4 percent believe the rapture will occur during the tribulation (which would fit midtribulation or prewrath) and 4 percent believe the church will be raptured before the wrath of God is poured out on the earth (which sounds like prewrath but would also fit a midtribulation understanding of the point at which the wrath of God is poured out during the tribulation). There was no record of any in this survey affirming a partial rapture. See Smietana, "End times, rapture & Antichrist focus of new study," https://www.baptistpress.com/resource-library/news/end-times-rapture-antichrist-focus-of-new-study/.

[50] Hays, Duvall, and Pate, "Rapture," 328.

[51] Compare Richard R. Reiter, ed., *Three Views on the Rapture: Pre-, Mid-, or Post-Tribulational?* (Grand Rapids: Zondervan, 1984) with Alan Hultberg, ed., *Three Views on the Rapture: Pretribulation, Prewrath, or Posttribulation* (Grand Rapids: Zondervan, 2010). See also Hultberg, "Introduction," in *Three Views on the Rapture*, 22nn19–20 for several recent defenses of the prewrath position.

[52] A cursory online search found only two books each that feature the midtribulation and partial rapture view, none by established or well-known presses.

Prewrath Position

According to Alan Hultberg, "The prewrath position rests on two major theses: that the church will enter the last half of Daniel's seventieth week [the final seven years of world history] and that between the rapture of the church and the return of Christ to earth will be a significant period of extraordinary divine wrath."[53] In his presentation of the prewrath position, Marvin Rosenthal breaks Daniel's seventieth week into three major sections: "the beginning of sorrows," which lasts the first three and a half years; "the great tribulation," which begins with the abomination of desolation and continues for an undefined length of time; and "the day of the Lord," interpreted as the time of God's wrath. The church is raptured before the day of the Lord. He further sees "the cosmic disturbances associated with the sixth seal" of Rev 6:12–14 as signaling "the approach of the Day of the Lord," but that day does not actually begin until the opening of the seventh seal (Rev 8:1).[54]

For the first thesis, Hultberg argues that Matthew (Matthew 24), Paul (primarily 2 Thessalonians 2) and John (Revelation 7 and 13) all agree "that the rapture of the church will occur after the middle of Daniel's seventieth week," because they "expect the church to see the eschatological Antichrist," with Matthew and Paul describing the church's witnessing of the "abomination of desolation" (Matt 24:15; 2 Thess 2:4), and Matthew and John expecting the church to experience something of the eschatological tribulation.[55]

Thus far, the prewrath position has much in common with the posttribulation position. Both see the church as still on earth for much of the time of tribulation. In fact, one assessment of the prewrath position thinks it faces the possibility of "shifting into posttribulationism."[56] But here is

---

[53] Alan Hultberg, "A Case for the Prewrath Rapture," in Hultberg, *Three Views on the Rapture*, 109.

[54] Marvin J. Rosenthal, *The Prewrath Rapture of the Church* (Nashville: Thomas Nelson, 1990), 60.

[55] Hultberg, *Three Views on the Rapture*, 141.

[56] Hays, Duvall, and Pate, "Rapture," 352.

where the prewrath position moves closer to the pretribulation position by arguing "that the church avoids God's *parousia* wrath by being raptured."[57] Hultberg agrees that some references to being saved from God's wrath refer to salvation from God's eternal wrath (Rom 5:9, for example). But he argues that in 1 and 2 Thessalonians Paul sees a special outpouring of wrath in the latter half of the seventieth week of Daniel; he calls this "*parousia* wrath" from which the church is rescued via the rapture.[58] He argues that the *parousia* should be seen as a complex of events: the rapture, divine wrath, then the Second Coming to earth. He acknowledges this sequence is not explicit in Paul but thinks it is the best interpretation of Paul, strengthened by the fact that this pattern is explicit in Revelation: "The church will be raptured immediately prior to the outpouring of God's wrath in the day of the Lord, some time before the end of the tribulation period, and will return with Christ to earth at the end of that extended period of wrath."[59]

Midtribulationism

The central difference between this position and the prewrath position is the contention of mid-tribulationists that no other view, including prewrath, gives "a convincing explanation for the emphasis on the midpoint of Daniel's seventieth week."[60] It is true that Dan 7:25 and 12:7 refer to "a time, times, and half a time," which can be seen as three and a half years. Daniel 9:27 refers to some event in the middle of Daniel's seventieth week, and Rev 11:2 refers to an event happening after forty-two months. Additionally, at least one important presentation of the midtribulational view gives five objections to the posttributional view.[61] Some of these objections were not

---

[57] Hultberg, *Three Views on the Rapture*, 182.

[58] Hultberg, 142, 182.

[59] Hultberg, 153.

[60] Gleason L. Archer Jr., "The Case for the Mid-Seventieth Week Rapture Position," in Reiter, *Three Views on the Rapture: Pre-, Mid-, or Post-tribulational?*, 115.

[61] Archer, "The Case for the Mid-Seventieth Week Rapture Position," 116.

mentioned in the presentation of the prewrath position, such as the white-clad saints who come with Christ at his return and the need for "flesh-and-blood believers in the millennium." Both are seen to require a lapse of time between rapture and return.[62] But these arguments are in no way contrary to the prewrath position. The only truly distinctive aspect of the midtribulation view is the placing of the time of the rapture squarely in the middle of Daniel's seventieth week. However, it can also be noted that while some attention is called to the middle of Daniel's seventieth week, there is no explicit evidence of the rapture at that point.[63]

Partial Rapture

The last of the minority perspectives is the partial rapture view. This view argues that not all believers are raptured at the same time. Some are raptured before the seven-year tribulation, some partway through that period, and others after. The time of one's rapture "depends on one's spiritual maturity and preparedness." Being raptured is seen as a "reward for obedience."[64] But there are numerous objections to this position. This view sees watchfulness as a characteristic only of mature believers, whereas in the New Testament watchfulness characterizes all true Christians. Moreover, seeing the tribulation as a time of purgation for immature believers alive at the time of the rapture seems to demand a purgatory for immature believers who died before the rapture, thus requiring multiple resurrections of believers.[65] In 1 Thess 4:17, those raptured are simply "we who are still alive"; in 1 Cor 15:51, "we will all be changed." There is no indication of any distinction between mature and immature believers. This view has the weaknesses of both the pretribulation and posttribulation views, without the strengths of either, along with numerous

[62] Archer, 119–22.

[63] Hays, Duvall, and Pate, "Rapture," 286.

[64] Hays, Duvall, and Pate, 328.

[65] Gundry, *The Church and the Tribulation*, 201.

weaknesses of its own, and thus this view is by far the least favored by students of eschatology.[66]

Posttribulationism

The strongest argument for posttribulationism is at the same time the strongest argument against all the other views. The New Testament seems to know only one second coming of Christ, while all the other views separate the rapture and the Second Coming into two second comings—the first his coming for the church and the second his coming with the church. According to one student of the subject, this "two-comings objection has been the most substantial and long-standing" objection to the pre-tribulation rapture position,[67] but would also apply to all the other positions, as all involve a distinction between the rapture and Second Coming. One common response to this objection is that the Old Testament does not clearly point out that Christ would have two comings to earth, the incarnation and his return. Only in the light of the New Testament do we see those two comings. However, there is nothing beyond the New Testament to justify splitting the Second Coming into two events.

There is also a historical argument on this point. According to Alan Hultberg, in the early church, "The rapture, when it was discussed at all, was assumed to be contemporaneous with the return of Christ to earth to establish his kingdom; that is, to be posttribulational." For the rest of church history up to the nineteenth century, he adds of all the eschatological

---

[66] For the only two arguments for the partial rapture view I could find, see J. W. White, *The Partial Rapture Theory Explained: Escaping the Coming Storm* (Maitland, FL: Xulon, 2008) and Paul Shonebarger, *The Partial Rapture and the Left-Behind Church* (self-published, 2020).

[67] See the dissertation defending the pretribulation rapture from the two-comings objection by Jason Whitlock, "The Coming of the Lord as an Extended Unified Complex of Events: A Proposed Response to the Two 'Second Comings' Objection to Pretribulationism" (PhD diss., Southeastern Baptist Theological Seminary, 2015).

traditions that developed, "The issue of the timing of the rapture was a nonquestion in these traditions."[68] It seems likely the reason why it was a nonquestion is that the assumption from the days of the early church continued. Hays, Duvall, and Pate say that before the rise of pretribulationism in the mid–nineteenth century, "the vast majority of Christians throughout church history favored the posttribulation view."[69] This may be true, but it is only fair to recognize that there was very little discussion of the rapture at all for most of church history, especially following the patristic period. In any case, contemporary posttribulationists do not make their case from church history but from their reading of Scripture.

Douglas Moo begins his case by clarifying the key terms "rapture" and "tribulation."[70] He notes that in the key rapture passage, 1 Thess 4:17, "the rapture is not a movement to escape something but a movement to be joined to something,"[71] or better, to be joined to someone: "to meet the Lord." This is confirmed by a look at the context and concern of the larger passage of which this verse is a part, 1 Thess 4:13–18. The comfort and encouragement Paul is giving the Thessalonian believers is not that they will escape the time of tribulation on earth but that they and their departed loved ones will both be with Jesus when he comes.

Moo also speaks at length about the meaning of tribulation. He thinks we too quickly link tribulation with a future time, while the overwhelming majority of occurrences of the word for tribulation in the New Testament (*thlipsis*) "indisputably refer to the 'tribulation' that believers experience

---

[68] Hultberg, "Introduction," in Hultberg, *Three Views on the Rapture*, 15.

[69] Hays, Duvall, and Pate, "Rapture," 340.

[70] Moo makes the case for the posttribulation view in two prominent three-view books: Douglas Moo, "The Case for the Posttribulation Rapture Position," in *Three Views on the Rapture: Pre-, Mid-, or Post-Tribulational*, ed. Richard R. Reiter (Rapids: Zondervan, 1984), 169–211; and Douglas Moo, "A Case for the Posttribulation Rapture," in *Three Views on the Rapture: Pretribulation, Prewrath, or Posttribulation*, ed. Alan Hultberg (Grand Rapids: Zondervan, 2010), 185–239. The presentation above will draw heavily from the work of Moo in the second of these two books.

[71] Moo, "A Case for the Posttribulation Rapture," 186.

throughout this age." He does not deny that there will be "an especially intense and worldwide time of suffering for God's people that will come at the end of history," and "a climactic experience of God's wrath." But he does think we should see these events not as belonging only "to a new period of salvation history but as the climax to an era already begun."[72] If then tribulation has always been experienced by believers, he wonders if it makes sense that the last generation of believers would be exempt from tribulation. He sees nothing in the texts on the last intense time of tribulation that suggests the suffering of that time will be "greater in degree than what many believers throughout the age must suffer." Moo knows that some who hold other views acknowledge that believers may suffer persecution; what they deny is that believers will suffer the wrath of God.

So, he questions the notion that "references to the wrath of God require that believers be physically absent during the final tribulation."[73] He believes only in Revelation are there possible references to the wrath of God associated with the final tribulation (Rev 6:16–17; 11:18, 14:10, 19; 15:1, 7; 16:1, 19; 19:15). Of these, he thinks many relate to a final judgment after the final tribulation, especially if, as he sees it, Revelation follows a "'recapitulative' structure," in which the same events are referred to multiple times. Thus, it is not clear to Moo that the wrath of God falls during the final tribulation; perhaps it falls during a final judgment after the final tribulation. But even if the wrath of God falls during the final tribulation, Moo thinks we must take account of "the selective nature of God's judgments and wrath."[74] This is found in Rev 9:4, when the locust swarm harms "only those people who do not have God's seal on their foreheads," or Rev 16:2, where the bowls of God's wrath produce painful sores "on the people who had the mark of the beast and who worshiped its image." While it may or may not be speaking of final tribulation wrath, Isa 26:20–21 has the same idea of wrath falling selectively.

---

[72] Moo, "A Case for the Posttribulation Rapture," 187–88.

[73] Moo, 192.

[74] Moo, 192–93.

After beginning with the more general arguments—namely, there is nothing that leads us to separate the Second Coming into two events and to believe there must be a rapture to allow believers to avoid the wrath of God that falls during the final tribulation—Moo proceeds to more specific textual arguments. Three will be included here.

The first argument is from the vocabulary used for the Second Coming. All three of the key Greek terms (*parousia*, *apokalypsis*, and *epiphaneia*) are clearly used for the posttribulational return of Christ,[75] but all are also used for the rapture.[76] There is no vocabulary used for the rapture not also used for the posttribulational Second Coming. Moreover, these three terms are used for an event that is the hope and expectation of believers.[77] Moo concludes, "If, then, believers are exhorted to look forward to this coming of Christ, and this coming is presented as posttribulational, it is natural to conclude that believers will be present through the tribulation."[78]

The second step deepening this argument is to examine the texts claimed by pretribulationists as "the three principal Scriptures revealing the rapture—John 14:3; 1 Corinthians 15:51, 52; and 1 Thessalonians 4:13–18."[79] John 14:3 says nothing more than that we will be with the Lord. No specific details are given as to when that will occur, especially in relation to an end time tribulation. Thus John 14:3 does not constitute an argument for a rapture separate from the Second Coming. In 1 Cor 15:51–52, the reference to the "last trumpet" is suggestive. Moo says the parallel passage to this account found in Matt 24:31 with Jesus teaching on the sound of the trumpet "can hardly be ignored." That trumpet is "manifestly posttribulational."

---

[75] Moo cites Matt 24:3 for *parousia*; 2 Thess 1:7 for *apokalypsis*; and 2 Thess 2:8 for *epiphaneia*.

[76] Moo, 195.

[77] See 1 Thess 2:19; 1 Cor 1:7; 1 Tim 6:14.

[78] Moo, 195. See n. 5 for others who make this same point, including G. E. Ladd, *The Blessed Hope: A Biblical Study of the Second Advent and the Rapture* (Grand Rapids: Eerdmans, 1956), 63–68.

[79] John F. Walvoord, *The Blessed Hope and the Tribulation: A Study of Posttribulationism* (Grand Rapids: Zondervan, 1976), 50.

Together with the use of trumpets in the Old Testament, this background suggests that the trumpet in 1 Cor 15:52 marks "the time when the Jewish nation experiences its eschatological salvation (Isa 27:12–13) after the final tribulation (Matt 24:31)."[80]

Neither of these first two texts gives any clear evidence of a rapture separate from and preceding the Second Coming. But by common consent, 1 Thess 4:13–18 is the key text for the rapture. In that text, Moo sees "four indications that indicate a posttribulational setting."[81] First are the numerous parallels with Matthew 24 and the Olivet Discourse (angels, clouds, a trumpet, and gathering of believers). Since Matthew 24 and the *parousia* of the Olivet Discourse are clearly posttribulational, it suggests that the same would be true of the *parousia* in 1 Thessalonians 4. Second is the reference to the trumpet, which Moo claims is "an established symbol for the ushering in of the time of Israel's salvation and judgment." Third are the parallels with Dan 12:1–2 (dead as sleeping, presence of Michael, resurrection and deliverance of God's people). But in Daniel 12, the resurrection is clearly after the final tribulation. Fourth is the use of the word *apantēsis* to describe the meeting of the saints with the Lord in the air in 1 Thess 4:17. The word was used in the culture of Paul's day to describe citizens of a city who would go out to meet a visiting dignitary and accompany him back to their city. In the two other places where the word is used in the New Testament it has this meaning (Matt 25:6; Acts 28:15). Craig Blomberg says that, in view of all the other "imperial language" Paul uses for Christ in 1 Thessalonians, "it would be amazing if Paul was not also thinking of an imperial *apantēsis* when he used that word."[82] Alan Hultberg suggests that the return to the point of origin may not be immediate, thus making a separation between

[80] Moo, "A Case for the Posttribulation Rapture," 198. See the concurring view of Gundry, 148.

[81] Moo, 199–200.

[82] Craig L. Blomberg, "The Posttribulationism of the New Testament: Leaving 'Left Behind' Behind," in *A Case for Historic Premillennialism: An Alternative to 'Left Behind' Eschatology*, ed. Craig L. Blomberg and Sung Wook Chung (Grand Rapids: Baker Academic, 2009), 79.

rapture and return possible.[83] Evidence of such a separation is not found in this or the other two principal texts (John 14:3 and 1 Cor 15:51–52), which some claim as teaching a rapture that is distinct from the Second Coming.[84] All the evidence points to one Second Coming.

Moo's second line of specific textual argument includes a consideration of 1 Thess 5:1–11, 2 Thessalonians 1–2, the Olivet Discourse, Rev 3:10 and Revelation as a whole. Of these, 2 Thessalonians 2 seems to be a strong support for the posttribulational position. Paul begins with announcing his concern as the *parousia* of Christ and our being gathered to him, words that seem to describe the rapture. He then connects that event with the "day of the Lord" (v. 2) and the possibility that the Thessalonians may have become fearful that the day of the Lord had come, and they had missed it. What is instructive is the way Paul seeks to allay their fears. If the rapture was to precede the day of the Lord, Paul could easily have pointed out to them they had not been caught up to meet the Lord in the clouds. Instead, he gives events that must take place first, at least one of them, the revelation of the man of lawlessness (whom Moo calls "the Antichrist"), an event that is to take place during the final tribulation.[85] There are a number of interpretive challenges in this text (particularly the identity of the restrainer of v. 6) but none that obstruct the support of this text for the posttribulational position. For how could the Thessalonians possibly have been worried that the day of the Lord had already come if they had been taught they would be raptured before it came, as claimed by other views?

A third line of argument for the posttribulation view is the "remarkable degree of consistency" of the order of end time events in "every important New Testament depiction of the end" under the posttribulation view; Moo gives a chart showing that order of events.[86] Numerous advocates of

---

[83] Hultberg, "A Case for the Prewrath Rapture," 143.

[84] Moo, "A Case for the Posttribulation Rapture," 201.

[85] Moo, 210; Blomberg, "The Posttribulationism of the New Testament," in Blomberg and Chung, *A Case for Historic Premillennialism*, 80–81.

[86] Moo, "A Case for the Posttribulation Rapture," 233; the chart is given on 240–41.

the pretribulation position have claimed otherwise, namely that there are numerous differences between rapture passages and Second Coming passages.[87] Moo responds that once we do not require every author to mention every event but recognize that the authors exercise some selectivity in mentioning only the events appropriate for their concern, those differences melt away and what is left is remarkable coherence.

Of course, the advocates of the other positions see weaknesses in Moo's position. Craig Blaising thinks Moo has not given the biblical theme of the day of the Lord sufficient consideration,[88] and Alan Hultberg differs with him on the issue of chronology in Revelation,[89] and Moo acknowledges that their criticisms are not without some merit.[90] He adds that there is a reason why evangelicals disagree on this issue: "The evidence is simply not clear-cut."[91]

In my opinion, the posttribulation position seems the best reading of the biblical teaching for three reasons. First, the other views separate rapture and Second Coming into two events when no text clearly distinguishes them and when such a separation also requires other twos (two trumpet blasts, two angelic announcers, etc.). Second, the other views understand Daniel and Revelation as giving us something of a chronology for end-time events, but I have increasingly wondered in recent years if we are not reading

---

[87] See, for example, Akin, "A Rapture You Can't Miss," 55–56, who lists nine differences between the rapture and the Second Coming "that are consistent with a pretribulational understanding of the rapture event."

[88] Blaising, "A Pretribulation Response," in Hultberg, *Three Views on the Rapture*, 255.

[89] Hultberg, "A Prewrath Response," in Hultberg, *Three Views on the Rapture*, 257–63.

[90] Moo, "A Rejoinder," in Hultberg, *Three Views on the Rapture*, 272. In response to Blaising's critique that he did not give sufficient consideration to the day of the Lord theme: "He is probably right; I should have spent more time here" (272). On his difference with Hultberg over Revelation, he says, "I hate to engage Hultberg in debate over the meaning of Revelation: he knows the book far better than I" (270).

[91] Moo, "A Rejoinder," 270.

the seventy sevens of Daniel 9 and especially the seventieth week of Daniel from a particularly Western and modern mindset and missing the symbolic nature of numbers that are more common in other cultures. The same is true of finding a chronology of events in Revelation. John is reporting a series of visions, and the number seven keeps reappearing. Should we not see some symbolism and overlapping or recapitulation in these series of sevens? Such interpretations do not call our doctrine of inerrancy into question; we are simply seeking to read these texts as the original authors and audiences would have read them. Third, 2 Thessalonians 2 seems very hard to reconcile with a pretribulational position; perhaps a prewrath position could be argued, but posttribulationism clearly fits it, and the other two reasons elevate the posttribulation position over all the other options for me.

At the same time, I want to acknowledge the possibility that I have not presented the arguments for the other views as fully and strongly as they could be presented. That was not my intention. I have tried to present each view as fully and fairly as possible in the limited space of one chapter, but I am aware that I devoted more time and space to the view I favor and so want to urge my readers to read for themselves the arguments for the other views. Only then should they make their decision on this issue.

We have devoted considerable attention to this issue, but we should close by acknowledging that little attention is given to the rapture and its relationship to a future time of tribulation outside of premillennial and dispensational circles. All who affirm the Bible should accept 1 Thessalonians 4 and the reality of the rapture, but historically, for those in the amillennial and postmillennial traditions, "the issue of the timing of the rapture" has been "a nonquestion."[92] We think it is a valid and important question for a book on eschatology to address, but we acknowledge that it is dwarfed by the importance of the next issue on the eschatological timeline: the return of Christ to earth. That will be the topic of the next chapter.

---

[92] Hultberg, "Introduction," 15.

CHAPTER 5

The Second Coming of Jesus

Introduction

Christ's return is the most prophesied event in the New Testament (more than 250 times) and has been included in the great historic creeds of the church since the beginning. The significance of his return is monumental. We think of Jesus's first coming as incredibly transformative, the very turning point of history. Yet it is the Second Coming that will bring us full salvation (Heb 9:26). At his second coming, we will receive our resurrected and glorified bodies (1 Cor 15:52), as part of his "making everything new" (Rev 21:5). It makes everything now temporary and intermediate. This world is subject to immediate and drastic interruption.

The reality of his return has not been an issue of controversy among orthodox theologians. In a recent survey, 97 percent of the pastors of evangelical and historically black churches affirmed belief in a literal, personal

Second Coming,[1] though certain details regarding his return remain controversial. We will survey this doctrine by asking four questions:

1. What is the return of Christ (the nature of this event)?
2. When will he return (the timing)?
3. Why will he return (the purpose)?
4. What should be our response (the application)?

The Nature of Christ's Return

It may seem obvious, but we need to say at the outset that Christ's return will be a future event. This is because there are two positions that oppose the idea of a future return of Christ. Full preterists, like those in the International Preterist Association, believe that "the final events of the redemptive drama came to pass in the first century within the apostles' generation (before A.D. 70)." Christ's return was "in some sense in connection with the Fall of Jerusalem at 70 AD."[2] While we do attach some importance to a possible coming of Christ in judgment in AD 70, many other events associated with the return of Christ have not happened. The preterist view remains very much a minority view.[3]

Others in the school of what is called realized eschatology insist that the New Testament emphasis is that in Jesus, the kingdom of God has already come. They want to highlight the reality of Christ's presence with his people now.[4] But Christ's presence now, mediated by his Spirit (John 14:18), does

[1] Aaron Earls, "Vast majority of pastors see signs of end times in current events," Lifeway Newsroom, April 7, 2020, https://news.lifeway.com/2020/04/07/vast-majority-of-pastors-see-signs-of-end-times-in-current-events/#:~:text=A.

[2] See the position of the International Preterist Association at https://www.preterist.org/about-us/what-is-preterist-view/, accessed July 20, 2023.

[3] Though they claim that their view is "capturing significant media attention," it is still largely unknown, and their claim that the Second Coming, resurrection, and judgment have already been fulfilled is not considered viable by most students of eschatology.

[4] See the discussion in G. M. Burge, "Realized Eschatology," in *Evangelical Dictionary of Theology*, 3rd ed., ed. Daniel J. Treier and Walter A. Elwell (Grand Rapids: Baker Academic, 2017), 724.

not rule out a fuller, personal presence in the future. Those who disbelieve in the "literal future return of Christ" could suggest that Christ's return was the resurrection, or Pentecost.[5] However, this cannot be, for his return is prophesied after these events throughout the New Testament, by Jesus himself before his death (Matt 24:30; 25:31; John 14:3), by angels after his ascension (Acts 1:11), by Paul as our "blessed hope" (Titus 2:13) and as our comfort in the face of death (1 Cor 15:51–52; 1 Thess 4:16–17), by Peter in the face of doubters (2 Pet 3:4, 10), and by John as the last prophecy of Scripture (Rev 22:20).

It will be a personal, visible return, in "the same manner" as his ascension (Acts 1:11; 1 Thess 4:16: "the Lord himself"). We need to state this clearly, for some advocates of realized eschatology could view the return of Christ as his coming into the heart of a believer. But the three terms commonly used for the return of Christ all have this personal, visible idea.[6]

For example, the word *parousia* is found twenty-four times in the New Testament referring to Christ's return (see Matt 24:3; 1 Thess 2:19; and others). The word literally means "presence," but by the time of the New Testament it had developed a special significance, sometimes used for the arrival of a king.[7] As a result of his arrival, he was present, and thus *parousia* means the presence of the one who has arrived. The expectation is clearly that of a personal, visible return.

The second word, *apokalupsis*, means "revelation" (1 Cor 1:7; 2 Thess 1:7; Rev 1:1). This word may signify that, while Christ is present in the world today (through the Spirit, the Word, and his church, as well as his own divine omnipresence), he is not physically revealed yet. Again, that future revelation will be of a more personal and visible nature. His true nature was

---

[5] See Anthony A. Hoekema, *The Bible and the Future* (Grand Rapids: Eerdmans, 1979), 295. He cites C. H. Dodd as a representative of realized eschatology who does not believe in a literal future coming of Christ.

[6] Hoekema, 171.

[7] Anthony C. Thiselton, *Life after Death: A New Approach to the Last Things* (Grand Rapids: Eerdmans, 2012), 90–91; Georg Braumann, "Present," in *NIDNTT*, ed. Colin Brown (Grand Rapids: Zondervan, 1976) 2:898.

hidden during his first coming in humiliation; his second coming will be in glory, and his true nature will be revealed to all.[8] For this reason, the last book of the Bible, which is occupied with his return, is sometimes called "The Apocalypse," from "the *apokalupsis* of Jesus Christ" (Rev 1:1).

The third word, *epiphaneia* (Titus 2:13; 2 Tim 4:8), was used in Greco-Roman culture for the appearing of a deity who came to help his people.[9] Our English word "epiphany" is derived from this Greek word and is used to describe an encounter with God. Christ will appear physically, visibly, and personally in order to come to our aid and accomplish our final deliverance. This is our blessed hope.

It is important to balance this affirmation of the future coming of Christ with the belief in his presence in the world today (Matt 28:20), through means such as the Word, the Spirit, and the body of believers. While some may overemphasize the absence of Christ, surely the greater danger among most believers is neglecting or even denying the return of Christ. For example, the Catholic Church has historically emphasized the presence of Christ now, in the Eucharist and in his body, the Church. The Catholic Church has also historically had a very weak emphasis on eschatology and the return of Christ.[10] The danger for most evangelicals may be to rest satisfied with our experience of his presence now through his Spirit and in his Word. Do we deeply desire his full presence? Does the prayer of the early church, "*Maranatha*!" spontaneously burst from our hearts? The best of evangelical piety and theology has always sought an intimate, personal relationship with Christ that desires an abundance of his presence. This fullness of his presence is one of the blessings his return will bring.

Among modern liberal theologians, the tendency has been to dismiss Christ's return entirely, with an attitude remarkably similar to that of

---

[8] Thiselton, *Life after Death*, 91.

[9] Thiselton, 91; Buckhard Gärtner, "Revelation," in *NIDNTT* (Grand Rapids: Zondervan, 1978) 3:317.

[10] G. C. Berkouwer, *The Return of Christ*, trans. James Van Oosterom, ed., Marlin J. Van Elderen (Grand Rapids: Eerdmans, 1972), 144–45.

2 Pet 3:4, specifically scoffing. For Rudolf Bultmann, the Second Coming is another one of the myths of the New Testament that must be demythologized and recast in terms of existential philosophy to be relevant to modern people. We may acknowledge with G. C. Berkouwer that some aspects of Christ's return are difficult to conceptualize.[11] For example, when Matt 24:30 says he will come "on the clouds," is that a literal description or symbolic (for clouds have often been symbols of God's presence in Scripture)? When Rev 1:7 says every eye will see him, how is that to be accomplished? After all, a good portion of the earth will be experiencing nighttime when Christ returns, and millions will be sleeping. When 1 Thess 4:15–17 says we will rise to meet the Lord in the air, how will millions and millions of believers all get close enough to really be with him? Yet, despite these questions, most believers have steadfastly accepted the New Testament's ringing promise that he will return. Only then will we understand.

Alongside "future," "personal," and "visible," one other adjective should be included to describe the nature of Christ's second coming—"glorious."[12] Christ humbled himself at his first coming (Phil 2:7–8), but at his second coming every knee will bow and every tongue confess that Christ is Lord (Phil 2:10–11). They will do so because he will be unveiled, and every eye will see "the appearing of the glory of our great God and Savior" (Titus 2:13). Moses asked God, "Please, let me see your glory" (Exod 33:18). At that time, Moses's request could only be partially answered, but when Christ returns, he will be seen "with power and great glory" (Matt 24:30). This prospect led the early Christians to cry, *Maranatha* (1 Cor 16:22)!

The Time of Christ's Return

In the previous chapter, we mentioned the intense sense of expectation for the return of Christ in the New Testament and the controversy over whether the return of Christ is imminent, in the sense that it could happen

[11] Berkouwer, *The Return of Christ*, 163–65.

[12] Hoekema, *The Bible and the Future*, 172.

at any moment, or whether it is imminent in the sense that it could happen very soon with the caveat that some events must happen first. The New Testament word for the time of Christ's coming is "soon" (Rev 22:20), or "near" (Jas 5:8), but this teaching of the soon return of Christ exists in tension with two other biblical teachings.

First, the time of Christ's return is unknown, even by Christ (Mark 13:32). If it is unknown, how can the biblical writers say it is "soon"? For contemporary Christian believers, how can an event that has not happened in nearly 2,000 years still be described as "soon"?

Second, how can the return of Jesus be described as "soon" if there are events that must happen before his return? In the previous chapter, I argued that an "apostasy" and the appearing of a "man of lawlessness" associated with the end time tribulation must happen before Christ's return (2 Thess 2:3); I also wonder if the proclamation of the gospel to all nations has happened, as it must happen before "the end will come" (Matt 24:13). Moreover, if signs must happen first, how can Christ's return be unexpected (Matt 24:44; 1 Thess 5:2–3; 2 Pet 3:10), like the coming of a thief at night?

These three biblical teachings—the nearness of Christ's return, the unknown time of Christ's return, and the sign events that must take place before Christ's return—all call for further comment.

The Nearness of Christ's Return

It is clear that the New Testament rings with a vibrant and joyful expectation of Christ's return, but two questions are not so clear. First, does the New Testament teach that Jesus's return *would* occur very soon, in fact, within the first generation of those living after the resurrection? If we say yes, then we must see error in the New Testament.[13] If we say no, we must find an explanation for Matt 24:34 and the attitude of expectancy regarding the

[13] Such a claim would be error unless we side with the International Preterist Association. As mentioned earlier in the chapter, it claims that Jesus did say he would return within the first generation and did so, in AD 70. But this view of the

nearness of Christ's return that pervades the New Testament. Second, does the New Testament teach that Jesus *could* return at any moment, including today, or does the eager expectation of his coming soon not rule out the prior fulfillment of certain signs? Answering these questions requires consideration of two issues that have been the subject of much discussion over the last hundred years.

The first is known among scholars as the problem of the delay of the *parousia*, but it is by no means limited to scholars. The average Bible reader may be troubled by passages, especially in the Synoptic Gospels, in which Jesus seems to say his return will be imminent in the sense of very soon, even within the lifetime of some standing there. In Matt 10:23, Jesus tells the Twelve they will not finish their preaching mission of going through all the towns of Israel "before the Son of Man comes." Matthew 16:28 is more specific, stating that some standing in the presence of Jesus would not die before seeing "the Son of Man coming in his kingdom." The language of Matt 24:34 seems to indicate that the coming of the Son of Man would be within a generation of the time when Jesus was speaking. This is important, for if Jesus did predict his return within the lifetime of his first followers or within a generation of his first coming, he was mistaken, which would in turn raise even more important questions about the deity of Christ and the inerrancy of the Scriptures.

Evangelical New Testament scholars have not been unaware of the questions raised by these texts and have provided cogent interpretations that see the prophesied "coming" in these texts not as the Second Coming but as his coming back from death via resurrection or his coming in judgment that happened in AD 70 with the destruction of Jerusalem.[14] Those interested can find these explanations in commentaries and other studies

---

Second Coming denies its personal and visible character, and the events surrounding Christ's second coming did not occur in AD 70.

[14] It is worth noting that none of the three verses usually mentioned in connection with the delay of the *parousia* (Matt 10:23; 16:28; and 24:34) contain the word *parousia*.

of eschatology.[15] I prefer here to focus on some more obvious reasons for concluding that these texts do not prophesy that Jesus would return within a generation or the lifetime of his original hearers, the most obvious being the second of the biblical teachings we mentioned above—namely, Jesus's clear statement that he did not know the time of his return (Mark 13:32). If he did not know the time of his return, he could not have said it would be within the lifetime of his hearers or within one generation.

In addition, these three sayings must be interpreted in light of other sayings within the Synoptic Gospels that indicate Christ's second coming might be delayed and still other texts which stress the uncertainty of the timing of the Second Coming.[16] Following the principle of interpreting each text in light of other texts provides further reason for concluding that Jesus did not erroneously teach that he would return within a generation.

Still, there is an undeniably vibrant expectancy in the New Testament concerning Jesus's return, with the promise that he is coming "soon" in the next-to-last verse of the book of Revelation (22:20). There is no time specified, but this promised "soon" coming led to questions being raised as early as 2 Pet 3:4, where scoffers asked, "Where is this 'coming' he promised?" Today, after nearly 2,000 years, the question of delay is even more pressing. This leads to further consideration of the second strand of biblical teaching, the unknown time.

---

[15] Numerous commentaries on Matthew provide the grammatical and exegetical reasons for not seeing these verses as referring to the second coming of Jesus. See, for example, D. A. Carson, "Matthew," in *EBC*, vol. 8 (Grand Rapids: Zondervan, 1984) and Charles L. Quarles, *Matthew*, EBTC (Bellingham, WA: Lexham Academic, 2022). Books on eschatology that give possible resolutions of these passages include Hoekema, *The Bible and the Future*, 112–19, and Berkouwer, *The Return of Christ*, 86–95.

[16] See G. E. Ladd, *A Theology of the New Testament* (Grand Rapids: Eerdmans, 1974), 207–8. Texts indicating a possible delay in Christ's return include Mark 13:7, Luke 19:11, and Matt 25:19. Uncertainty about the time of Christ's return is seen in Mark 13:36, Matt 24:44, and Matt 25:13.

The Unknown Time of Christ's Return

The clear statement of Jesus that he himself did not know the time of his return prompts two questions and an observation. The first question is how can Jesus, who the Bible teaches is true God and true man, not know the time of his return, since one of the attributes of God is omniscience? This is answered by biblical teaching on what is called the *kenōsis*, or "emptying" of Christ, taught in Phil 2:6–7. While the teaching that Christ "emptied himself" in the incarnation has been taken by some to deny or limit Christ's full deity,[17] we believe the formulation of Daniel Akin accurately captures Paul's meaning. Jesus did not lose any of the attributes of deity; rather, he "voluntarily forfeited . . . the free use of his divine attributes, depending instead on his Father and the Holy Spirit."[18] As fully human seeking to identify with humans, he accepted human limitations. He would know only what the Father gave him to know and do only what the Father enabled him to do. For reasons known only to God, among the things not given to Jesus to know was the time of his return; Christ chooses not to exercise his own omniscience, again, in order to identify with us.

The second question we briefly raised earlier. If no one, including Jesus, knows the time, how can biblical writers teach that Christ's return is "soon"? Here 2 Pet 3:8 is helpful as the reminder that God's time scale is not like ours. If with the Lord a thousand years is like a day, it's only been slightly less than two days that we have been waiting for Christ's return. An even more expansive meaning of "soon" can be seen when one considers what time is like to an eternal being. Maybe even a thousand years like a day does not capture the reality of the situation. Perhaps to an eternal being like God, any finite period of time is soon.

---

[17] See the discussion of historical and contemporary formulations of kenotic Christology that pose challenges to orthodox Christology in Stephen J. Wellum, *God the Son Incarnate: The Doctrine of Christ* (Wheaton; Crossway, 2016), 355–93.

[18] Daniel L. Akin, "The Person of Christ," in *A Theology for the Church*, rev. ed., ed. Daniel L. Akin (Nashville: B&H, 2014), 405.

Finally, the statement of Jesus concerning the unknown time of his return prompts the observation that no one today knows the hour of his return, yet many in church history have made the attempt. The most recent well-publicized instance was that of radio pastor Harold Camping, who claimed he had calculated the date of Christ's return to be May 21, 2011. When that day came and passed, he recalculated it to October 21, 2011. When Jesus did not return on that day, he admitted his foolishness saying we are not meant to calculate the time of Christ's return.[19] Yet, the attempt of Camping and others does raise a further question. If we are not to calculate the time of Christ's return, what it the purpose of the signs which must precede his return? This leads to the third strand of biblical teaching with which we began this section on the time of Christ's return—the purpose of the signs.

The Purpose of the Signs

In the previous chapter, we considered the position of dispensationalists who say that no signs must precede Christ's return. They reject these signs because dispensationalism splits Christ's return into two events—a coming for the church and a coming with the church—and says that any unfulfilled signs will be fulfilled in the period between these two comings. We considered more briefly the position of Ben Merkle, who says that whatever signs remain to be fulfilled may be fulfilled already without our knowledge of it. He says, "We must also admit that the precise fulfillment of many verses of Scripture is ambiguous to us. This ambiguity, I believe, is of God's design."[20] Merkle thinks such ambiguity applies to the fulfillment of signs that he himself affirms must take place before Christ returns. What he does not want

[19] See Robert D. McFadden, "Harold Camping, Dogged Forecaster of the End of the World, Dies at 92," *New York Times*, December 18, 2013, https://www.nytimes.com/2013/12/18/us/harold-camping-radio-entrepreneur-who-predicted-worlds-end-dies-at-92.html.

[20] Benjamin L. Merkle, "Could Christ Return at Any Moment? Rethinking the Imminence of the Second Coming," *Trinity Journal* 26, no. 2 (2005): 292.

is the lack of fulfillment of signs to dull our expectation and anticipation of Christ's return. He writes, "If certain events have yet to be fulfilled, might the church become lackadaisical knowing that Jesus' return is not imminent?"[21]

If the purpose of the signs is not to dull our expectation nor to enable us to calculate the date of Christ's return, what is their purpose? It seems they are intended first not to dull our expectation but to focus it. The time of Christ's return is not only unknown but will be unexpected for some, like the coming of "a thief in the night" (1 Thess 5:2). But it is not to be unexpected by believers. Since they "know the time," they wake up from their sleep, recognizing that their "salvation is nearer than when we [they] first believed" (Rom 13:11). Here is where Merkle's caution may be appropriate. Because the events we see might be the fulfillment of the remaining signs, we do not calculate but remain watchful and hopeful.

Second and perhaps surprisingly, another function of unfulfilled signs is to prevent us from being deceived or made anxious by claims that Christ has already returned. In 2 Thess 2:1–4, Paul calms the fears of those who feared they had missed Christ's return by pointing out that at least one important preceding event had not happened. Matthew 24:6–8 prepares the disciples for a delay, for though many ominous events may have occurred, these are just "the beginning of labor pains." Alongside the eager expectation of a soon return there is also acknowledgment of a delay, that certain things have to happen first. Therefore, believers should not be worried that they have somehow missed his return or have been left behind, nor should they be deceived by frauds who claim to be Jesus. Christians should be prepared to persevere for the long term (Matt 24:48), neither burning out through not caring for their body, nor rusting out through laziness, but wearing out through faithful, fruitful service. We may relate this to the interesting note by G. C. Berkouwer that the effect of the hope of Christ's return in the New Testament is not fanaticism but sobriety and watchfulness (1 Pet 1:13; 4:7).[22] One function of the signs is to calm overanxious believers.

---

[21] Merkle, 279.

[22] Berkouwer, *The Return of Christ*, 21.

A final function of the signs is to serve as a call to action. If we see some of the signs very evidently being fulfilled around us today, should we sell our belongings and go up on a mountainside to await Christ? No; instead, we should be filled with an urgency to live out his will for us, whatever it is. We do not know how much more time we will have to complete the ministry he has given us. Our watching is thus directed, not to the signs, but to the Lord, and while we watch, we work, fulfilling his calling in our lives.

The Purposes of Christ's Return

A skeptic could raise the question as to why Christ should need to return. He or she could ask, Why did he not finish the job at his first coming? While Scripture cautions us not to expect to understand all of God's purposes in his plans (Isa 55:8–9; Rom 11:33), one reason for why he has not returned yet is given in 2 Pet 3:9. He is "not wanting any to perish but all to come to repentance." Had Christ completed all his work at his first coming, and thus left no need for a second coming and no time between a first and second coming, there would be a multitude too large to count who would never have come to know and worship him. There would be an untold number of Christians who would never have the joy of serving and sharing in his purpose to "make disciples of all nations" (Matt 28:19). We have good reason to agree with Jesus when he said it was good for him to go away for a time. He sent the Holy Spirit to live and work through us while we await his return to complete the work entrusted to him by the Father. We will offer four reasons why Christ will return.

To Consummate Our Salvation

While it is true that we have been saved from the penalty of sin by justification and that we are being saved from the power of sin by sanctification, there is a future component of salvation that is called glorification. That is why Heb 9:28 can say that at Christ's second coming he will "bring salvation to those who are waiting for him." But of what does this glorification or consummation of salvation consist?

Bruce Demarest sees glorification as consisting of four phases.[23] We discussed the first of these phases of glorification earlier in connection with the intermediate state. This first phase is the glorification of the soul or spirit. For those still alive at Christ's return, John describes this glorification in these words: "We know that when he appears, we will be like him because we will see him as he is" (1 John 3:2). But for those who die before Christ's return, this change seems to have already happened, as those now in the heavenly Jerusalem are described as "the spirits of righteous people made perfect" (Heb 12:23). The other three phases are clearly connected to Christ's return.

The second phase of glorification will be the perfecting of our bodies. At Christ's return, "God will raise, transform, and glorify the bodies of Christians."[24] This is specifically connected to Christ's return in numerous places in Scripture (1 Cor 15:52; Phil 3:20–21; 1 Thess 4:16) and was included in the earliest Christian creeds.[25] Indeed, the resurrection of the body is such an important topic that we will defer further consideration of it until the following chapter.

The third phase of glorification posited by Demarest is vindication before the judgment seat of Christ.[26] But not all agree with Demarest on this. Some conclude that believers will appear before the judgment seat of Christ "immediately after the believer's death"; still others believe there will be multiple acts of judgment at different times.[27] This too demands more detailed consideration in the chapter to come.

---

[23] Bruce Demarest, *The Cross and Salvation: The Doctrine of Salvation* (Wheaton: Crossway, 1997), 469.

[24] Demarest, 474.

[25] See, for example, the Apostles' Creed: "I believe in . . . the resurrection of the body," or the Nicene Creed: "I believe in . . . the resurrection of the dead."

[26] Demarest, *The Cross and Salvation*, 471.

[27] J. Daniel Hays, J. Scott Duvall, and C. Marvin Pate, *Dictionary of Biblical Prophecy and End Times* (Grand Rapids: Zondervan, 2007), 236, 258. They cite

The fourth phase of glorification offered by Demarest is our full entry into our life in the new creation. After the somber scene of judgment before the great white throne (Rev 20:11–15), the new creation is only described as "coming down out of heaven" (Rev 21:2). Prior to Christ's return, believers enjoy fellowship with Jesus in paradise as perfected spirits; now they enjoy the fuller blessings of God dwelling in their midst in the new creation as embodied spirits. Demarest suggests "perfected and perpetual worship . . . sharing in Messiah's royal reign and serving his kingdom purposes" and experiencing "the great joy of fellowship with ethnically diverse believers of all centuries" as among the blessings of this phase of glorification,[28] a phase that will never end. Indeed, life in the new creation may involve much more as we will explore in a chapter later in this book on heaven.

To Reveal Christ's True Nature

During his earthly life, Christ's true nature was veiled, except for the moments on the Mount of Transfiguration (Matt 17:1–6; Mark 9:2–7; Luke 9:28–35). Indeed, his entire earthly life follows a trajectory of humility: the incarnation itself, life as a servant, obedience unto death, even death on a cross (Phil 2:7–8). Some of the revelation of Christ's true nature began with his resurrection and ascension, but every knee has not yet bowed; every tongue has not yet confessed. He is not yet honored or recognized as he should be. At his return, that will change.

Jesus himself describes his return as "coming on the clouds of heaven with power and great glory" (Matt 24:30); Paul describes it as "the revelation of the Lord Jesus from heaven with his powerful angels" (2 Thess 1:7). He will return to be "glorified by his saints and to be marveled at by all those who have believed" (1:10). His return will be "the appearing of the glory of

---

John F. Walvoord, *The Millennial Kingdom: A Basic Text in Premillennial Theology* (Grand Rapids: Zondervan, 1971), 276–95 as arguing for seven acts of judgment at differing times for differing groups.

[28] Demarest, *The Cross and Salvation*, 478–79.

our great God and Savior, Jesus Christ" (Titus 2:13). The entire last book of the Bible is "the revelation of Jesus Christ" (Rev 1:1), and it culminates with his return, at which he vanquishes his enemies (Rev 19:19–21). Indeed, he puts "all his enemies under his feet" (1 Cor 15:25). There will no longer be any doubt as to who is Lord. Jesus will receive the recognition due him.

To Judge the World

In addition to the judgment of individuals, which we will consider further in the next chapter, there is also a larger sphere of judgment: that of the world or the world system and the evil powers behind it (Satan and his angels). This will be our focus here.

Leon Morris argues that in the Bible, "Judgment is the process whereby one discerns between the right and the wrong, *and takes action as a result*."[29] God is the one who defines what is right and the one responsible to judge that which is not right. The action he takes is often but not always punishment. The goal is to establish justice. Judgment is both present and future, but we will limit our consideration here to final judgment, which takes place after Christ's return.

In the Old Testament, God is affirmed as the judge of all the earth (Gen 18:25). In the New Testament, the Father "has given all judgment to the Son" (John 5:22). While judgment was not the Son's purpose in coming into the world (John 3:17), his coming does precipitate something of a judgment in that he is light, and light both attracts and repels (John 3:19). Even though his judgment of the world began with the cross (John 12:31), it is not yet complete as the world system is still obviously in power in our world today.

That power ends with the judgment of Babylon the Great in Revelation 18. Numerous commentators think Babylon is best interpreted as "not confined to any one historical manifestation," but as "the archetypal head of all

---

[29] Leon Morris, *The Biblical Doctrine of Judgment* (Eugene, OR: Wipf & Stock, 2006), 17. Emphasis in original. Morris is speaking specifically of judgment in the Old Testament, but that statement is true of judgment throughout the Bible.

entrenched worldly resistance to God."[30] Grant Osborne says Babylon "symbolizes seductive Rome and all self-centered empires of history."[31] At the same time, others believe it will appear in history as "the final and intensified expression of worldly power,"[32] with the beasts described in Revelation 13 as persons who will lead this empire in its end-time manifestation.[33] Whatever is meant by Babylon, the fall of Babylon is explicitly seen as God's judgment (Rev 17:1; 19:2).

That act, along with the defeat and judgment of the beast, the false prophet, Satan, and all the enemies of God (Rev 19:19–21; 20:10), makes way for the end of "the old order of things" (Rev 21:4 NIV). This end of the old order is the goal and ultimate importance of the judging work of Christ at his return. Not only is justice served in the punishment of all that is evil, but true judgment establishes the good. The old order of things is judged and ended so a new, just order can be put into effect. While we are not told the details of the new order, we are given hints that are wonderful almost beyond description. There will be an end to tears, death, grief, crying, and pain (Rev 21:4), and thus all that caused those painful effects in the old order

---

[30] Alan Johnson, "Revelation," EBC (Grand Rapids: Zondervan, 1981), 12:554.

[31] Grant R. Osborne, *Revelation*, BECNT (Grand Rapids: Baker Academic, 2002), 629.

[32] Robert H. Mounce, *The Book of Revelation*, NICNT (Grand Rapids: Eerdmans, 1977), 308.

[33] Osborne, *Revelation*, 495, 510. He sees the first beast as an Antichrist figure and the military leader of this empire, while the second beast seems to have more a religious function. G. K. Beale, *The Book of Revelation: A Commentary on the Greek Text*, NIGTC (Grand Rapids: Eerdmans, 1999), 681, 707–8, acknowledges the debate over seeing the beasts as persons or evil spirits and opts for seeing the first beast as "the leader of opposition to God's people at a future time before the end," while the second beast may be false teachers within the church of that time. In "Revelation" (530), Johnson sees Babylon and the two beasts of Rev 13:1 and 11 as "the worldwide anti-God system of Satan and its manifestation in periodic, historical human antichrists". Mounce says in *The Book of Revelation* that the first beast "has always been, and will be in a final intensified manifestation, the deification of secular authority" (251), while the second beast he sees as "a religious power" (259).

must have been removed and ended. That is the scope of the judgment of Christ upon the world. The summary description of his work of judgment is the true hope of all God's people: "I am making everything new" (Rev 21:5).

To Inaugurate the Millennial Kingdom

This fourth possible purpose would be rejected by many. Only premillennialists would see the inauguration of a millennial kingdom as a purpose of Christ's return, but as premillennialism is still the majority view in many evangelical circles, this purpose warrants mention here.[34] Evaluation of the premillennial position which assumes this purpose, and the alternative views which reject it, will be given in a later chapter.

Our Response to Christ's Return

We should not leave the topic of Christ's return without asking the application question: What should our response be to this glorious truth? In short, our response should be to allow this hope to fuel our lives today. But how that hope impacts us is a multi-faceted thing. It begins by following Peter's counsel to set our hope "completely on the grace to be brought to you at the revelation of Jesus Christ" (1 Pet 1:13). Every other hope will, in the end, not be enough; center your hope fully on Christ's return. Chris Davis contrasts our usual posture toward Christ's return as "hopefully" with Peter's admonition to set our hope fully on Christ's return. Davis says, "We hope fully when that hope transforms how we live today."[35]

---

[34] A 2016 survey of 1,000 Protestant senior pastors found 48 percent affirmed premillennialism compared to 31 percent amillennialism and 11 percent postmillennialism. Among Baptists, 75 percent affirmed premillennialism. See Bob Smietana, "Pastors: The End of the World Is Complicated," Lifeway Newsroom, April 26, 2016, at https://news.lifeway.com/2016/04/26/pastors-the-end-of-the-world-is-complicated/.

[35] Chris Davis, *Bright Hope for Tomorrow: How Anticipating Jesus' Return Gives Strength for Today* (Grand Rapids: Zondervan, 2022), 4.

It transforms how we see all of life. It is the hope that sustains us when we grieve the death of a loved one (the "hope" Paul mentions in 1 Thess 4:13 is described in verses 14–18 as the return of Christ). It is the hope that despite all the senseless mass shootings that seem to happen every day, despite the unjust wars and persecution of the weak and vulnerable (including believers) all around the world, despite all the oppression, suffering, and injustice we see all around us—despite all this, it is the hope that one day the prayers of believers that, "Your kingdom come. Your will be done on earth as it is in heaven," (Matt 6:10) will be fully answered. It is the hope that one day Jesus will not be mocked, scorned or ignored, but worshipped by many and acknowledged as Lord by all.

But hope is not purely future-oriented. Davis points out how we are to keep the hope for Christ's return clear in the midst of daily life here and now by practicing what he calls "rhythms of anticipation."[36] For example, the call to practice regular gathering with God's people to encourage each other is motivated by keeping the coming of Christ's return in view: "encouraging one another—and all the more as you see the Day approaching" (Heb 10:24–25 NIV). The practice of fasting can serve as a reminder that the Bridegroom is gone (Matt 9:15), and the very pain of his absence can "create more space to nurture a love for Jesus' appearing."[37] The practice of a Sabbath rest can be preparation for the final Sabbath rest that Jesus will bring at his return.[38]

Scripture also points to the ways that hope can transform our lives now. To those troubled by the fear that their faith will fail, Scripture abounds with promises that God will hold us and keep us "blameless" all the way until Christ returns.[39] Paul says to the Corinthian Christians: "He will also

---

[36] Davis, 113.

[37] Davis, 136. Helpfully, Davis adds that fasting can be not just from food but "from anything good but distracting" (139), such as fasting from electronic media.

[38] Davis, 146. Davis sees this final rest that Christ brings at his return as the Sabbath rest that remains for the people of God, mentioned in Heb 4:9.

[39] "When you look through the New Testament for texts that specifically connect our purity of life with the return of Christ, you discover a beautiful dynamic.

strengthen you to the end, so that you will be blameless in the day of our Lord Jesus" (1 Cor 1:8), and he prays for the same blamelessness for the Thessalonians on two occasions (1 Thess 3:13; 5:23), adding his assurance that God will answer this prayer on the second occasion: "He who calls you is faithful; he will do it " (1 Thess 5:24). Jude tells us the same truth in slightly different terms, that God "is able [and willing!] to protect you from stumbling and to make you stand in the presence of his glory, without blemish and with great joy" (Jude 24).

The promise that God will keep us blameless is connected with the exhortation to live a blameless life, and that exhortation is linked to the expectation of Christ's return. John says when Christ appears, we will be like him. He then joins that prospect with holy living now: "And everyone who has this hope in him purifies himself just as he is pure" (1 John 3:3). Paul gives the proper response to the hope of his coming in these words: "Therefore, put to death what belongs to your earthly nature: sexual immorality, impurity, lust, evil desire, and greed, which is idolatry" (Col 3:5). He adds that while we wait for Christ's appearing, we are "to deny godlessness and worldly lusts and to live in a sensible, righteous, and godly way in the present age" (Titus 2:12). Peter concludes his description of what will happen at Christ's return with this charge: "Therefore, dear friends, while you wait for these things, make every effort to be found without spot or blemish in his sight, at peace" (2 Pet 3:14).

There is one final surprising response that the hope of Christ's coming fuels in our lives. In the description mentioned in the previous paragraph of events of "the day of the Lord," Peter gives a clear implication: "Since all these things are to be dissolved in this way, it is clear what sort of people you should be in holy conduct and godliness as you wait for the day of God and hasten its coming" (2 Pet 3:11–12a). The surprise is in the last phrase. How can our holy conduct hasten the coming of the day of the Lord? Is that not something set by the Father's will alone? The answer seems to be found in

---

About half the texts emphasize how we are to live, and the other half contain promises that God will keep us to the end." Davis, *Bright Hope for Tomorrow*, 166–67.

recognizing some of the factors the Father tells us will affect his decision as to when that final day will come.

One factor is mentioned in 2 Pet 3:9. God is patient, not wanting any to perish but all to come to repentance. If we call people without faith in Jesus to repentance, perhaps we will hasten the coming of the day of the Lord, since that is one reason given. Matthew 24:14 records Jesus saying something similar, "This good news of the kingdom will be proclaimed in all the world as a testimony to all nations, and then the end will come." If our holy conduct is Great Commission conduct, obeying the command Jesus gave us to make disciples of all nations, then this other prerequisite to Christ's return may also be met.

Thus the hope we have in the promise and prospect of Christ's coming is not just a hope that calms and cheers us in the midst of a world filled with reason for despair; it is also a hope that needs to be nurtured by practices like gathering, fasting, and resting. It is a hope that challenges us both to trust God to keep us blameless and moves us to seek a life of holy conduct, including calling lost people to repentance and making disciples of all nations.

CHAPTER 6

Resurrection and Judgment

Introduction

The second coming of Christ is the great watershed of eschatology, with everything since his first coming pointing ahead to it and other important events being ushered in by it. Of the two such events we discuss in this chapter, the resurrection of the body and final judgment, there is some disagreement as to which comes first. Of course, God has always been "the Judge of the whole earth" (Gen 18:25) and one can find acts of divine judgment throughout Scripture, from casting Adam and Eve out of the garden (Gen 3:23–24) to striking Ananias and Sapphira dead in the days of the early church (Acts 5:1–11).[1] But do acts of eschatological judgment occur before the resurrection of the dead?

Dispensationalists see multiple eschatological acts of judgment, with at least one, the judgment of the church before "the judgment seat of Christ"

---

[1] See Leon Morris, *The Biblical Doctrine of Judgment* (1960; repr., Eugene, OR: Wipf & Stock, 2006), 44, who characterizes judgment in the New Testament as "a present reality."

(2 Cor 5:10), occurring "immediately after the rapture and prior to the return of Christ to the earth."[2] Some go further and see 2 Cor 5:10 as referring to a "'particular judgment' occurring immediately after the death of each individual Christian."[3] Stan Gundry says, "Premillennialists generally distinguish four judgments: of believers, of Israel, of the nations, and the 'great white throne' judgment."[4] But John Walvoord sees seven future judgments "related in some sense to end-time events,"[5] while progressive dispensationalist Daniel Akin mentions only two separate judgments.[6] They all agree on one act of judgment described in Rev 20:11–15 as the great white throne judgment. Indeed, most scholars acknowledge other possible acts of judgment, such as that occurring before the judgment seat of Christ (2 Cor 5:10) or the judgment of the sheep and goats (Matt 25:31–46), as all included within the great white throne judgment.[7] This act of judgment clearly follows the resurrection of the dead. Thus, we will treat the resurrection of the body first here and consider the case for an act or acts of

---

[2] John F. Walvoord, *The Millennial Kingdom: A Basic Text in Premillennial Theology* (Grand Rapids: Zondervan, 1959), 276. Daniel Akin acknowledges some uncertainty as to the exact time of the judgment seat of Christ but affirms that it will be "after the rapture and before the Second Coming." Danny Akin, "A Rapture You Can't Miss (1 Thessalonians 4:13–18); A Judgment You Must Face (2 Corinthians 5:10); A Supper You Will Want to Attend (Revelation 19:1–10)," in *The Return of Christ: A Premillennial Perspective*, ed. David L. Allen and Steve W. Lemke (Nashville: B&H Academic, 2011), 57.

[3] Murray J. Harris, *Raised Immortal: Resurrection & Immortality in the New Testament* (Grand Rapids: Eerdmans, 1983), 157. Hebrews 9:27 also mentions judgment as following death, but that verse is not explicit as to whether judgment comes immediately after death or not.

[4] S. N. Gundry, "Judgment of Nations," *Evangelical Dictionary of Theology*, 3rd ed., ed. Daniel J. Treier and Walter A. Elwell (Grand Rapids: Baker Academic, 2017), 453.

[5] Walvoord, *The Millennial Kingdom*, 276.

[6] Akin, "A Rapture You Can't Miss," 57–58.

[7] "Most scholars see the Great White Throne Judgment as a general judgment of the entire human race, righteous and unrighteous alike." J. Daniel Hays, J. Scott Duvall, and C. Marvin Pate, *Dictionary of Biblical Prophecy and End Times* (Grand Rapids: Zondervan, 2007), 195.

eschatological judgment before that event of resurrection in a later section of this chapter.

The Resurrection of the Body

We mentioned the resurrection of the body in the previous chapter as part of the consummation of our salvation that Christ's return brings. Salvation includes our past justification, the present process of sanctification, and the future prospect of glorification. While it seems that our spirits experience something of the blessing of glorification at death (Heb 12:23) since we will be in Christ's presence, which is transforming (1 John 3:2), John Murray thinks that we do not receive the blessing of glorified bodies at death, but rather we have to wait and then partake of this blessing together with all believers: "It is as a body that the whole company of the redeemed will be glorified." He believes this is meant to bring together our final glorification with the final glorification of Christ: "The glorification of the elect will coincide with the final act of the Father in the exaltation and glorification of the Son."[8] More simply, the delay of the resurrection and glorification of our bodies until the return of Christ may be another way to honor him.

We will consider the biblical teaching on the resurrection of the body under four headings. First, who are to be raised bodily? Second, what will be the nature of our resurrected bodies? Third, what is the importance of the resurrection of the body, both theologically and practically, for Christian life and practice? Finally, we will have to raise the question of when; specifically, is there one general act of resurrection at Christ's return, or will there be multiple resurrections at different times? This question is linked to the issue of multiple acts of judgment, and both are tied to the issue of the millennium.

---

[8] John Murray, *Redemption Accomplished and Applied* (Grand Rapids: Eerdmans, 1955), 176–77. Murray does not think that what we called the first phase of glorification (the perfecting of the spirit) should be seen as part of glorification, but we concur in what he says about the glorification of the body.

Full resolution of these questions will have to await the next chapter on the millennium, but we will seek to clarify the issues and options in this chapter.

Who Will Be Raised?

The first question is the easiest to answer. The subjects of resurrection will be everyone, believers and nonbelievers. Paul specifically says that his hope was in the resurrection "both of the righteous and the unrighteous" (Acts 24:15). The language of the sea, death, and Hades giving up the dead that were in them in Rev 20:13 is widely interpreted as referring to the "general resurrection of all."[9] Some attempt to limit the resurrection described in Rev 20:13 to unbelievers, but that is based on seeing the resurrection of believers as already described in Rev 20:4–6,[10] a passage we will have to examine in detail in the next chapter in connection with the millennium. Whether in one resurrection or multiple resurrections, the final result is the same: all are raised.

This may be surprising to some. Does the fact that nonbelievers are raised indicate that they are given the gift of eternal life? Several verses make it clear that resurrection to eternal life is conditional and that resurrection for some may be to condemnation.[11] John 5:29 is the most explicit biblical text on this matter. Those who have "done good things" will come out of their graves "to the resurrection of life," while those who have done "wicked things" will come out of their graves "to the resurrection of condemnation." Daniel 12:2 is similar. Some will rise from the dust to "eternal life"; others, "to disgrace and eternal contempt." Finally, whether those raised in Rev 20:13 are nonbelievers only or both believers and nonbelievers, their resurrection does not guarantee a resurrection to life. Only those whose names are in the Book of Life escape the sentence of condemnation; the rest are thrown into the lake of fire.

---

[9] Anthony A. Hoekema, *The Bible and the Future* (Grand Rapids: Eerdmans, 1979), 243.

[10] Harris, *Raised Immortal*, 179.

[11] Harris, 172.

What Will Be the Nature of Our Resurrected Bodies?

Our second question—the nature of our new, resurrected, and glorified bodies—has attracted the most attention from scholars, and here, the discussion is limited to the resurrected bodies of believers, as we have very little biblical data on the nature of the bodies in which nonbelievers will be raised. We are given one clue as to the nature of our resurrection bodies in Phil 3:21: they will be "the likeness of his [Christ's] glorious body." Thus, some look to the Gospel accounts of the resurrection appearances of Jesus to help answer this question. Luke 24:39–43 tells us that Jesus's resurrected body was not ghostly but had "flesh and bones" that could be touched. He even ate a piece of fish. Thus, it seems we should see some continuity between our present and future bodies.[12] Further evidence for continuity is found in the very language of resurrection. As Anthony Hoekema says, "There must be continuity, for otherwise there would be little point in speaking of a resurrection at all."[13] To that may be added the fact that the Bible refers to our present bodies as one day "being clothed with" our new resurrected bodies (1 Cor 15:53).

But there are also obvious discontinuities between Jesus's resurrected body and our bodies. The New Testament repeatedly speaks of Jesus appearing to his followers,[14] even within a locked room (John 20:19) and then suddenly disappearing from their sight (Luke 24:31). Was Jesus's apparent ability to appear and disappear at will "the result of his glorified resurrection body or his divinity"?[15] Murray Harris connects this ability to the "spiritual body" of 1 Cor 15:44, which he sees as "a form of corporeality . . . unfettered by time and space."[16] Also, the difficulty the disciples experienced

---

[12] M. Jeff Brannon, *The Hope of Life After Death: A Biblical Theology of Resurrection* (Downers Grove: IVP Academic, 2022), 157.

[13] Hoekema, *The Bible and the Future*, 251.

[14] Acts 1:3 speaks of Jesus "appearing" to his disciples for a period of forty days following his resurrection; Paul lists five post-resurrection appearances of Jesus to one or more of his disciples.

[15] Brannon, *The Hope of Life After Death*, 157.

[16] Harris, *Raised Immortal*, 57.

sometimes in recognizing Jesus cautions us against seeing too much continuity. N. T. Wright connects this to the incorruptibility of the resurrected body (1 Cor 15:53). He says that Jesus's body was strange to the disciples because they "were looking at the first, and so far the only, piece of incorruptible physicality."[17]

The duality of continuity and discontinuity is also seen in Paul's illustration of the body that dies as a seed that God creatively transforms into a plant. There is some continuity in that we should not expect the seed of a human body to be raised with the flesh of an animal, a bird, or a fish (1 Cor 15:39), but the emphasis in Paul is more on discontinuity. In 1 Cor 15:42–44, Paul describes the nature of the resurrection body in four contrasts with our present body. The first contrast, corruptible versus incorruptible, is poorly translated according to Anthony Thiselton. He says, "imperishable," (or "incorruptible") is "simply not good enough." The translation needs to include more positive terms such as "flourishing," something to convey "a dynamic, ever-increasing condition."[18] At the least it means the end of our vulnerability to the multitude of maladies that afflict our bodies now.

Harris connects imperishability with the next two contrasts (dishonor/glory, weakness/power) and sees all three (imperishable, glorious, powerful) as the work of the Spirit in the nature of the resurrection body as a "spiritual body." In fact, there is something of a consensus on the fourth contrast: natural body/spiritual body. Harris, Anthony Hoekema, N. T. Wright, and Anthony Thiselton all insist that "spiritual body" does not mean a body consisting of spirit.[19] That would be an oxymoron. Rather, in

---

[17] N. T. Wright, *Surprised by Hope: Rethinking Heaven, the Resurrection, and the Mission of the Church* (New York: HarperOne, 2008), 160.

[18] Anthony C. Thiselton, *Life after Death: A New Approach to the Last Things* (Grand Rapids: Eerdmans, 2012), 121.

[19] Harris, *Raised Immortal* (120) points out that Greek adjectives ending in *ikos*, as *pneumatikos* (1 Cor 15:44) carry "a *functional* or *ethical* meaning," as opposed to a "*substantial* or *material* sense." Emphasis in original.

the words of Thiselton, spiritual body "denotes a mode of existence or form animated, motivated, and controlled by the Holy Spirit."[20] Such a Spirit-controlled body would imply other qualities mentioned in the contrasts in 1 Corinthians 15: "Because it is constantly renewed by the Spirit, the spiritual body is *imperishable*. . . . Because it is completely suffused with the Spirit . . . the spiritual body is *glorious*. . . . And because it is permanently energized by the Spirit, the spiritual body is *powerful*."[21]

From elsewhere in 1 Corinthians 15, 2 Cor 5:1, and Luke 20:34–36, Harris derives three additional characteristics of the resurrected body. First, it is provided by God (1 Cor 15:38), with God "as its architect and builder." Second, it is "angel-like and without physical instincts." Harris derives this from Jesus's discussion with the Sadducees (Luke 20:34–36). He believes "like angels" means "without sexual passions or procreative powers," but not sexless.[22] Bruce Demarest goes further, affirming that we will retain "gender and ethnic characteristics."[23] Finally, from 2 Cor 5:1 and 1 Cor 15:47, we should think of the resurrection body as heavenly, in that its "natural habitat . . . is heaven."[24]

Of all the points on the nature of the resurrection body, the point most often emphasized is this idea of the spiritual body. Thiselton is worth quoting at length here:

> [T]he post-resurrection mode of being will be *ongoing, moving ahead, dynamic, and on-the-move*. It will be more like a flowing stream or river than a lake or a canal. We cannot dream of what

---

[20] Thiselton, *Life after Death*, 123. Compare Hoekema, *The Bible and the Future*, 250; Wright, *Surprised by Hope*, 156; and Harris, *Raised Immortal*, 120. Harris differs slightly in seeing the *pneuma* in *pneumatikos* as "the human spirit as revitalized by the divine Spirit."

[21] Harris, *Raised Immortal*, 121. Emphasis in original.

[22] Harris, 124.

[23] Bruce Demarest, *The Cross and Salvation: The Doctrine of Salvation* (Wheaton: Crossway, 1997), 477.

[24] Harris, *Raised Immortal*, 123–125.

> the Holy Spirit will yet do, in us and through us, in the mode of existence characterized by the Holy Spirit of Christ.[25]

The other side of the nature of the resurrected body that we have not yet discussed is its nature as a body and its continuity with the believer's present body. Are we to think that the body God raises for the believer has the exact same molecules as the body which died? Stephen Davis says this was the majority interpretation among church fathers in the patristic era, but, as he notes, there are some long-standing objections to this view. Suppose a believer is lost at sea, with his body eaten by sea creatures whose bodies are, in turn, eaten by fishermen who catch these sea creatures. At the resurrection, whose molecules will they be?[26] Davis offers several possible sophisticated philosophical responses to this objection,[27] but Murray Harris notes two ideas that seem to point to a simpler solution. The first is the observation of biochemists "that during a seven-year cycle the molecular composition of our bodies is completely changed."[28] We are constantly sloughing off old cells and adding new ones, and yet we are the same persons. Continuity of person does not seem to require material continuity. The second point is the teaching of 1 Cor 15:50 that our bodies will undergo radical transformation: "Flesh and blood cannot inherit the kingdom of God."

Together, these two points suggest that our continuity is personal, but not material. Just as we are the same person despite the change in molecules during our lives on earth, so our present body and the resurrection body can be connected by possessing "the same identifiable ego"; that is, there will be "an identity of identifiable personal characteristics." As Harris puts it, "One and the same person find expression in two successive but different types of

---

[25] Thiselton, *Life after Death*, 128. Emphasis in original.

[26] Stephen T. Davis, "Eschatology and Resurrection," in *The Oxford Handbook of Eschatology*, ed. Jerry L. Walls (Oxford: Oxford University Press, 2008), 391.

[27] Davis, 391–93.

[28] Harris, *Raised Immortal*, 126.

body. There are two dwellings but only one occupant."[29] Scripture does not seem to give more detail than this.

What Is the Importance of the Resurrection Body?

One point of importance worth noting with respect to the resurrection of the body is the way it highlights the ministry of the Spirit in the lives of believers. Murray Harris identifies four such functions in the teaching of Paul. He sees the presence of the Spirit in our lives now as "the pledge [or "down payment"] of a future resurrection and transformation" (2 Cor 1:22; 5:5; Eph 1:14); he argues that the Spirit "is the means God will use to effect a future resurrection transformation" (Rom 8:10–11); he identifies the Spirit as the one who "sustains resurrection life" (2 Cor 3:6);[30] and he contends that the Spirit "represents the continuity between the pre- and post-resurrection states of the believer."[31] The argument for this last point is tied to the first one. If the Spirit in us now is the "down payment," the fullness of the Spirit should be our experience in the age to come. Both Harris and Thiselton were persuasive in convincing this author of the significance of the role of the Spirit in the resurrection of the body.

A more obvious point of importance to the resurrection of the body is the fact that it tells us that God's intention is for us to live eternally as embodied beings, that the body is not the prison of the soul, that it is not to be despised or disregarded. N. T. Wright says, "According to the early Christians, the purpose of the new body will be to rule wisely over the new

---

[29] Harris, *Raised Immortal*, 126.

[30] Harris (147) acknowledges that the evidence on this point is not explicit, but consists of inferences from other statements identifying the Spirit as the one whose principal characteristic is "that he perpetually imparts the physical and spiritual life of which he is the source" (146). Thiselton, *Life after Death* (122), agrees, linking the resurrection body to "the ongoing work of the Spirit."

[31] Harris, *Raised Immortal*, 143–48.

world. Forget those images about lounging around playing harps. There will be work to do and we shall relish doing it."[32]

This robust expectation may be linked to a third point. In the New Testament, the hope that is to sustain us is not the expectation that we will die and be with the Lord in the intermediate state, but that we will be raised. Jeff Brannon argues that Christians should see the resurrection "as the goal of the Christian life" and as the "basis for hope in the midst of trial, tribulation, suffering, and persecution."[33] This is evidenced in the conclusion Paul draws to his lengthy exposition about the resurrection of the body in 1 Corinthians 15 in the last verse of that chapter: "Therefore, my dear brothers and sisters, be steadfast, immovable, always excelling in the Lord's work, because you know that your labor in the Lord is not in vain" (1 Cor 15:58).

Finally, the resurrection of the body is the final confirmation of the Bible's high view of the body. That high view is indicated in the fact that we were created as embodied; it is strengthened by the fact that Christ became incarnate in a fully human body; and it is confirmed by the resurrection of the body. This leads to at least two practical applications.

First, we are called to minister holistically, that is to the whole person, and not disregard people's embodied nature. God models this for us in his treatment of the prophet Elijah. After his great triumph on Mount Carmel (1 Kgs 18:20–46), Elijah somewhat surprisingly becomes fearful and even suicidal in the face of threats from Queen Jezebel (19:1–4). God, recognizing Elijah is emotionally and physically exhausted, does not reprimand the prophet; rather, he sends an angel and gives him food, water, sleep, and forty days to travel and recover (19:5–8).[34] Only then does God confront and recommission Elijah (19:9–18).

Second, we live now as embodied creatures and are called to "glorify God" with our bodies (1 Cor 6:20) and "to present" our bodies "as a living

---

[32] Wright, *Surprised by Hope*, 161.

[33] Brannon, *The Hope of Life after Death*, 165, 167.

[34] It is hard to resist suggesting that what the angel baked for Elijah (v. 6) must have been angel food cake.

sacrifice" to God (Rom 12:1). Sadly, there is little reflection of this in how Christians in the United States take care of their bodies, as a 2006 study revealed that "church members tend to be more overweight than the general population, and Baptists, including Southern Baptists, have the distinction of being the most overweight religious group in the study."[35] Fortunately, in recent years evangelical theologians have given attention to developing a theology of the body, with several books addressing that topic.[36] Hopefully, the concerns addressed in those books will lead to more thoughtful living with respect to our bodies in coming years.

One group that has special difficulty in glorifying God with their bodies is those suffering from gender dysphoria, who feel a sharp conflict between what they see in their bodies and what they sense in their minds. They feel as if they are a woman trapped in a man's body or vice versa, and some feel such intense pain that they attempt suicide. Others seek to alter the biological sex of their body to align with their perceived gender identity, becoming transgendered. The literature on this issue is large and growing but intersects with our concern in one specific point.[37] In a perceptive article, Matthew Mason notes that the doctrine of the resurrection of the body "speaks to questions of gender dysphoria and especially to ethical questions surrounding gender reassignment."[38] The first word it speaks, he confesses,

---

[35] Wendy Ashley, "Obesity in the Body of Christ," Baptist Press, January 1, 2007, https://www.baptistpress.com/resource-library/sbc-life-articles/obesity-in-the-body-of-christ/. Ashley sees support for this finding from a screening at the 2005 Southern Baptist Convention meeting, which found 75 percent of the 1,472 participants to be overweight, compared to the national average of 65 percent.

[36] See, for example, Gregg R. Allison, *Embodied: Living as Whole People in a Fractured World* (Grand Rapids: Baker, 2021); Timothy C. Tennent, *For the Body: Recovering a Theology of Gender, Sexuality, and the Human Body* (Grand Rapids: Zondervan Reflective, 2020); and Nancy R. Pearcey, *Love Thy Body: Answering Hard Questions about Life and Sexuality* (Grand Rapids: Baker, 2018).

[37] See the discussion in John S. Hammett and Katie J. McCoy, *Humanity*, Theology for the People of God, ed. David S. Dockery, Nathan A. Finn, and Christopher W. Morgan (Brentwood, TN: B&H Academic, 2023), 393–402.

[38] Matthew Mason, "The Wounded It Heals: Gender Dysphoria and the Resurrection of the Body," in *Beauty, Order, and Mystery: A Christian Vision of*

is "a hard word," yet he seeks to speak it with "sensitivity, gentleness, and patience." He says that the resurrection of the body "speaks clearly about the appropriate form of our bodies." That is, "My body's biological sex at birth is also the biological sex of the body in which I shall be raised. It therefore defines my body now." So glorifying God with one's body involves accepting the sex of that body, not seeking to change it, however painful that may be. The resurrection of the body also speaks a word of hope and comfort, for that resurrection will involve complete renewal and integration: "For those who experience gender dysphoria but cling to Christ for mercy and hope, surely one of the glories of the new creation will be to receive back the body they were originally given, transformed and glorified, to inhabit that body as their Creator and Redeemer's loving gift, and finally to be at rest." Gender dysphoria will be no more.

When Are Our Bodies Resurrected?

At first glance, this question may seem easily answered. The dead are raised at Christ's return. Both 1 Thess 4:16 and 1 Cor 15:52 seem to clearly connect the two events of return and resurrection. But some interpret 1 Thess 4:16 as describing the rapture, an event they see as happening seven years before the Second Coming. Dispensationalists affirm multiple resurrections, with the first resurrection including only the church at the rapture, with 1 Thess 4:16 as their support.[39] Thus they see what is referred to as "the first resurrection" in Rev 20:4–5 as actually a second resurrection, limited to those martyred for their faith in Christ during the seven-year tribulation. This resurrection is of those who are called tribulation saints.[40]

Human Sexuality, ed. Gerald Hiestand and Todd Wilson (Downers Grove: IVP Academic, 2017), 144. The quotations in the rest of this paragraph are taken from this same article, 144–145.

[39] Walvoord, *The Millennial Kingdom*, 277. There are some differences of interpretation among dispensationalists on some fine points, but the overall picture is much the same. Walvoord is a classic exemplar of dispensational thought.

[40] Walvoord, 278.

There is some difference of opinion among dispensationalists as to when Old Testament saints are resurrected. While some believe they are resurrected at the same time as the church (the rapture), Walvoord argues for their resurrection as separate and occurring just before the establishment of the millennial kingdom.[41] There is widespread agreement that Rev 20:11–15 gives a final resurrection event, but premillennialists understand this resurrection as only or at least primarily of unbelievers,[42] while amillennialists see it as describing "a general resurrection of all the dead,"[43] believers and nonbelievers.

Thus most dispensationalists argue for a four-stage resurrection, with each stage occurring at a different time. Historic premillennialists see a two-stage resurrection, based almost entirely on the mention of a first resurrection in Rev 20:4–5. This first resurrection takes place at the second coming of Jesus (Rev 20:4–5; 1 Thess 4:16; 1 Cor 15:52); then the second resurrection is after the millennium (Rev 20:11–15). Amillennialists and postmillennialists affirm only one event of resurrection; believers and unbelievers, indeed, all who have ever lived, are included in that resurrection.

On the side of the amillennials and postmillennials is the fact that Scripture commonly refers to one time of resurrection, with believers and nonbelievers resurrected together. They claim Dan 12:2, John 5:28–29, and Rev 20:11–15 in support of this position.[44] In response, premillennialists admit that these passages do not indicate the separation of the resurrection into two groups, with the resurrection of believers separated from that of nonbelievers. But they would also add that there is nothing in those verses that would prohibit the separation of the resurrection into two stages.

---

[41] Walvoord, *The Millennial Kingdom*, 284.

[42] Hoekema, *The Bible and the Future* (239n3) notes that some historic premillennialists hold that there will still be death during the millennium. Thus, the resurrection of Rev 20:11–15 may include some believers who lived and died during the millennium, but it will be primarily a resurrection of nonbelievers.

[43] Hoekema, 243.

[44] Hoekema, 240.

The case for the four-stage resurrection of dispensationalists rests largely on their larger schema, with the rapture preceding and separated from the Second Coming, with a seven-year tribulation between the rapture and the Second Coming, and with a sharp separation between Israel and the church. Those who find their overall position convincing may see a plausible rationale for the four-stage resurrection, but there is little explicit textual support.

In support of the two-stage resurrection, one can find some possible support in Paul's mention of three stages in 1 Cor 15:23–24. Christ's resurrection would be distinct, as the "firstfruits." Then the next stage would include the resurrection of believers, described in verse 23 as happening "at his [second] coming," and limited to "those who belong to Christ." Verse 24 is interpreted as a second event of resurrection for those who do not belong to Christ. The problem is that verse 24 does not explicitly mention the resurrection, so even premillennialists do not argue for this as strong support. They do, however, view Rev 20:4–5 as strong support. They see the explicit mention of a "first resurrection" as strongly implying a second resurrection in Rev 20:11–15.

By common consent, Revelation 20 is the key textual battleground. Those who want to maintain only one resurrection must provide an interpretation of the "first resurrection" of verses 4–5 as not a literal, bodily resurrection and as something before the Second Coming, for they interpret Rev 20:11–15 as describing the resurrection, which happens after the Second Coming. They think there are plausible interpretations that meet those criteria. G. K. Beale argues that the "first resurrection" is a spiritual resurrection: "It is reasonable to interpret the ascent of the soul at the time of death into the Lord's presence as a form of spiritual resurrection."[45] Similarly, other amillennialists argue that the first resurrection is "a heavenly exaltation with Christ after death during the intermediate state."[46] Premillennialists see any-

[45] G. K. Beale with David H. Campbell, *Revelation: A Shorter Commentary* (Grand Rapids: Eerdmans, 2015), 443.

[46] Hays, Duvall, and Pate, *Dictionary of Biblical Prophecy and End Times*, 371.

thing other than a literal, bodily resurrection as a very strained and unnatural interpretation.[47]

The interpretation of Revelation 20 is complex, involving issues like one's overall approach to the book of Revelation and events described in Revelation 20, such as the binding of Satan (vv. 1–3) and the already mentioned "first resurrection" of verses 4–5, as well as the need to understand Revelation 20 in the light of the rest of New Testament teaching. Thus, we will forego further discussion of the timing of the resurrection (or resurrections) until we examine Revelation 20 more thoroughly in the chapter to come on the issue of the millennium.

Judgment

As we mentioned at the start of this chapter, God's judgment is a pervasive theme throughout the Bible, both as a "present reality" and "future certainty."[48] Of these two, Leon Morris argues that in the Old Testament the emphasis was on future judgment: "The most significant thing about judgment was the eschatological judgment of the Lord" that will fall on all people on "the day of the Lord."[49] And while the New Testament lays emphasis on the idea of present judgment, references to future judgment "are so frequent, and so basic to the thought of the biblical writers, that no theology which fails to do justice to it can be reckoned as true to the New Testament faith."[50] Our concern in this section of this chapter will be eschatological judgment (or judgments). As with the resurrection of the body, we will address this doctrine of judgment

---

[47] See the critique of such interpretations of Rev 20:4–5 by G. E. Ladd, "An Historic Premillennial Response," in *The Meaning of the Millennium: Four Views*, ed. Robert G. Clouse (Downers Grove: InterVarsity, 1977), 190–91.

[48] Morris, *Biblical Doctrine of Judgment*, 44, 54.

[49] Morris, 24, 42. Morris mentions that the key verb for "judge" (*shophet)* is found 135 times in the Old Testament, with sixty-five applying to God's judgment. Of these sixty-five, forty-one refer to future judgment (24n1).

[50] Morris, 58.

via several questions: Who will be judged? What will be judged? How will we be judged? When will we be judged? Why will we be judged?

Who Will Be Judged?

There is widespread agreement among students of eschatology that all—living and dead—will be subject to final judgment. Indeed, "all human beings who have ever lived" will be judged.[51] The Bible uses phrases like "all the nations" (Matt 25:32), "the living and the dead" (Acts 10:42; 2 Tim 4:1), and "the great and the small" (Rev 20:12) and describes God as "the Judge of the whole earth" (Gen 18:25; cf. Heb 12:23). Even wicked angels will be included in final judgment (2 Pet 2:4–10; Jude 6), and 1 Cor 6:3 suggests that believers may play a role in their judgment. Paul specifically includes believers in the judgment that will take place before the judgment seat of Christ (2 Cor 5:10); they too must face judgment. Hebrews 9:27 sees death, and after death, judgment, as something appointed for all humans. It is inescapable.

What Will Be Judged?

There is likewise little controversy in church and academy concerning what will come under God's judgment—everything we have done. The phrase "according to his/their works" is common (Ps 62:12; Prov 24:12; Rom 2:6; Rev 20:12–13), but works includes our thoughts, even those we keep secret (Rom 2:15–16) and "the intentions of the heart" (1 Cor 4:5). Jesus specifically mentions "every careless word" we speak as something for which we will be held accountable on the day of judgment (Matt 12:36). Hebrews 4:13 is all inclusive: "All things are naked and exposed to the eyes of him to whom we must give an account." Judgment will be of our "deeds, words, and thoughts."[52]

---

[51] Hoekema, *The Bible and the Future*, 257.

[52] Hoekema, 258.

Some may raise the question of whether the sins of believers will be mentioned on the day of judgment. After all, they have been forgiven, cast "into the depths of the sea" (Mic 7:19). But the biblical text is clear; we are judged for all that we have done in the body, "whether good or evil" (2 Cor 5:10). But, as Anthony Hoekema emphasizes, the sins of believers "will be revealed in the judgment as *forgiven sins*, whose guilt has been totally covered by the blood of Jesus Christ."[53]

Leon Morris gives both the comfort and challenge of this comprehensive judgment: "It is the far-reaching and all-inclusive nature of the judgment that makes it so frightening. At the same time, the thought that all we do matters in God's sight helps make life worth living. It gives a dignity to even the most insignificant action, the most unimportant word."[54]

How Will We Be Judged?

By this question, we mean by what standard will we be judged? Whether a deed, word, or thought is good or evil depends on its agreement with the character of God and the revealed will of God. The fullest revelation of God's character and will is in the written Word of God, but not all have the written Word, and so we find a principle in Scripture: one's standard for judgment is in keeping with the degree of revelation given to them (Luke 12:48).

Everyone has been given the light of universal revelation in the created order, and thus they may be justly judged for what they could have known by that revelatory light; all are "without excuse" (Rom 1:18–20). Some have the written law of God and will be "judged by the law" (Rom 2:12). But even those who do not have the written law of God have the law "written on their hearts" (Rom 2:15), confirmed by their conscience, and may be justly judged by their response to that law. All may be justly judged based on their knowledge of and obedience to the law and will of God that they did have.

[53] Hoekema, 259. Emphasis in original.

[54] Morris, *Biblical Doctrine of Judgment*, 64.

Jesus performed miracles in order to give additional light, for those miracles revealed Jesus as God's Messiah. For that reason, he said that it would be more tolerable on the day of judgment for cities where he did no miracles (Tyre, Sidon, Sodom) than for the cities where most of his miracles were done (Chorazin, Bethsaida, Capernaum). Jesus says that the former cities would have responded to the revelation given through miracles with repentance if they had seen them (Matt 11:20–24). More light means more accountability and stricter judgment. There is even a warning given to those who become teachers, that they "will receive a stricter judgment" (Jas 3:1). While the rationale for that "stricter judgment" is not given, it seems likely that teachers would be those given more understanding of the revelation of God, and with that gift would come additional accountability. Indeed, reading the Bible in which we grow in our knowledge of God's character and will, and even reading books like this present one, results in increased accountability.

When Will We Be Judged?

Leon Morris says categorically, "The New Testament makes it clear that God is engaged upon a present activity of judging."[55] It is seen in the deaths of Ananias and Sapphira (Acts 5:1–9), the sickness and deaths of those who shared in the Lord's Supper in an unworthy manner (1 Cor 11:30), and in the somber phrase repeated three times in Romans 1 as an expression of God's judgment of sin: "God gave them over" to their sinful desires (Rom 1:24, 26, 28 NIV). And while divine judgment may not be behind all the suffering experienced by individuals and nations down through history, Morris suggests "that there are occasions when God's chastening hand is to be discerned in the judgments which come upon men and nations."[56] But the question we are dealing with here does not involve discerning the

---

[55] Morris, *Biblical Doctrine of Judgment*, 45.

[56] Morris, 47n1. Morris cites Abraham Lincoln, who saw the judgments of the Lord in the sufferings of the Civil War.

judgments of God in present-day situations. We are asking about the time (or times) of eschatological judgment, which will occur at the end of the present age, most often referred to as "the day of the Lord."[57]

Here we encounter the same division of opinions we discussed earlier on the issue of the resurrection of the body. Those who affirm one general resurrection of the dead after Christ's return see one final judgment following that resurrection; those who argue for multiple acts of resurrection see multiple times of judgment. Stan Gundry states, "Premillennialists generally distinguish four judgments: of believers, of Israel, of the nations, and 'the great white throne' judgment,"[58] but there is certainly variation among premillennialists. John Walvoord affirms seven future judgments: the judgment of the church before Christ in heaven following the rapture (2 Cor 5:10); the judgment and rewarding of tribulation saints (Rev 20:4); the judgment of Old Testament saints following Christ's return (Dan 12:2); judgment of Gentiles living on earth at the time of Christ's return (Matt 25:31–46); judgment of those of Israel living at the time of Christ's return (Ezek 20:33–38); the judgment of Satan (Rev 20:1–3); and the great white throne judgment of the unrighteous dead (Rev 20:11–15).[59] Some would say Walvoord represents "the more classic form of dispensationalism,"[60] and changes in dispensational thought may be seen in the treatment of judgment by progressive dispensationalist Daniel Akin. He mentions only two events of judgment: the judgment of believers at the judgment seat of Christ (happening between the rapture and Second Coming or after the

---

[57] Morris sees Amos 5:18 as the earliest reference to this eschatological day of the Lord, but since Amos mentions it with no explanation, as if it was a well-known concept, Morris believes that the day of the Lord as a day of future judgment "was evidently a very early idea," (42). He adds later a variety of New Testament phrases referring to that day: "the day of God" (2 Pet 3:12), "the day of Christ" (Phil 2:16); "the day of our Lord Jesus Christ" (1 Cor 1:8), "the last day" (John 6:39), "the day of God's wrath" (Rom 2:5), "the day of judgment" (1 John 4:17) and others (60).

[58] Gundry, "Judgment of Nations," 453.

[59] Walvoord, *The Millennial Kingdom*, 276–95.

[60] Hays, Duvall, and Pate, *Dictionary of Biblical Prophecy and End Times*, 257.

Second Coming) and the great white throne judgment of unbelievers only, after the millennium.[61]

For amillennialists and postmillennialists, there is no eschatological time for multiple judgments. There is no seven-year time of tribulation between the rapture and the Second Coming, and there is no thousand-year millennium after Christ's second coming. They see the New Testament as teaching a simple timeline of Christ's second coming, followed by a general resurrection of all, and the general judgment of all.[62] And most scholars have seen the great white throne scene as depicting "a general judgment of the entire human race."[63]

For premillennialists, there is time for multiple acts of judgment, for the great white throne judgment will not happen until after the millennial reign of Christ following his return, and acts of judgment involving him may well have already happened by then. But is there more positive grounding in Scripture, not just for the possibility of multiple acts of judgment, but for the reality of such acts?

Walvoord's advocacy of seven future judgments has not been widely accepted and seems to deny that two texts of Scripture could include different elements and still refer to the same act of judgment. For example, the judgment scene in Matt 25:31–46 differs from that of Rev 20:11–15, leading Walvoord to interpret Matt 25:31–46 as a judgment just of Gentiles living at the time of Christ's return,[64] yet most scholars understand the two texts as referring to the same event. David Turner says that most read the Matthew text as referring to "the final judgment of all humanity"; with Grant Osborne adding "almost certainly," a universal judgment is in view.[65] R. T. France posits a link between the two texts in evaluating the genre of

---

[61] Akin, "A Rapture You Can't Miss," 57–58.

[62] See Hoekema, *The Bible and the Future*, 254–55.

[63] Hays, Duvall, and Pate, *Dictionary of Biblical Prophecy and End Times*, 195.

[64] Walvoord, *The Millennial Kingdom*, 284–85.

[65] David L. Turner, *Matthew*, BECNT (Grand Rapids: Baker Academic, 2008), 605; Grant R. Osborne, *Matthew*, ZECNT (Grand Rapids: Zondervan, 2010), 934.

Matt 25:31–46, saying it "is closer to the majestic visions of judgment in the book of Revelation than to the Synoptic parables."[66]

But the case for interpreting 2 Cor 5:10 as describing a separate act of judgment is stronger. Where Rev 20:11–15 and Matt 25:31–46 may describe an act of universal judgment, numerous commentators give reasons that lead them to interpret 2 Cor 5:10 as referring only to the judgment of believers.[67] While acknowledging that there is some division among scholars on the point, Murray Harris, George Guthrie, and Philip E. Hughes all point to the context and language of 2 Cor 5:10 as limiting those who appear before the judgment seat of Christ to believers,[68] and this is the majority view on this text.[69] As to when this act of judgment will take place, there may not be enough in the text to determine this point. Options include immediately after the death of each believer or at or after the rapture or return of Christ.[70] Despite the uncertainty on the precise matter of time, Hays, Duvall, and Pate believe one thing is clear: "Believers will be judged when they appear before Christ."[71] And from texts like Luke 23:43, 2 Cor 5:8, and Phil 1:23, it seems that believers will be with Christ from the moment of their death. Thus it seems likely to this author that believers appear before the judgment seat of Christ at their death.

What about an act (or acts) of eschatological judgment connected with the return of Christ? Both Matt 25:31–46 and Rev 20:11–15 seem to describe such as act of judgment, but Eckhard Schnabel contends that Rev 19:11–21 describes the judgment occurring at Christ's second coming,

---

[66] R. T. France, *The Gospel of Matthew*, NICNT (Grand Rapids: Eerdmans, 2007), 960.

[67] See the table of differences between the judgment seat of Christ and the great white throne judgment in Akin, "A Rapture You Can't Miss," 58.

[68] Murray J. Harris, *The Second Epistle to the Corinthians*, NIGTC (Grand Rapids: Eerdmans, 2005), 406; George H. Guthrie, *2 Corinthians*, BECNT (Grand Rapids: Baker Academic, 2015), 287; P. E. Hughes, *Paul's Second Epistle to the Corinthians*, NICNT (Grand Rapids: Eerdmans, 1962).

[69] Hays, Duvall, and Pate, *Dictionary of Biblical Prophecy and End Times*, 236.

[70] Harris, *The Second Epistle to the Corinthians*, 409; Hays, Duvall, and Pate, 236.

[71] Hays, Duvall, and Pate, 236.

with that of Rev 20:11–15 describing an act of judgment following the millennium. He realizes that this goes against the scholarly consensus that the great white throne judgment is universal, but he sees the language of Rev 20:11–15 as speaking "only of the judgment of Satan's followers, that is, the unrepentant, while the judgment of the saints is not mentioned."[72] Of course, Schnabel's position assumes the premillennial view; he knows that amillennialists see no thousand-year time between the return of Christ in Rev 19:11–21 and the judgment scene of Rev 20:11–15.[73] Thus, final adjudication of the question of when judgment will occur must await our consideration of the issue of the millennium, the topic of our next chapter. Before moving to that contentious topic, one more important question needs attention.

Why Will We Be Judged?

There are three parts to this question. First, why will be judged at all? Second, why will we be judged for what we have done (deeds, thoughts, and words) when Scripture makes it clear that we are not saved by what we have done, but by grace through faith? Third, what are we to make of the differing rewards given to believers based on this judgment?

To the first part of this question, we are judged because we are responsible moral agents; we are judged by God because it is right for God to do so. He is just and the judge of all the earth, responsible for upholding and maintaining justice. He judges, punishing sin and evil and rewarding good, because that is what is just. He does not view good and evil as equivalent, and he will see to it that in the end, justice prevails. As Paul Barnett says, judgment "preserves the moral seriousness of God."[74] We are morally

---

[72] Eckhard Schnabel, *40 Questions about the End Times* (Grand Rapids: Kregel Academic, 2011), 289.

[73] Schnabel, 289n5.

[74] Paul Barnett, *The Second Epistle to the Corinthians*, NICNT (Grand Rapids: Eerdmans, 1997), 277.

responsible creatures. While we may be affected by forces beyond our control (which God knows and takes into account), we still make responsible choices. We are given a life for which we are accountable, making choices for which we are accountable. Without judgment, we would be like students whose schoolwork is never graded, rendering their work meaningless. Our lives before God are not meaningless; all we do matters to God. Judgment is the necessary result.

As to the second part of the question, is the fact that we will be judged by what we have done contrary to our belief that we are saved not by works but by what Christ has done for us? Justice and grace are both present in the character of God and come together in his acts of judgment as well.[75] They come together, first, in that the deeds we do in the body reflect the reality of the work that Christ has done in our lives. This is seen in the insistence of James that true faith is made evident in one's works, and that the absence of works is an indication of dead faith, not saving faith (Jas 2:14–26).[76] Salvation by grace through faith and judgment based on deeds done in the body also fit together when we realize that what one receives for the deeds done in the body is not salvation but some reward in addition to salvation. This is most clearly seen in 1 Cor 3:10–15.

In that text, Paul sees the foundation of every Christian's life as Christ (vv. 10–11). Christ alone saves and makes one a Christian. But Christians diverge on how they build upon that foundation. Paul says that some build on it with "gold, silver, costly stones" (v. 12), signifying the type of persons who put their all into serving Christ, while others use "wood, hay, or straw" (v. 12),[77] indicating those who "build carelessly," offering Christ "shoddy

[75] See verses like Jer 9:24, which affirm that God shows "faithful love, justice, and righteousness on the earth" and that he delights in them.

[76] "Faith must reveal itself in works, and works, in turn, are the evidence of true faith." Hoekema, *The Bible and the Future*, 260.

[77] David Garland, *1 Corinthians*, BECNT (Grand Rapids: Baker Academic, 2003) 116–17. The list of materials contrasts those of "exceptional quality," which will endure, with those of "inferior quality," which will not endure.

and half-hearted" service.[78] Paul warns the Corinthians that the quality of each one's work will be tested by the fire of judgment (v. 13). Those whose work survives the fire "will receive a reward" (v. 14), but the reward received is not salvation, for those whose work "is burned up" in the fire of judgment will experience loss of reward, but not loss of salvation: "He himself will be saved—but only as through fire" (v. 15).

As to the third part of the question, we are told little of the reward given to those whose service to Christ survives the test of judgment. Indeed, it is difficult to imagine what could be added to the gift of eternal life in the presence of God in a resurrected body in a new creation. The New Testament writers refer to various crowns given to believers for various types of service: "an imperishable crown" for exercising self-control (1 Cor 9:25); "a crown of boasting" or joy over those we helped to bring to Christ (1 Thess 2:19); a "crown of righteousness" to those who love Christ's appearing in his return (2 Tim 4:8); the "crown of life" for enduring trials (Jas 1:12); and an "unfading crown of glory" for faithfully shepherding God's flock (1 Pet 5:4). These may be the crowns we lay before the throne of God in worship (Rev 4:10), but it seems more likely they are symbolic, not literal crowns. What could be a fitting reward for faithful service?

It should be said that differing rewards do seem fair, for it is clear that some serve Christ with zeal and whole-heartedness over an entire life, while others may come to Christ near the end of their life or serve Christ half-heartedly through their entire life. On the one hand, even our service to Christ is the result of his work in us (Phil 2:13; 1 Cor 15:10), yet it is Jesus himself who taught the principle of differing rewards based on service (Luke 19:16–19; Matt 5:12). What could such a reward be?

I cannot cite a biblical text in support of this idea, but it has long seemed to me that a greater or lesser capacity to enjoy heaven would be a fitting reward. Every saved individual would be equally in heaven; every saved individual would be equally enjoying themselves to 100 percent of their capacity, but that capacity for enjoyment would vary in keeping with

[78] Morris, *Biblical Doctrine of Judgment*, 67.

one's service to Christ. Anthony Hoekema sees this as a fitting and "organic" connection between our works and reward:

> When one has studied music and has attained some proficiency in playing a musical instrument, his capacity for enjoying music has been greatly increased. In a similar way, our devotion to Christ and to service in his kingdom increases our capacity for enjoying the blessings of that kingdom, both now and in the life to come.[79]

If this is true, then judgment should be a tremendous incentive to the believer. Not only will it clearly show to the world that justice prevails, but it will also manifest the eternal value of one's faithful service to Christ. Every day, the believer is shaping their capacity for eternal joy. It is not that we serve the Lord for what we get out of it; love prompts our service, but it is fitting and tremendously encouraging that the reward for love-prompted service is a greater capacity to enjoy the one we love.

---

[79] Hoekema, *The Bible and the Future*, 264. Morris, *Biblical Doctrine of Judgment* (67), makes a similar observation, that those who serve the Lord wholeheartedly know more of the joy of the Lord now than the half-hearted, and that we have no reason to think it will be any different in heaven.

CHAPTER 7

The Mystery of the Millennium

Introduction

Of all the topics in eschatology, none is more difficult than that of the millennium; that is, the idea that there will be a thousand-year period of Jesus's rule on the earth following his return. It is difficult biblically, for while there are many texts that have some bearing on the millennium, the key text is Revelation 20, a difficult text in what most would affirm as the most difficult book in the Bible to interpret.[1] It is difficult theologically, with the history of interpretation showing one approach dominant for a time, only to lose that place to another. It is difficult practically, in that there seems to be little difference regarding how one's millennial view changes the way one

[1] This is seen in the fact that there is an entire book devoted to different methods of interpreting the book of Revelation (C. Marvin Pate, ed., *Four Views on the Book of Revelation* [Grand Rapids: Zondervan, 1998]), as well as lengthy sections on these different methods of interpretation found in commentaries on Revelation.

lives a Christ-honoring life. Yet, because it is considered important in some theological circles, it demands attention in a book like this.

For ease in following the discussion below, it may be helpful to give a brief introduction to the major views of the millennium before examining the arguments offered in defense of each of these views.[2] The first major view is premillennialism, so called because in this view Christ's second coming *pre*cedes the millennium. The millennium is understood as a time when Christ will reign on the earth with believers. Many take that time to be literally a millennium, 1,000 years; others take the number as symbolic for simply a significant time period.[3] Within premillennialism itself, there are two major approaches to the millennium. One school is called historic premillennialism because it is well represented in early church history. The second is called dispensational premillennialism, because part of the argument for premillennialism rests on the arguments for dispensationalism as a theological system. Both agree on the central point: Christ's second coming precedes the millennium, which will be a future time on earth.

The second major view of the millennium is called amillennialism, though some of its advocates prefer to call it realized millennialism. In this view, there is no expectation of a future millennium preceded by Christ's second coming. Rather, the millennium is "the present reign of the souls of deceased believers with Christ in heaven."[4] The reign is spiritual, and the millennium involved is not a literal thousand years;

---

[2] For an excellent survey and overview of these major views, see Thomas R. Schreiner, *Revelation*, BECNT (Grand Rapids: Baker Academic, 2023), 664–76.

[3] For two defenses of premillennialism, see G. E. Ladd, "Historic Premillennialism," in *The Meaning of the Millennium: Four Views*, ed. Robert G. Clouse (Downers Grove: InterVarsity, 1977), 17–40; and Craig A. Blaising, "Premillennialism," in *Three Views on the Millennium and Beyond*, ed. Darrell L. Bock (Grand Rapids: Zondervan, 1999), 157–227.

[4] Anthony A. Hoekema, *The Bible and the Future* (Grand Rapids: Eerdmans, 1979), 174. Hoekema defends amillennialism in the book just cited and in "Amillennialism," Clouse, in *The Meaning of the Millennium: Four Views*, 155–87. Perhaps even more influential has been the work of G. K. Beale, both in his commentary on Revelation (*The Book of Revelation*, NIGTC [Grand Rapids: Eerdmans,

rather, the number is symbolic for all the time between Christ's first and second advents.

The third major view is called *post*millennialism, because it views the second coming of Christ as following (post-) the millennium. It sees the millennium as in one sense present, but primarily still to come. Postmillennialist Kenneth Gentry Jr. gives the following as its basic idea:

> Postmillennialism expects the proclaiming of the Spirit-blessed gospel of Jesus Christ to win the vast majority of human beings to salvation in the present age. Increasing gospel success will gradually produce a time in history prior to Christ's return in which faith, righteousness, peace, and prosperity will prevail in the affairs of people and of nations.[5]

After this "time in history," which will be a significant era but not a literal thousand years, Christ will return to conclude history.

While the issue of the millennium touches on many issues, from theological systems to individual texts, there seem to be three key issues. Different interpretations of these three issues lead to these differing positions.

Three Key Issues

Interpretation of Old Testament Prophecy

The first major issue is how one interprets Old Testament prophecy. It is evident in reading the Old Testament that there are many prophecies that look to a glorious future time of peace and prosperity with manifold blessings. In Isaiah alone, one reads of the prophecy of a time when nations will no longer train for war against each other (2:1–4), of the time to come when even the violence of predator and prey among animals will be gone, when

---

1999]) and in a more recent article ("An Amillennial Response to a Premillennial View of Isaiah 65:20," *JETS* 61, no. 3 [2018]: 461–92).

[5] Kenneth L. Gentry Jr., "Postmillennialism," in Bock, *Three Views of the Millennium and Beyond*, 13–14.

the earth will be filled with the knowledge of the Lord (11:6–9), and even of the coming creation of a new heaven and new earth (65:17–25). The question is how one should interpret these passages.

Dispensational premillennialists make much of these prophecies as support for their position. They insist that these prophecies should be interpreted literally. If they make promises of an earthly kingdom to Israel, then those promises must be kept to Israel.[6] John Walvoord asserts that "it is conceded by practically all parties that the Old Testament presents premillennial doctrine if interpreted literally." They take the length of this kingdom (a thousand years) and the timing (after Christ's return) from Revelation 20, but the nature of the kingdom is fleshed out in these Old Testament prophecies. For them, premillennialism is not derived from Revelation 20 alone, but their view "offers the only possible literal fulfillment for the hundreds of verses of prophetic testimony."[7]

Postmillennialists see many of these prophecies as already fulfilled "in the *permanent establishing* of Christianity in God's judgment on Israel when he destroyed the old Jewish order in 70 A.D."[8] For example, postmillennialists see the prophecy of Isa 65:17–25 "as a description of blessings that are promised for the present millennial age."[9] But due to the failure of Israel, these blessings now come to the church. The future kingdom prophesied

[6] The larger issues of the relationship of the church to Israel, and of a future for ethnic Israel in God's eschatological plans, lie underneath this more specific issue, but space limitations preclude a full treatment of these issues. For a presentation of contrasting positions on these issues, see Marten H. Woudstra, "Israel and the Church: A Case for Continuity," and Robert L. Saucy, "Israel and the Church: A Case for Discontinuity," in *Continuity and Discontinuity: Perspectives on the Relationship Between the Old and New Testaments*, ed. John S. Feinberg (Wheaton: Crossway, 1988), 221–59, and Chad O. Brand, ed., *Perspectives on Israel and the Church: Four Views* (Nashville: B&H, 2015).

[7] John F. Walvoord, *The Millennial Kingdom: A Basic Text in Premillennial Theology* (Grand Rapids: Zondervan, 1959), 114.

[8] Kenneth L. Gentry Jr., "A Postmillennial Response," in Bock, *Three Views on the Millennium and Beyond*, 234. Emphasis in original.

[9] Keith Mathison, *Postmillennialism: An Eschatology of Hope* (Phillipsburg, NJ: P & R, 1999), 87.

by the Old Testament prophets will come, but not to Israel by "premillennial catastrophism," but to the church by "*gradualistic* development of the kingdom of God in history."[10]

Amillennialists think that we are given the proper approach to Old Testament prophecies in the New Testament. Robert Strimple asserts,

> the proper *Christian* preunderstanding in reading Old Testament prophetic passages is the authoritative apostolic, post-Pentecost New Testament interpretive pattern, which consistently sees these prophecies as fulfilled in Christ and his messianic kingdom, both in its present, partially realized phase and in its future, fully realized phase.[11]

While following Strimple in taking interpretation of the Old Testament prophecies from their New Testament interpretations, fellow amillennialist Anthony Hoekema sharpens the point of fulfillment. He is aware of the criticism of the amillennial position by dispensationalists: that it spiritualizes prophecies which should be taken literally.[12] He says,

> Dispensationalists commonly say that we amillennialists spiritualize prophecies of this kind by understanding them as being fulfilled either in the church of this present age or in heaven in the age to come. I believe, however, that prophecies of this sort refer neither primarily to the church of this age nor to heaven, but to *the new earth*.[13]

We shall argue in a future chapter that the new earth is one way the Bible refers to heaven, and so both Strimple and Hoekema may be referring

---

[10] Gentry, "Response," 235. Emphasis in original.

[11] Robert B. Strimple, "An Amillennial Response," in Bock, *Three Views on the Millennium and Beyond*, 267. Emphasis in original.

[12] This critique is seen in dispensationalists from John F. Walvoord, *The Millennial Kingdom*, 59–67, to David L. Allen, "The Millennial Reign of Christ," in *The Return of Christ: A Premillennial Perspective*, ed. David L. Allen and Steve W. Lemke (Nashville: B&H Academic, 2011), 75.

[13] Hoekema, *The Bible and the Future*, 205.

to the same idea—that Old Testament prophecies should be seen as being fulfilled in the future, final phase of the messianic kingdom, which will be the new earth. Either way, they decisively differ from the dispensational understanding that a proper understanding of the Bible demands that a promise made to Israel be kept to Israel. They think the New Testament gives grounds for seeing the church as inheriting the promises made to Israel and the kingdom promises being fulfilled to all God's people.

The difficulty in choosing an interpretive position on this matter may be seen in consideration of just one of these Old Testament passages, Isa 65:17–25. The opening words, referring to the creation of a new heavens and new earth, call to mind the same phrase from Rev 21:1, and so one may think that this prophecy refers to the new creation that will be the final home of all God's people. But Isa 65:20 refers to death, which has no place in the new creation. So, is this prophecy a reference to an earthly millennial kingdom? John Walvoord splits the text, with Isa 65:17–18 referring to the eternal state and verses 20–25 referring to the conditions of life in the millennial kingdom.[14] Hoekema admits, Isa 65:20 "is a difficult text to interpret."[15] Schreiner, however, gives several reasons for suggesting that verse 20 should be interpreted as "rhetorical and poetic" language. For example, verse 19 says there will be no more "weeping and crying." Would Isaiah include that if he also thought people were still dying?[16] The interpretation of this and other Old Testament texts is not an easy matter.

To this author, the key issue seems to be the New Testament guidance on how we are to interpret Old Testament prophecies. Normally, conservative Christians want to take the Bible literally; we do not want to spiritualize miracles and make Bible stories into fairy tales. But what if the Bible itself seems to set something of a different pattern? Take, for example, the prophecy of a new covenant (Jer 31:31–34). Verse 31 says this is the covenant God will make "with the house of Israel and with the house of Judah"; verse 33

[14] Walvoord, *The Millennial Kingdom*, 325, 318–19.

[15] Hoekema, *The Bible and the Future*, 202.

[16] Schreiner, *Revelation*, 717.

reiterates that this covenant will be made "with the house of Israel." But clearly, Jesus instituted this new covenant with the church (Luke 22:20; Heb 8:8–13). In 1 Pet 2:9, Peter takes four phrases used of Israel in the Old Testament and applies them to the church; in Gal 3:29, all who belong to Christ are called Abraham's seed, which is not true literally but spiritually. It does seem that the New Testament justifies understanding promises made to Israel as fulfilled to the church.

This conclusion does not fully determine one's millennial position. In addition to dispensational premillennialists, there is a growing camp of what are called historic premillennialists. One representative of that camp, G. E. Ladd, concludes from his own study of Scripture that "the New Testament applies Old Testament prophecies to the New Testament church and in so doing identifies the church as spiritual Israel." He recognizes that an alert reader may say, "This sounds like amillennialism."[17] But there are other factors that leave Ladd "a convinced premillennialist."[18] We move now to consideration of these other factors.

Revelation 20

By common consent Revelation 20 is the key text for the issue of the millennium. It is the only text in the Bible that specifically mentions the period of a thousand years in connection with this rule of Christ with his people,[19] and thus is responsible for the term "millennium." There are numerous issues on which interpreters differ concerning this text.

1. Do the events described in Rev 20:1–6 follow the events described in Rev 19:11–21? The answer to this question is shaped in large part by one's

---

[17] G. E. Ladd, "Historic Premillennialism," 25, 27.

[18] G. E. Ladd, "An Historic Premillennial Response," in Clouse, *The Meaning of the Millenium*, 191.

[19] While Revelation 20 is the only text that mentions the one thousand years, it does use the phrase "a thousand years" six times in Rev 20:1–7.

overall approach to the book of Revelation. Premillennialists take a futurist approach to the book of Revelation; that is, they believe "that the events of Revelation are largely unfulfilled, holding that chapters 4–22 await the end times for their realization."[20] They interpret Rev 19:11–21 as describing the future second coming of Christ, with the events of Revelation 20, particularly the millennium, following the Second Coming. Craig Blaising gives six arguments for seeing this order, with perhaps the most often discussed argument being the phrase *kai eidon*, "then I saw," in Rev 19:11, 17, 19; 20:1, 4 and 11; and numerous times throughout Revelation. Blaising views this phrase as tying together the visions of Revelation 19–20 "in a unified sequence." He acknowledges that the phrase is not "determinative in itself of a chronological sequence," but it is "a recognized structural marker," especially when "the content of the visions helps to determine the chronology."[21] Thomas Schreiner and Grant Osborne both share the premillennial understanding of Revelation 19 and 20 following each other sequentially, but not based on this understanding of *kai eidon*. Both cite other places in Revelation where the phrase introduces events which are not "clearly sequential temporally";[22] Schreiner affirms that the book of Revelation "is often recursive and recapitulatory." He believes that the sequential nature of Revelation 19 and 20 "must be established on other grounds," such as the contents of Rev 20:1–6.[23]

A second approach to the book of Revelation, favored by postmillennialists, is the preterist approach. Whereas the futurist approach sees most of Revelation prophesying events still in the future, the preterist view "holds that the bulk of John's prophecies occur in the first century,"[24] with the fall of

---

[20] C. Marvin Pate, "Introduction to Revelation," in Pate, *Four Views on the Book of Revelation*, 17.

[21] Blaising, "Premillennialism," 215.

[22] Schreiner, *Revelation*, 683; Grant R. Osborne, *Revelation*, BECNT (Grand Rapids: Baker Academic, 2002), 699.

[23] Schreiner, *Revelation*, 683. See also Osborne, *Revelation*, 699.

[24] Kenneth L. Gentry Jr., "A Preterist View of Revelation," in Pate, *Four Views on the Book of Revelation*, 37.

Jerusalem in AD 70 being an important time of fulfillment.[25] To be specific, the coming of Christ in Rev 19:11–21 is seen by postmillennialists in the preterist sense, as a coming in judgment that was fulfilled in AD 70.[26] The events of Revelation 20 are something of an exception to the preterist view as postmillennialists understand the millennium as the entire era between the two advents of Christ, and thus past, present, and future.[27] The final return of Christ concludes the millennial era and is thus postmillennial.

The approach to the book of Revelation most common among amillennialists is called recapitulation or "progressive parallelism," in which "the book of Revelation consists of seven sections which run parallel to each other, each of which depicts the church and the world from the time of Christ's first coming to the time of his second coming."[28] Amillennialists believe Rev 19:11–21 describes Christ's triumphant return at the end of history, bringing final judgment on his enemies. The events of Revelation 20, however, do not describe things to happen following Christ's return; rather, "Revelation 20:1 takes us back to the beginning of the New Testament era."[29] It is the beginning of the last of the seven sections of Revelation. In the words of G. K. Beale, Rev 20:1–6 "describes the course of the church age and temporally precedes the final judgment, which has been narrated in chs. 17–19."[30] Beale especially argues against using the phrase *kai eidon* in Rev 20:1 as evidence that Rev 20:1 narrates events sequentially after the events of Rev 19:11–21.[31] But as we noted earlier, some premillennialists grant that *kai eidon* does not settle the question of temporal sequence; thus, they point

---

[25] Mathison, *Postmillennialism*, 140. The preterist view "teaches that many if not most of the prophecies within the book pointed to the destruction of Jerusalem in A.D. 70."

[26] Gentry, "A Preterist View," 81.

[27] "The 'millennial' era has already lasted almost two thousand years; it may continue another thousand or ten thousand more, for all we know." Gentry, "Postmillennialism," 55.

[28] Hoekema, *The Bible and the Future*, 223.

[29] Hoekema, 227.

[30] Beale, *Revelation*, 972.

[31] Beale, 974–76.

to other elements in the content of Rev 20:1–6. The first such element in that content is the binding of Satan in Rev 20:1–3.

2. The binding of Satan. The question here is the timing and extent of the binding of Satan; the two matters are intimately related. If Satan is bound to an extent that we have not seen in the time since the first advent of Christ, then the binding of Rev 20:1–3 must be future and the idea that it follows the events of Rev 19:11–21, the second coming of Jesus, makes sense. On the other hand, postmillennialists and amillennialists believe the binding of Satan occurred at Jesus's first coming; it is the binding that has prevented Satan from deceiving the nations during the church age. Postmillennialists add the idea of increasing boundness during the church age—"Christ bound Satan with the result that his deceptive power over the nations is fading as the gospel advances into all the world—" but they still see Christ's life, death, and resurrection as the crucial beginning.[32] Amillennialists focus on the binding that occurred in Jesus's first coming and see two results: Satan's ability to deceive the nations is curtailed or restricted, and he is not able to gather Christ's enemies together to attack the church, as in Rev 20:7–10.[33]

Amillennialists are sensitive to the charge that to many, Satan does not seem to be bound in this age. They qualify the extent of Satan's binding carefully. Beale says, "That Satan is 'cast out' (*ekballō)* by Christ's death does not restrict Satan in every way."[34] Hoekema adds, "This [binding] does not imply that Satan can do no harm whatever while he is bound."[35] Beale in particular argues that this limited understanding of binding is consistent with what the New Testament says elsewhere about the results of Christ's death and resurrection.[36] But the binding of Rev 20:1–3 is far more comprehensive than the binding mentioned in texts like Matt 12:29, for in the

---

[32] Gentry, "A Preterist View," 83–84.

[33] Beale, *Revelation*, 984–85; Hoekema, *The Bible and the Future*, 228–29.

[34] Beale, *Revelation*, 985.

[35] Hoekema, *The Bible and the Future*, 228.

[36] See the lengthy discussion in Beale, *Revelation*, 984–91.

former text Satan is not just bound but thrown into the abyss, which is locked and sealed over him. In this age, Satan still deceives some (2 Tim 3:13; Titus 3:3) and blinds the minds of unbelievers (2 Cor 4:4). Rather than being locked in an abyss, he is described as "prowling around like a roaring lion" (1 Pet 5:8). Rather than being shut away from the world, he is described as having the whole world "under his sway" (1 John 5:19). Even if we accept a symbolic understanding of the abyss and the thousand years during which Satan is bound and locked away, the language "does not fit the current situation. Rather, it demands a later period after the *parousia*."[37] The language of Rev 20:1–3, the language elsewhere in the New Testament of the devil's activity in the world today, and present evidence of Satanic activity (the resistance of many nations to the gospel) all seem inconsistent with the amillennial idea of a partial binding of Satan now or the postmillennial claim that he is being gradually bound. The premillennial claim of a comprehensive binding that has not yet happened appears to be well founded.

3. The resurrection and reign of the righteous with Christ. Another crucial element of the content of Revelation 20 that impacts whether we should interpret verses 1–6 as happening now or in the future is the description of some who "came to life and reigned with Christ for a thousand years" (Rev 20:4). How could that phrase describe something happening now? Some postmillennialists argue this first resurrection is simply salvation, a spiritual resurrection, and cite John 5:24–29 as evidence that John "parallels spiritual resurrection unto present salvation and physical resurrection unto eternal destiny."[38] Most amillennialists see this first resurrection as the translation of believers upon death to life with Christ in heaven in the intermediate state.[39] This amillennial view of "came to life" seems preferable to the view which understands it as simply salvation because the latter would apply to

[37] Osborne, *Revelation*, 703.

[38] Gentry, "A Preterist View," 85. According to Beale, *Revelation* (1011), this was also the "classical Augustinian perspective."

[39] Hoekema, *The Bible and the Future*, 233, and Beale, *Revelation*, 1010–11.

all believers, living and dead, whereas the group referred to in Rev 20:4 seems limited to those who had died, indeed, had "been beheaded."

By contrast, the premillennial view insists that "came to life" in Rev 20:4 must refer to a literal, physical resurrection. They point to the similar phrase, "come to life," in verse 5, which almost all commentators agree refers to a physical resurrection.[40] If the word in verse 5 means physical resurrection, then the same word in the previous verse should be understood as a physical resurrection. The words of the nineteenth-century exegete Henry Alford are often quoted: "If, in a passage where two resurrections are mentioned . . . if in such a passage the first resurrection may be understood to mean *spiritual* rising with Christ, while the second means *literal* rising from the grave;—then there is an end of all significance in language, and Scripture is wiped out as a definite testimony to anything."[41] Further support for the premillennial view is the fact that the Greek term for resurrection, *anástasis*, occurs forty-one times in the New Testament and refers to a physical resurrection in every case except Luke 2:34 and John 11:25.[42]

G. K. Beale acknowledges both of these arguments, yet makes what is perhaps the most extensive counter-argument for the amillennial understanding that the first resurrection in Rev 20:4 is spiritual and that of Rev 20:5 is physical.[43] He contends that the key terms ("come to life" and "resurrection") are used in an interchangeable manner for spiritual and physical resurrection in Rom 6:4–13 and John 5:24–29. He builds on the argument of Meredith Kline and adds additional arguments of his own, showing, for example, that other "first-second" language in Scripture (first/last Adam; old/new covenant) does not demand that both refer to things that are

[40] "On this all commentators apparently agree." Beale, *Revelation*, 1003.

[41] Henry Alford, *The Greek Testament* (Boston: Lee & Shepard, 1872), IV, 732. Emphasis in original. This passage is cited by premillennialist G. E. Ladd, "Historic Premillennialism," 37–38, and by amillennialist G. K. Beale, *Revelation*, 1003–4, as "one of the most substantial arguments in favor of the premillennial interpretation," (1003).

[42] Beale, *Revelation*, 1004; Osborne, *Revelation*, 718.

[43] Beale, *Revelation*, devotes 1004–17 to a defense of the amillennial view.

identical and that existence in the intermediate state is often described with the language of life and coming to life (Rev 2:10–11; Luke 20:37–38).[44]

Premillennialist Grant Osborne surveys Beale's arguments and calls them "well presented and viable," yet not "compelling."[45] Thomas Schreiner goes further, acknowledging that he had at one time supported the amillennial interpretation, but then presents ten objections that he believes "make it ultimately implausible."[46] To the claim that Rom 6:4–13 and John 5:24–29 refer to spiritual and physical resurrection interchangeably, G. E. Ladd responds that in those passages there are clear clues in the context pointing to variation in interpretation, while "in Revelation 20 *there is no such contextual clue for a similar variation of interpretation*."[47] A physical resurrection better fits the near universal meaning of *anástasis*, the context in Revelation 20, and the hope for believers.[48]

The premillennial understanding that Rev 20:4–6 refers to the physical resurrection of certain ones who had been beheaded that occurs after the return of Jesus seems the clearly preferable understanding of this passage. When combined with other texts that teach the resurrection of all believers after the return of Christ (1 Cor 15:51–52; 1 Thess 4:16), we have grounds for seeing the martyrs referenced in Rev 20:4 as representing the whole church, "all who have remained faithful to Jesus, not only during this final period of history but throughout the ages."[49] This also sheds light on two questions we left open from the previous chapter: Is there only one general resurrection or are there multiple events, and is there only one general judgment or are there multiple acts of eschatological judgment? The language of Rev 20:4–5 of the first resurrection of some and of a later coming to life of

[44] Meredith G. Kline, "The First Resurrection," *Westminster Theological Journal* 37, no. 3 (1975): 366–75.

[45] Osborne, *Revelation*, 718.

[46] Schreiner, *Revelation*, 671. The ten objections are found on 671–74.

[47] Ladd, "Historic Premillennialism," 37. Emphasis in original. Osborne, *Revelation*, 718, and Schreiner, *Revelation*, 671–72, concur.

[48] Schreiner, *Revelation*, 673.

[49] Osborne, *Revelation*, 705.

others strongly suggests two acts of resurrection. The question of multiple eschatological judgments is not as clear, but if there is a gap of time between the return of Christ and the final judgment of Rev 20:11–15,[50] it would open up time when an act of judgment on Christ's part (the "judgment seat" of 2 Cor 5:10 or the throne judgment of Matt 25:31–46) could take place, but again, the case for multiple acts of judgment is not as clear.

The Return of Christ

The third factor that strongly shapes one's view of the millennium is the belief some have that Christ's return is the climax of God's plan of redemption; it is the point at which everything should be concluded—the dead are all resurrected, all face judgment, and we move to the eternal state. Many would say a thousand-year delay seems pointless and contrary to biblical teaching on all that is associated with Christ's return.

For example, amillennialists say Dan 12:2 and John 5:28–29 strongly imply that all are resurrected at the same time; John 6:39 adds that this resurrection occurs "on the last day." How can that be if there is a thousand-year period following the last-day resurrection? Moreover, 1 Cor 15:51–52 teaches that we are raised at Christ's second coming and at that time the prophecy of Isa 25:8 will be fulfilled, "Death has been swallowed up in victory." But how can that be if there is a period of a thousand years of history, with births and deaths continuing? Sam Storms notes the problem premillennialists face in explaining what happens to believers who die during the millennium. How can they die if death has been swallowed up in victory? If they die, are there individual bodily resurrections for each one of these believers? Storms sees this scenario as "bizarre."[51] Far better is the view that sees Christ's return as bringing the resurrection of all, and the end of death.

---

[50] The "thousand years" of Rev 20:1–7 may be symbolic or figurative, but some length of time would seem to be indicated.

[51] Sam Storms, *Kingdom Come: The Amillennial Alternative* (Ross-shire, Scotland: Christian Focus, 2012), 551–52.

A second event linked to the return of Christ is eschatological judgment. Jude 15 speaks of the Lord coming "to execute judgment on all"; Paul speaks of the day when Christ returns as the time when he gives relief to those who have suffered for the kingdom and to take vengeance "on those who don't know God and on those who don't obey the gospel" (2 Thess 1:6–8). Jesus himself describes a scene of judgment when "the Son of Man comes in his glory" (Matt 25:31), a scene that is interpreted by most scholars as "almost certainly" referring to a universal and final judgment,[52] though dispensationalists would dispute this, seeing it as a judgment only of Gentiles who are living at the time of Christ's return.[53]

A text that has occasioned much discussion and disagreement is Rev 20:11–15. It may be accurate to say that most understand this great white throne judgment "as a general judgment of the entire human race, righteous and unrighteous alike,"[54] but the verdict is far from unanimous. In addition to objections from dispensationalists, who interpret this text as describing the resurrection and judgment of only the wicked dead,[55] non-dispensationalist Thomas Schreiner concurs that in Rev 20:11–15, "only unbelievers are in view."[56] By contrast, amillennialists find in this text both the general resurrection and judgment of all and see it preceded by the return of Christ in Rev 20:7–10, which they view as a recapitulation of the earlier description of Christ's return in Rev 19:11–21.[57]

Much of the disagreement centers around the phrase describing the dead who come to stand before the throne for judgment as "the great and the small" (v. 12). It could be read as a phrase to indicate the whole human race, but Schreiner cites places in Revelation where this phrase

---

[52] Grant R. Osborne, *Matthew*, ZECNT (Grand Rapids: Zondervan, 2010), 934; David Turner, *Matthew*, BECNT (Grand Rapids: Baker Academic, 2008), 605.

[53] Walvoord, *The Millennial Kingdom*, 284–85.

[54] J. Daniel Hays, J. Scott Duvall, and C. Marvin Pate, *Dictionary of Biblical Prophecy and End Times* (Grand Rapids: Zondervan, 2007), 195.

[55] Walvoord, *The Millennial Kingdom*, 332.

[56] Schreiner, *Revelation*, 700n2.

[57] Beale, *Revelation*, 1031.

is used for those who fear God (11:18; 19:5) and other places where it refers to nonbelievers (13:16; 19:18). He argues that the phrase here is probably referring only to unbelievers, since there is no reference to any whose names *are* found in the Book of Life and who are *not* thrown into the lake of fire.[58]

A final text joining the return of Christ to final judgment is 2 Pet 3:10. Here, "the day of the Lord," a phrase intimately linked to judgment and to Christ's return,[59] is said to be the day when the present creation gives way to the new heavens and new earth. Whether the present creation is totally destroyed or is purified and transformed into the new creation is an interesting question;[60] either way, it seems like the present creation will not be available for an earthly millennium after Christ's return. His return will mean judgment even on the created order.

While there is some disagreement, a fairly strong case can be made that the coming of final judgment is associated with the return of Christ and to delay that judgment for a thousand-year millennium is contrary to that biblical link (see Matt 25:31; John 5:28–29; 2 Pet 3:10). The early church saw that link, as the description of Christ's ascension and being seated at the right hand of God in the Apostles' Creed is immediately followed by the phrase, "from thence he shall come to judge the quick and the dead." There is a similarly strong, though mostly implicit, argument that Christ's return is also the time when both believers and unbelievers are raised. Many premillennialists grant that the case for the amillennial view is strong, and some say that were it not for Rev 20:1–6, they could be amillennialists. Amillennialists think that to allow one passage, in the book of the Bible most difficult to interpret, to overturn this repeated association in Scripture of the end of this age with the return of Christ is poor hermeneutics.

---

[58] Schreiner, *Revelation*, 701.

[59] Morris, *The Biblical Doctrine of Judgment*, 43, 60; Hays, Duvall, and Pate, *Dictionary of Biblical Prophecy and End Times*, 110.

[60] Hoekema, *The Bible and the Future* (280–81) calls the options annihilation or renewal and gives four reasons why he thinks renewal is the better interpretation.

Of these three key issues, the interpretation of Old Testament prophecy is of vital importance to the case for dispensational premillennialism and is claimed to be of importance for postmillennialism,[61] but it does not figure significantly in the case for historic premillennialism or amillennialism. The second key issue, Revelation 20, is central to historic and dispensational premillennialism; amillennial and postmillennial readings of this key text are subject to some serious objections. The third key issue, the association of the return of Christ with universal resurrection and final judgment, is supportive of amillennial views and fits with postmillennialism (though it does not figure significantly in arguments for it). It presents a major challenge to premillennialists.

Evaluation

Thus far I have sought to speak mostly in descriptive terms, giving what the key issues are and what the various views claim. The time has come now for evaluation. Which view has the strongest claim for our affirmation? I will begin with the view I see as least compelling and explain why, then proceed to views which I see as stronger and conclude with the view I see as most in keeping with all biblical teaching.

The key claim of postmillennialism is that the proclamation of the gospel will "win the vast majority of human beings to salvation in the present age," and that "increasing gospel success will gradually produce a time in history prior to Christ's return in which faith, righteousness, peace, and prosperity will prevail in the affairs of people and of nations."[62] This claim is sharply challenged by observable reality and by biblical and theological teaching.

---

[61] Gentry, "Postmillennialism" (31–32), even finds it necessary to deny that postmillennialism is "primarily an Old Testament-dependent system without New Testament support." He claims numerous texts in both Testaments support his position. Mathison devotes a significant section of his book *Postmillennialism* (57–100) to what he sees as Old Testament support for postmillennialism.

[62] Gentry, "Postmillennialism," 13–14.

Some think a simple look at the realities of history is sufficient to disprove postmillennialism. While we rejoice at the spread of Christianity around the world as the only truly global religion, we are far from seeing the majority of human beings embrace the gospel. Craig Blaising says that the one who insists increasing gospel success will transform our world now "owes us an explanation of the history of the last two thousand years."[63] After all this time, we should be able to see more progress. It is instructive to note that postmillennialism was the dominant view among evangelicals during periods "in which the church appeared to be succeeding in its task of winning the world,"[64] with advocates such as Jonathan Edwards during the First Great Awakening and major theologians such as Charles Hodge and Baptist A. H. Strong in the nineteenth century, often called the Great Century of the modern missionary movement. Since then, postmillennialism has become by a large margin the least popular view,[65] and not just because of where history appears to be heading now. If that were the only objection, postmillennialists could accuse their opponents of prematurely judging the direction of history, and they could possibly be right. But there are also reasons to critique postmillennialism on more secure grounds than the shifting tides of history.

---

[63] Blaising, "A Premillennial Response," in Bock, *Three Views on the Millennium and Beyond*, 75.

[64] Millard Erickson, *Christian Theology*, 3rd ed. (Grand Rapids: Baker Academic, 2013), 1108.

[65] A 2011 story reported that the January Evangelical Leaders Survey found 65 percent of evangelical leaders identify with some form of premillennialism, 13 percent with amillennialism, and only 4 percent with postmillennialism. See "Premillennialism Reigns in Evangelical Theology," National Association of Evangelicals, January 1, 2011, https://nae.org/premillennialism-reigns-in-evangelical-theology/. A broader survey of 1,000 Protestant pastors, both evangelical and mainline pastors, found 11 percent affirmed postmillennialism, still significantly less than the number who affirmed premillennialism (48 percent) and amillennialism (31 percent). See Bob Smietana, "Only One-Third of Pastors Share 'Left Behind' End Times Theology," *Christianity Today*, April 26, 2016, https://www.christianitytoday.com/2016/04/sorry-left-behind-pastors-end-times-rapture-antichrist/.

Amillennialist Robert Strimple critiques postmillennialism on biblical grounds, giving his "most fundamental objection to postmillennialism" as its lack of any biblical text teaching or proving it. He cites with approval the assessment that biblical support for postmillennialism simply does not exist.[66] On the contrary, the claim that we are to expect a golden age before Christ returns contradicts biblical teaching that speaks only of two ages, this present evil age and the new age, which only comes with the return of Christ.[67] Craig Blaising reviews all the texts Gentry claims as support for postmillenialism and finds none of them as truly supportive of the postmillennial view; he finds Gentry's postmillennial view of Revelation 20 "the most disappointing part of his article."[68] My evaluation is that postmillennialism deserves to be the least popular option among millennial views.

The case for the amillennial view is much stronger. Historically, it was dominant from Augustine till the eighteenth century, a period of around 1,400 years. Today, while it is less widely believed than premillennialism, especially among evangelicals and Baptists, support for it is still significant and rising, especially among the younger generation.[69] Moreover, I find myself much in agreement with what amillennialist Robert Strimple calls the "two crucial factors" in his presentation of amillennialism; namely, that

---

[66] Robert Strimple, "An Amillennial Response," in Bock, *Three Views on the Millennium and Beyond*, 69.

[67] Strimple, "An Amillennial Response," 63.

[68] Blaising, "A Premillennial Response," 79.

[69] See the number of amillennialists among evangelical leaders (13 percent) and Protestant pastors (31 percent) from "Premillennialism Reigns," and Smietana, "Only One-Third of Pastors." Smietana also reports that 75 percent of Baptists are premillennialists. I have no statistical evidence for the rise in amillennialism among those under forty, but in twenty-five years of teaching students at Southeastern Baptist Theological Seminary, the trend toward amillennialism has been clear among my students. Trevin Wax offers a similar observation in a May 5, 2014 blog on The Gospel Coalition, "5 Observations about Younger Southern Baptists." See https://www.thegospelcoalition.org/blogs/trevin-wax/5-observations-about-younger-southern-baptists/.

we should follow the New Testament in how we interpret Old Testament prophecies and that we should notice the New Testament teaching concerning the second coming of Christ "and the events that will accompany that coming."[70] The New Testament's application of prophecies given to Israel to the church (such as the promise of the new covenant in Jer 31:31–34) strongly weakens the dispensational claim of Old Testament support for dispensational premillennialism as well as their overall separation of Israel and the church. We previously discussed the importance of the clustering of major events like judgment and the resurrection of believers around the return of Christ. These two factors have been sufficient in the past to cause me to sometimes describe myself as "49 percent" amillennial. It is a very attractive position, but like Thomas Schreiner, who says he "previously supported this view," it fails in its interpretation of Revelation 20. Even though the interpretation "that the coming to life and the first resurrection refer to the reign with Christ that begins at death in the intermediate state" is defended ably by numerous amillennialists, Schreiner points out objections that, in the end, make it "ultimately implausible."[71] Those objections were discussed earlier in our examination of Revelation 20 and need not be reviewed again here, but they are sufficient to make me reluctantly back away from the amillennial view.

The remaining view is premillennialism. It is the dominant view among evangelicals and Baptists, but it comes in two distinct versions, as discussed above. Statistics are lacking, but few would dispute that among Southern Baptists, the dispensational variety of premillennialism has been the dominant view for decades. Few also would dispute that among younger Southern Baptists, "dispensationalism is on the decline."[72] It is still ably

---

[70] Robert Strimple, "Amillennialism," in Bock, *Three Views on the Millennium and Beyond*, 84.

[71] Schreiner, *Revelation*, 671. For presentations of the amillennial view, see Meredith G. Kline, "The First Resurrection," *Westminster Theological Journal* 37, no. 3 (1975): 366–75; G. K. Beale, *Revelation*, 1003–15; and Hoekema, *The Bible and the Future*, 223–38.

[72] Wax, "5 Observations."

defended today,[73] but ground is being lost to amillennialism and historic premillennialism. I have friends and many I respect among dispensationalists, but I see three weaknesses with this still strongly held position.

The first weakness is the firm separation of Israel and the church in dispensational premillennialism. We noted above that the New Testament sees promises made to Israel inherited by the church (such as the new covenant). The New Testament applies titles given to Israel in the Old Testament to the church (1 Pet 2:9), and it even describes a Jewish person in terms that fit Christians (Rom 2:28–29). Thus, the relationship of Israel and the church is more promise (or type) and fulfillment than separation. The Old Testament prophecies of blessings to come to Israel are not support for an earthly millennium where these prophecies are fulfilled to ethnic Israel. Some are being fulfilled to the church now; others will be fulfilled in the new heavens and new earth to come.

Revising this separation of Israel and the church to a promise/fulfillment understanding lessens the need for dividing eschatological judgment into seven events,[74] a division which seems to come more from the assumptions of the dispensational system than from exegetical findings.

A second weakness is not directly related to the view of the millennium in dispensational premillennialism but to their view of the rapture and Second Coming, which affects their view of events related to the millennium. This weakness is their separation of the rapture and return of Christ into two second comings, with the rapture being a coming *for* the church and the Second Coming a coming *with* the church. A variety of positions

---

[73] See David L. Allen and Steve W. Lemke, ed., *The Return of Christ: A Premillennial Perspective* (Nashville: B&H Academic, 2011). Though the subtitle only says "premillennial," the book consistently presents dispensational positions, though some of the contributors are progressive dispensationalists.

[74] Walvoord, *The Millennial Kingdom*, 276, lists seven future judgments; Gundry, "Judgment of Nations," *Evangelical Dictionary of Theology*, 3rd ed., ed. Daniel J. Treier and Walter A. Elwell (Grand Rapids: Baker Academic, 2017), 453, states that premillennialists "generally distinguish four judgments," but this is truer of dispensational premillennialists than historic premillennialists.

separate the rapture from the Second Coming, based on the relationship of the rapture to a coming seven-year tribulation: Is the rapture before this tribulation (pretribulational), at some point during this tribulation (prewrath or midtribulational), or after the tribulation and part of the event of the Second Coming (posttribulational)?[75] We examined these positions and the arguments for and against them in chapter 4 of this volume and will not repeat that discussion here, except to repeat the key argument against all views that separate the rapture and Second Coming: the New Testament knows only one Second Coming. To separate the rapture from the Second Coming goes contrary to this uniform teaching.

A third weakness, like the previous one, is concerned with the dispensational aspect of dispensational premillennialism. There is a lack of clear historical evidence for dispensational premillennialism before the nineteenth-century work of John N. Darby. Some of the ideas central to dispensationalism, such as the separation of Israel and the church and the rapture as separate from the Second Coming, have little to no historical precedents before the nineteenth century. On the contrary, there is abundant evidence for premillennialism in the early church, with advocates such as Justin Martyr, Irenaeus, and Tertullian, but not for dispensational premillennialism. This weakness is not fatal to dispensational premillennialism, for we do not see history as infallible, only Scripture. But history is the record of how other believers interpreted Scripture, reading the same Scriptures we read and having the illumination of the same Spirit we have. If we come to a position no other believers came to for the first 1,800 years of the church's history, then that position bears a heavy burden of proof.

And so I come to the second version of premillennialism, historic premillennialism, so called because, as just noted, it does have some historical support. It does not see support for its claim of an earthly millennium to be preceded by Christ's return in Old Testament prophecies; it

[75] See the helpful presentation of three of these positions in Alan Hultberg, ed., *Three Views on the Rapture: Pretribulation, Prewrath, or Posttribulation?* (Grand Rapids: Zondervan, 2010).

acknowledges that there is a clustering of events around the second coming of Jesus. But it sees the teaching of Rev 20:1–10 as sufficiently clear to justify inserting an interval of some length of time (the "thousand years" may be symbolic)[76] after Christ's return and before final judgment. It is troubling to rest a doctrine on one passage in a book as difficult to interpret as Revelation,[77] which is why humility and charity are especially important regarding this doctrine. For the reasons given above, the postmillennial and amillennial interpretations of Revelation 20 have seemed implausible to me, so I have in the past usually identified myself as a historic premillennialist, though I have sometimes qualified that as 51 percent historic premillennial and 49 percent amillennial.

The reason for my continuing reservations about the premillennial position is the difficulty of conceiving the conditions of millennial life that include the following scenario. Christ returns; believers are bodily resurrected and united with him. At the same time, earthly life continues. Are we to expect that alongside these resurrected believers there will be flesh-and-blood people still in their natural bodies? We are still awaiting the new heavens and new earth where death will be no more (Rev 21:1–4), so presumably some of those in their natural bodies will die during the millennium. What happens to believers who die during the millennium? Sam Storms think premillennialists must face the "bizarre" scenario either of thousands of individual resurrections or that those who die in Christ will exist for the rest of the millennium in an intermediate state awaiting their resurrection.[78]

This difficulty with historic premillennialism made me glad to see a new alternative offered by Thomas Schreiner called new creation millennialism,

---

[76] Schreiner, *Revelation* (674) says most premillennialists take the thousand years as a literal period while others see it as symbolic for a long period of time.

[77] Some see a hint at a period of time after Christ's return in the wording of 1 Cor 15:23–24, which gives the order of resurrections as "Christ, the firstfruits; afterward, at his coming, those who belong to Christ. Then comes the end . . ." But reading a period of time between the resurrection of those who belong to Christ and the end is far from clear.

[78] Sam Storms, *Kingdom Come*, 552–53.

a view that he thinks combines "the best features of amillennialism and the best features of premillennialism."[79] He says that "the millennium is the first age of the new creation" and not a part of the old creation, "where there is death and where unbelievers still reside on earth." Thus, in the millennium, "no one dies, weeps or sins."[80]

Schreiner goes on to give ten additional features of this new view. Some are simply affirmations of the traditional premillennial reading of Revelation 20 on the binding of Satan and the first resurrection. Other points resolve the problem of how some join with the devil in opposition to Christ after the millennium since all the enemies of Christ seem to be destroyed at Christ's return (Rev 19:19–21); namely, these enemies are those who are resurrected at the end of the thousand years. A final feature of this new view notices there are "good grammatical grounds" for seeing Rev 20:11 as describing the judgment and vindication of the righteous at the beginning of the millennium; verses 12–15 describe the judgment of the wicked that occurs after the millennium.[81]

I think Schreiner and the others he credits as pioneering this approach have made a real advance.[82] Like any new approach not seen by previous generations of students of Scripture, it faces the burden of having to prove itself, but I think it does so admirably. I see new creation millennialism as something of a modified version of historic premillennialism where Schreiner

---

[79] Schreiner, *Revelation*, 677.

[80] Schreiner, 677.

[81] Schreiner, 677–82.

[82] Schreiner, 677, cites works by J. W. Mealy, *After the Thousand Years: Resurrection and Judgment in Revelation 20*, Journal for the Study of the New Testament Supplement Series 70 (Sheffield, UK: Sheffield Academic, 1992) and "Revelation Is One: Revelation 20 and the Quest to Make the Scriptures Agree," in *Reconsidering the Relationship between Biblical and Systematic Theology in the New Testament: Essays by Theologians and New Testament Scholars*, ed. Benjamin E. Reynolds, Brian Lugioyo, and Kevin J. Vanhoozer, *Wissenschaftliche untersuchungen zum Neuen Testament* 2/369 (Tubingen: Mohr Siebeck, 2014), 131–53, and Eckhard Schnabel, "The Viability of Premillennialism and the Text of Revelation 20," *JETS* 64, no. 4 (2021): 785–95, and encouragement by Pastor Jeremy Sexton.

sees it as "a via media between amillennialism and premillennialism."[83] Regardless of the classification, I believe it to be the option that best explains all of biblical teaching on this topic.

Practical Application

A final difficulty in speaking of the millennium is seeing any application to one's daily life as a believer. Simply put, it does not seem vital to faith and practice. This is another of the reasons why Christians have been able to work and walk together while disagreeing on the millennium.[84] While there may be no positive application from one's position on the millennium, there may be a danger to be aware of in each position.

Postmillennialism may be overly optimistic concerning what can be accomplished in this world. To be sure, a careful formulation of postmillennialism accepts that change will be gradual and will only come through preaching the gospel in the power of the Spirit. But how does a postmillennialist understand the situation in a country like Japan where there has been little gospel progress after more than a hundred years of missionary service? Is the postmillennialist prepared to hold out for the long haul?

Similarly, do amillennialists overstate the boundness of Satan in this present evil age? Again, careful formulations of amillennialism limit the boundness of Satan to his inability to deceive the nations, but even with that limitation, do amillennialists pray with fervor for those still under Satan's deception? Are they on guard against Satan's schemes against them? The very language of Satan being bound may lead to unpreparedness for his attacks.

Premillennialism has been criticized for fostering a negative, pessimist, escapist attitude toward society and social action by its view of the end

---

[83] Schreiner, *Revelation*, 677.

[84] For example, the *Baptist Faith and Message 2000* is like most statements of faith in taking no position on the issue of the millennium. Trevin Wax, "5 Observations," adds that on this issue, among younger Southern Baptists, "diversity is the norm."

times. They are accused of seeing tribulation and judgment coming upon the world and taking the attitude that things are just going to get worse. Social action is viewed as doing as much good as rearranging deck chairs on the *Titanic*. Rather, the need is to evangelize in the hope that God will save some before judgment falls. Again, such an attitude is not a necessary implication of their position, and in many cases premillennialists, moved by the love of Christ, have been active in caring for the poor and needy around the world. But whereas the first two positions may be in danger of being overly optimistic in terms of what may be accomplished in this world and our vulnerability to satanic attack, premillennialism may be too pessimistic. Who is to say that God does not have a Third Great Awakening in store before the end-time day of the Lord arrives?

I hope the new position I am advocating, new creation millennialism, avoids all these dangers, but no theological position guarantees proper practice. In this area of eschatology, it behooves us to remind ourselves that the millennium is not the main thing; it is not our hope. Christ will come! He is the source of our hope. When he comes, we may see that all our millennial positions need revision.

CHAPTER 8

Finally Home: Heaven

We now come to the most serious issue in eschatology and, indeed, that which makes being a human such an incredibly serious matter. It is the issue of eternal destiny. Every human is going to exist forever, either in inexpressible glory or unimaginable horror. This is the weightiness of being a human. As the poet Longfellow wrote: "Life is real, life is earnest, and the grave is not its goal. 'Dust thou art, to dust returneth,' was not written of the soul."[1]

We are born, without asking to be born, and find thrust upon us the responsibility to make a decision that will have incredible, eternal consequences. Moreover, it is a decision which God allows some to make in a way that leads to eternal torment. It is a frightening, overwhelming freedom and responsibility, simply because the results are eternal and, once we pass beyond death, cannot be changed. Even steadily contemplating eternity is difficult. Apart from Christ, I would be terrified of anything eternal. Therefore, when we preach and teach about heaven and hell, about eternal destinies, we must do so with a proper sense of awe, reverence, and urgency,

[1] Henry Wadsworth Longfellow, "A Psalm of Life" (Wentworth Press, 2016).

and seek to awaken in others the same response. We begin with the destination which will be for Christians: the end of their status as aliens and exiles. They will be finally home. They will be in what we call heaven.

Introduction

It is becoming increasingly noticeable that our culture and the church have lost any significant vision of heaven. A recent survey found only 67 percent of Americans believe that heaven is a real place.[2] Peter Kreeft compares us to the medieval church and concludes that we have little faith, hope, and desire for heaven because we have lost sight of the wonder and glory of heaven and can imagine little better than our life here. Our view of heaven is strangely joyless. Kreeft contends that the glory of heaven never touches our hearts and so does not create a burning desire for heaven or even an interest in heaven. Yet heaven should either be the most fascinating reality in the world or the most fascinating falsehood in the world. We see neither, and live earthbound lives, like kids surrounded by toys but bored to death. The medievals, by comparison, had little material goods but lived in a world full of reason for gratitude, wonder, and praise.[3]

A. J. Conyers sees the loss of a vision of heaven as part of a larger loss of transcendence which is having a disastrous ripple effect in multiple areas of theology and life. Many have stopped asking the big questions (What is the meaning of life? Where are we going? Why are we here?) because they think there are no answers. But these are some of the questions that have occupied humans down through history.[4] We desperately need to recover a

---

[2] This is one of the findings of a 2014 survey conducted by Lifeway Research. See "Americans Believe in Heaven, Hell, and a Little Bit of Heresy," October 28, 2014, https://research.lifeway.com/2014/10/28/americans-believe-in-heaven-hell-and-a-little-bit-of-heresy/.

[3] Peter Kreeft, *Everything You Ever Wanted to Know about Heaven: But Never Dreamed of Asking* (San Francisco: Ignatius Press, 1990), 18–19.

[4] A. J. Conyers, *The Eclipse of Heaven: The Loss of Transcendence and Its Effect on Modern Life* (Downers Grove: InterVarsity, 1992), 21–22.

living, truly attractive doctrine of heaven. Fortunately, some are beginning to offer us some help here, with several recent works calling us to turn our hearts and thoughts toward heaven again.[5]

Randy Alcorn suspects Satan must be behind our lack of appreciation for heaven, but Alcorn also believes a major factor is the belief that heaven is so different from earth that we can know little of it. Alcorn agrees with C. S. Lewis that, while reason is the organ for grasping truth, imagination is the faculty that helps us grasp meaning, especially the meaning of transcendent realities like heaven. He advocates the use of imagination, starting from the biblical teaching that heaven is ultimately to become the new creation.[6] Thus, we are to imagine heaven starting from what we know of this creation, yet without all the effects of sin. But Scripture gives us not just the new creation but a variety of images for our imaginations to ponder. We will look at several biblical images for heaven, but we begin with the word "heaven," which is not as simple as it may seem.

Biblical Teaching on Heaven

We find the word "heaven" used in four senses in Scripture. First, heaven in the plural is used for one part of the created universe. As Gen 1:1 says, "God

[5] A short but helpful contribution is Kenneth Boa and Robert Bowman Jr., *Sense and Nonsense about Heaven and Hell* (Grand Rapids: Zondervan, 2007). More extended treatments are given by Dan C. Barber and Robert A. Peterson, *Life Everlasting: The Unfolding Story of Heaven* (Phillipsburg, NJ: P & R, 2012); N. T. Wright, *Surprised by Hope: Rethinking Heaven, the Resurrection, and the Mission of the Church* (New York: HarperOne, 2008); Randy Alcorn, *Heaven: Biblical Answers to Common Questions about Our Eternal Home* (Carol Stream, IL: Tyndale House, 2004); Christopher W. Morgan and Robert A. Peterson, eds., *Heaven*, Theology in Community (Wheaton: Crossway, 2014); Andrew M. Davis, *The Glory Now Revealed: What We'll Discover about God in Heaven* (Grand Rapids: Baker, 2021). A short response somewhat critical of the approach of Wright and Alcorn is Michael Allen, *Grounded in Heaven: Recentering Christian Hope and Life on God* (Grand Rapids: Eerdmans, 2018). Multiple views are presented and critiqued in Michael E. Wittmer, ed., *Four Views on Heaven* (Grand Rapids: Zondervan, 2022).

[6] Alcorn, *Heaven*, 10–17.

created the heavens and the earth." We should not pass over this phrase too quickly. It may refer simply to the earth's atmosphere, where we see the clouds and sun. The word may also signal to us that there is something more than our life here on earth that should cause us to look beyond what is earthly.[7] But the eclipse of heaven means we have little sense of something beyond us, no understanding that life here on this planet is incomplete in and of itself. We can scientifically analyze what is out "there," but we may miss the foreignness of it and what it should awaken in us. The very word "heavens" should remind us that there is more to life than what we see from our perspective.

Second, the word "heaven" can be used as a synonym for God. The prodigal son says: "I have sinned against heaven" (Luke 15:21). It can be used in this way because of the more common, third sense. "Heaven" most often refers to the dwelling place or habitation of God. Jesus described God as "the Father in heaven" (fourteen times in Matthew alone), and all the Bible agrees that God dwells in heaven (2 Chron 7:14; Ps 2:4; Eccl 5:2). Jesus descended from heaven and returned to heaven (John 3:13; Acts 1:11) and is now at the right hand of the Father.

Does this mean then that the teaching of the Bible commits us, as Rudolf Bultmann famously claimed, to a mythological three-story universe, in which hell is located somewhere within the earth and heaven is out there if we go far enough? Or do we say heaven is just a state of mind? Neither alternative is necessary or viable.

When we say heaven is the habitation of God, we must remember that God is a spirit and omnipresent, not located within or limited to any one physical place. Thus, while we affirm that heaven is a place (John 14:2–3; Heb 9:24), we should conclude that it is a special place, a spiritual place, the

---

[7] Philip E. Hughes, *Paul's Second Epistle to the Corinthians*, NICNT (Grand Rapids: Eerdmans, 1962), 433. Hughes suggests that Paul's language in 2 Cor 12:2 of the "third heaven" may show some idea of connection, with the first heaven being "the earth's atmosphere," the second heaven being the atmosphere of the stars, and the third heaven referring to a spiritual reality, what Paul calls in 2 Cor 12:4 "paradise."

logical dwelling for spiritual beings. We may even say that Scripture gives us hints that it does not belong to our dimensions. Hebrews 9:11 tells us that the true tabernacle, the dwelling place of God, is "not made with hands (that is, not of this creation)." It exists but as a spiritual place in another dimension. Thus, getting to it is not a matter of traveling far enough within our dimensions; we must leave this creation. Because the Bible was written in prescientific times to address all peoples of all times, it uses mostly phenomenological language (the language of appearance) to communicate with us and accommodate our limitations. Thus, the Bible speaks of Jesus descending from heaven and ascending upon his return, because that is how it could best be understood. Scripture does not require a woodenly literal, this-worldly understanding of heaven and even hints that we should think of it as not located within the bounds or dimensions of this created universe.

Finally, and most important for eschatology, is the fourth sense of heaven as the destination of believers after death on this earth. Even within this sense, there is something of a dual meaning. Randy Alcorn differentiates between what he calls "Present Heaven," the place believers go now when they die, which may also be called paradise (Luke 23:43), and "Eternal Heaven," which is the new creation, the new heavens and earth.[8] Both may be called heaven, because both are used to refer to the dwelling place of God. The dead in Christ are in his presence after death (Phil 1:23; 2 Cor 5:8), and as the dwelling place of God, such a place may be called heaven. But God's final and ultimate dwelling place will be the new creation of Rev 21:1–2, which is identified as God's dwelling place in verse 3 and thus may also be called heaven. The first heaven is present, temporary, and intermediate; the second is our final resting place.

There is some divergence of opinion concerning whether this new heaven and earth will be a totally new creation or a purification and restoration of this creation. The language of 2 Pet 3:10–12 would seem at first glance to point to a complete destruction of this creation and require a totally new one. Further, some might see the pollution of this planet as

[8] Alcorn, *Heaven*, 41–44.

putting it beyond repair. However, there are numerous reasons for understanding the language of 2 Peter 3 as referring only to destruction of all that is stained and evil in this world, and thus preparatory for a restoration and renewal of this creation.[9]

First, the word for "new" in the "new creation" descriptions in 2 Pet 3:13 and Rev 21:1 is *kainos* (new in kind) as opposed to *neos* (new in time). If the new creation was new in time, it would indicate that it did not previously exist and thus the new creation could not be a renewal of a previously existing creation. New in kind makes renewal of a previously existing creation possible.

Second, a comparison is made between the destruction awaiting creation with the destruction of the world in Noah's day (2 Pet 3:5–7). The same Greek root is used of the earlier destruction and the eschatological destruction to come, only a verbal form in the former (v. 6, *apōleto*) and a noun form in the latter (v. 7, *apōleías*). The destruction in Noah's day did not annihilate the creation; the destruction to come may properly be argued to be restorative rather than annihilative.[10]

Third, another important term, which is the last word in the key text, 2 Pet 3:10, leads many to think it does not teach the ultimate annihilation of this creation, even though it has been the subject of some debate. The King James Version translated the term from the Textus Receptus, *katakaēsetai*, as "shall be burned up." After discovery of better texts, modern translations work from the term *heurethēsetai*, translating it as "will be disclosed" (CSB) or "will be laid bare" (NIV) or "will be exposed" (ESV).[11] There is ongoing

---

[9] See Anthony A. Hoekema, *The Bible and the Future* (Grand Rapids: Eerdmans, 1979), 280–81, for a strong presentation of four reasons; Bruce Riley Ashford and Craig G. Bartholomew, *The Doctrine of Creation: A Constructive Kuyperian Approach* (Downers Grove: IVP Academic, 2020), 317–22, for a list of five reasons, most of them overlapping with those presented by Hoekema.

[10] Ashford and Bartholomew, *Doctrine of Creation*, 317. "Restorative" and "annihilative" are the terms used by Ashford and Bartholomew for the two views of what will happen to the created order in the end.

[11] All three of these translations acknowledge that some manuscripts have the term that would be translated "will be burned up."

discussion as to what it actually means for creation to be disclosed, laid bare, or exposed,[12] but it would seem at a minimum that the creation must still exist. Thus, the preceding phrases of 2 Pet 3:10 may indicate a fire, but one more restorative than annihilative.

Fourth is the promise of freedom from corruption given to nature in Rom 8:19–23. One could say that it will be fulfilled in a future earthly millennium, but the language of Romans 8 seems to fit better with a view of total restoration. Moreover, Col 1:20 sees the reconciling work of Christ as applying to "things on earth or things in heaven," also indicating a positive future for this creation, rather than annihilation.

A fifth argument concerns the original goodness of God's creation. Here the analogy with the resurrection body helps. Just as the goodness of God's creation of us as embodied creatures is validated by the resurrection of the body, so the goodness of God's creation (which is affirmed in Gen 1:31) is vindicated by its ultimate restoration. Others see a link to Christ's resurrection as well. N. T. Wright writes, "God will do for the whole cosmos, in the end, what he did for Jesus at Easter."[13] The resurrection of Jesus is the firstfruits for both humans and creation. It guarantees the resurrection of our bodies, vindicating the goodness of our bodies and the "resurrection" (perhaps "restoration" would be a better term) of the creation, vindicating the original goodness and reconciled status of creation.

Finally, if the creation is in the end destroyed, does this not give Satan a victory? He could claim that he has so perverted what God created as good that even God could not redeem it. This would be to overlook biblical teaching on the cosmic scope of Christ's atoning work. As we already noted, in the cross God was reconciling "everything to himself, whether things on earth or things in heaven" (Col 1:20). This suggests that the cross has some effect on the material creation, even if not visible now. As Christopher Wright puts

---

[12] See the review of various positions in Ashford and Bartholomew, *The Doctrine of Creation*, 318–20.

[13] N. T. Wright, *Simply Jesus: A New Vision of Who He Was, What He Did, and Why He Matters* (New York: HarperOne, 2011), 202.

it, "Ultimately all that will be there in the new, redeemed creation will be there because of the cross. And conversely, all that will not be there (suffering, tears, sin, sickness, oppression, corruption, decay and death) will not be there because they will have been defeated and destroyed by the cross."[14]

These points seem convincing to me, but some may still think the language of 2 Pet 3:10–12 and the description of the new Jerusalem as "coming down out of heaven" (Rev 21:2) require annihilation of this creation and a new *creatio ex nihilo*.[15] Either way, new creation is one image we are given to imagine what heaven is like, and it will be included in the list of images which will be discussed next.

Images for Heaven

Heaven is beyond our full capacity to comprehend (1 Cor 2:9). Therefore, Scripture uses images to communicate some idea of heaven to us. Since heaven is great and glorious, the Bible gives us numerous images for us to ponder and upon which we should exercise a sanctified imagination. We will consider eight such images here.

1. The tabernacle. We find the background for this image in the Old Testament worship setting. The tabernacle was the place where God met with the Israelites (Exod 29:44, also called the "tent of meeting"). The Old Testament tabernacles were shadows and temporary. They were easily dismantled and appropriate for a nomadic people. The image was enriched by the coming of Jesus. John 1:14 says he "tabernacled" with us, and one day we will roam no more. The final, true tabernacle will be set up in heaven (Rev 21:3). This tabernacle is not made by human hands but is the true tabernacle (Heb 9:11) and will never need to be dismantled or moved.

---

[14] Christopher J. H. Wright, *The Mission of God* (Downers Grove: IVP Academic, 2006), 315.

[15] Ashford and Bartholomew, *The Doctrine of Creation* (317–18) note Theodore Beza, some Lutherans, numerous classic dispensationalists, and some contemporary biblical scholars as among those supporting the annihilative view.

With this tabernacle, the eternal purpose of God is fulfilled. His motive throughout Scripture was to create a people whose God he could be and with whom he could dwell. Adam had run and hidden from God, but God's purpose persisted. Through Abraham (Gen 17:7–8), continuing through the children of Israel (Exod 6:7), to its culmination in a new covenant (Jer 31:33), God's purpose remained firm. Now it is fulfilled. God will dwell ("tabernacle") among his people, personally and permanently.

From this image, we can draw two implications about heaven. First, heaven is the reality behind all the earthly shadows and symbols. It is more real, more substantial than anything we have ever experienced. Second, heaven is the place where we will experience the presence of God in such a way that the merest hint of it now is astonishing. Indeed, what should be most attractive to the believer is not the place of heaven, but the person we meet there. Verses like John 14:3, Col 3:4, 1 Thess 4:16–17, and 1 John 3:2 underscore that what constitutes heaven is being with our Lord. If one finds the thought of being in God's presence unattractive, such a person should not plan on going to heaven; they would not like it there.

Peter Kreeft credits Augustine with a thought experiment to clarify what we truly desire.[16] Imagine God offered you a deal to give you power, wealth, whatever you wanted, along with a good conscience, peace of mind, and a life that would never end. You would never experience boredom, but there would be one limitation—you would never see God's face. Kreeft believes that Christians would instinctively recoil from such a deal, because what we want more than anything else is to be intimately in the presence of God.[17] That too is what God wants and what he has been working for throughout Scripture. The image of heaven as God's tabernacle is the promise of his personal, permanent presence.

---

[16] Peter Kreeft, *Heaven: The Heart's Deepest Longing* (New York: Harper & Row, 1980), 27. For the source in Augustine, Kreeft cites Augustine, *Ennarationes in Psalmos*, in *Corpus Christianorum*, Series Latina, vols. 38–40, ed. E. Dekkers and J. Fraipont (Turnhout, Belgium: Brepols, 2014), 127, 9.

[17] Kreeft, *Heaven*, 27.

2. The city. For us, the image of a city may not be too attractive. We think of traffic and crime and pollution. But in the time of the New Testament, a city was very attractive for numerous reasons. First, a city would mean heaven is a permanent place (Heb 11:9–10; 13:14). A city is a place with foundations, which indicates stability or permanence. Moreover, if the foundation for this city is the same as the foundation of the church (Jesus Christ; see 1 Cor 3:11), this too indicates its permanence, for Christ is the same yesterday, today, and forever (Heb 13:8). For those who had been wandering nomads, never staying very long in one place, this was a blessing almost too good to imagine.

Second, heaven as a city would have meant to first-century Christians a place of plenty, for the city was where all the vendors in the ancient world brought their wares to sell. In the desert, one had to make do with what he or she could find and carry, but in the city there was plenty. Revelation 21:24 and 26 give the application of the heavenly city: everything truly good on earth will be found there. I think this is the clearest clue we have to the multitude of questions as to what of earthly life will be found in heaven (sports, food, pets, etc.). Whatever is truly good is preserved and brought into the city.

Third, heaven as a city means it is a place of glory and splendor. This may be the implication behind the description of heaven as having precious stones in the walls and gates of pearls and streets of gold (Rev 21:18–21). Whether the streets are literally gold or John is using figurative language, the reality behind the language must be incredibly glorious.

Fourth, heaven as a city would imply a place of safety. We may think of cities as inherently dangerous places, but not so in the ancient world. This is the importance of the city's walls, described as 200 feet thick (Rev 21:17). A tent did not give much protection against marauders, but such a wall would. Fear, worry, and anxiety will not exist in heaven but rather perfect peace, safety, and security. It will be the first place we will ever live where we can fully relax, because it will be the first place where we will be completely safe.

Finally, heaven as a city means it is a place of service (Rev 22:3). A city requires many people working together to exist. The implication is that heaven will be more than an eternal day off; we take with us into heaven the capacities God has given us to serve and bless others. Some fear they will be bored in heaven, but why should that be, when we can continue to use those capacities in the new heaven and new earth to serve others and thus glorify God? Thus, while our relationship with God began in a garden, this image suggests it ends in a city, the new Jerusalem.

3. Our true homeland (Heb 11:13–16; Phil 3:20–21). Sometimes we want to feel at home in this world, but God has placed eternity in our hearts (Eccl 3:11), and we long for something more than earth provides. Thus, we remain strangers and pilgrims here. When Christians feel at home and fit in on earth, it is not a good sign. One of the positive by-products of the decay in American culture is that genuine Christians will begin to appear more and more alien and strange, and may thus begin longing for heaven, for it will be the place where we will finally and eternally fit in and feel at home. Until then, we are to be about "purging worldliness from our hearts" and "learning to wean ourselves from the preoccupations of this life."[18] Such an attitude toward the things of the world is commended to us in passages such as 1 Cor 7:29–31, 2 Cor 4:17–18, and 1 John 2:15–17. Because heaven is our true home, we need to learn to hold to the things of this world with a very loose hand.

4. A wedding feast (Rev 19:9; 21:2, 9–14; Eph 5:27). This image implies that heaven is a place of celebration, joy, and submissive and sacrificial love. Some are troubled by Jesus's statement in Matt 22:30 that earthly marriage relationships no longer apply in heaven. This is not an accurate understanding of this verse. Nor should we believe that we will be genderless in heaven. The verse says we will not marry nor be given in marriage, for one of the purposes of marriage (procreation of children) has ended and the other purposes (relationships, learning to love, intimate companionship) have been transcended. There is no reason to think we will not always have a special relationship with people who have been special to us here, but again,

[18] John MacArthur, *The Glory of Heaven* (Wheaton: Crossway, 1996), 63.

earthly marriages, as all earthly relationships, are the shadow.[19] Earthly life and earthly marriage are part of God's "school" in order to teach us how to love and how to be the bride of Christ. We will not love our earthly spouse less in heaven, but more, with that love extended most of all to our true Spouse, Christ, and to others. Special earthly relationships are given to us as schools where we learn to love. School may end, but the love goes on, only broader and wider and deeper.

Moreover, as Randy Alcorn notes, there will be one marriage in heaven, that of Christ and his bride, the church.[20] This is the real marriage, of which earthly marriage is the shadow. Even the sexual union in marriage is used in Scripture as a foreshadowing and illustration of God's love for his people.[21]

5. The kingdom. Those who live under democratic governments may not feel the force of this image. The implications of heaven as kingdom would include power and glory—namely, all true power and glory will be preserved in that kingdom (Rev 21:24, 26). Some might say the full establishment of God's kingdom is the best single phrase to sum up God's ultimate purpose in human history. In contemporary Western culture, virtually all ideas of power and authority are under attack. But by the image of heaven as a kingdom we are meant to imagine what life would be like in a place where every heart is gladly under the reign of the one whose power and authority are right and just and for our good.

6. A garden (Rev 22:1–3). Even though the word "garden" does not appear in Revelation 22, the tree of life that is in the paradise of God in Rev 2:7 is also in the middle of the city in Rev 22:2. But that tree of life was originally in a garden (Gen 2:9). After the fall, it is not the tree that is

---

[19] In Eph 5:22–33, Paul teaches extensively about how wives and husbands should treat each other in marriage, but he concludes that the true mystery of marriage is about Christ and the church (v. 32). It is the marriage of Christ and the church that is the original; earthly, human marriages are the shadow.

[20] Alcorn, *Heaven*, 350.

[21] See Ezekiel 16, Hosea 1–2, Jer 31:31–32 and according to typological interpretations of it, the Song of Songs too.

removed from the garden but humans. The picture this scene paints is of a park in the middle of the city, a park that resembles the garden of Eden, with the tree of life. The difference between the tree in Genesis and the tree in Revelation is that the people can now eat freely from it and its leaves will be "for healing the nations"—"There will no longer be any curse" (Rev 22:2–3). There will be a cure for all pains and all types of ills. Every result of sin and evil will be undone. All the scars of mind, body, and soul will be healed. There will be no more regret, no more fear, no unmet longing. The curse and all its ill effects will be undone. We will be whole. To this author, this image may be the most profound of all.

7. A family reunion (John 14:1–2). We are going to our Father's house, to the place our Elder Brother has been preparing for us. We will join a big family of brothers and sisters in Christ, with great joy in being together. Heaven is about perfected relationships or as Peter Kreeft calls it, "the communion of saints." He argues that one reason why heaven will not be boring is because "getting to know people is in one way or another the only thing we find inexhaustible here as well as there."[22] Often family reunions on earth involve new family members meeting each other for the first time without sufficient time for the relationships to develop. This will not be a problem at this family reunion.

8. New creation (Rev 7:16–17; 21:1, 4, 27). Craig Blaising contrasts two major models for heaven: the spiritual vision model, which emphasizes knowing God as the chief blessing of heaven, and the new creation model, which emphasizes a degree of continuity between this present creation and the new creation.[23] The new creation model can claim biblical grounding in the texts from the book of Revelation cited above, along with 2 Pet 3:13. In claiming some continuity between the new creation and this

[22] Kreeft, *Every Thing You Ever Wanted to Know about Heaven*, 53.

[23] Craig A. Blaising, "Premillennialism," in *Three Views on the Millennium and Beyond*, ed. Darrell L. Bock (Grand Rapids: Zondervan, 1999), 160–64. Blaising believes that one's model of heaven shapes how one sees the plausibility of an earthly millennium.

creation, this image seems to have given people help in imagining more clearly what heaven will be like. It will be like this creation, only restored, purified, redeemed.[24]

While helpful, the new creation image must be used with care. It points us back to the creation we know, but this creation is marred. It can only be an image for heaven if we subtract all the marks of the old order—tears, pain, crying, death, and sin and its effects. We must eliminate all these marks if the new creation image is to accurately reflect heaven. Moreover, while some speculation about various details of heavenly life may be unavoidable and helpful if disciplined by a biblically formed imagination, excessive speculation can lead to dangerously deformed views of heaven.[25] Finally, some think the new creation emphasis has already gone too far, leading us to turn from a "focus upon communion with Christ, the presence of God, or the beatific vision . . . to focus instead upon the resurrected body, the shalom of the city, and the renewal of the earth."[26] Michael Allen calls this earthly focus "eschatological naturalism."[27] While that phrase may be too harsh,

---

[24] Anecdotally, I can report that many seminary students who read Randy Alcorn's book *Heaven* for one of my classes report a transforming effect on their desire for and longing for heaven. Alcorn's book very strongly emphasizes the new creation model of heaven.

[25] While I find much to appreciate in *Heaven* by Randy Alcorn, there are examples of such excessive speculation, especially when not clearly presented as speculation. Alcorn includes chapters on questions such as "Will the New Earth Have Sun, Moon, Oceans, and Weather?" and "Will Animals, Including Our Pets, Live Again?" There is so little biblical material on these questions that the answers Alcorn offers are largely speculation, something he should acknowledge.

[26] Allen, *Grounded in Heaven*, 5.

[27] Allen, 8. Allen cites N. T. Wright, *Surprised by Hope*, J. Richard Middleton, *A New Heaven and a New Earth: Reclaiming Biblical Eschatology* (Grand Rapids: Baker Academic, 2015), and Michael E. Wittmer, *Heaven Is a Place on Earth: Why Everything You Do Matters to God* (Grand Rapids: Zondervan, 2004) as those he finds guilty of at least being in danger of moving perilously close to "eschatological naturalism." However, in responding to Middleton's presentation of the new earth view of heaven (see J. Richard Middleton, "A New Earth Perspective," in *Four Views on Heaven*, ed. Michael E. Wittmer [Grand Rapids: Zondervan, 2022], 65–94; Michael Allen, "Response to J. Richard Middleton," in *Four Views on Heaven*,

the new creation view runs the danger of underemphasizing how radically new the new creation will be and underemphasizing what will be the most important feature of that new creation, the presence of God. Allen is right to call for "recentering Christian hope and life on God."[28]

Historical and Cross-Cultural Illumination

While the Bible is the only normative source for theology, we interpret the Bible in a particular historical moment and within a specific cultural context. Thus, interpreting the Bible within a community of interpreters can be helpful. We pause here to consider if material from the history of thought and interpreters from other cultures can further illuminate heaven for us.

Help from History

It is somewhat surprising that there have not been many books on heaven in the history of theology. While there are certainly comments on heaven in the works of major authors like Augustine and Calvin, Augustine has no major work specifically on heaven, and Calvin has no chapter on heaven in the *Institutes*.[29] The Puritan Richard Baxter is an exception, with his 1650 work *The Saints' Everlasting Rest* as one of the few classics. There are, however, three recent books that explore the history of heaven and another group of books that signal movement toward one particular approach to heaven.

100–01), Allen finds the later presentation "far more balanced and serviceable" than the earlier book, though he adds, "I am still not sure to what extent I'd call this eschatology a theocentric one."

[28] Allen, *Grounded in Heaven*. The subtitle of the book is *Recentering Christian Hope and Life on God*.

[29] Some may see Augustine, *The City of God*, as having some relevance, but most see *The City of God* more as a theology of history than a study of heaven. In Calvin's *Institutes*, there is only one chapter on eschatology, entitled "The Final Resurrection" (3.25).

The three books on the history of heaven differ in several respects but agree on one main point that confirms the interpretation of Scripture adopted above: Christians have thought about heaven mainly through numerous images. Colleen McDannell and Bernhard Lang in *Heaven: A History* state that their book is not literally a history of heaven, but "a history of the images Christians use to describe what happens after death," and thus they seek to answer the question, "What will an eternity in heaven be like?"[30] Jeffrey Russell's book, *A History of Heaven: The Singing Silence*, is more limited in scope, tracing the development of Christian ideas of heaven from their origins through the completion of Dante's *Divine Comedy* in 1321, ending with Dante because of Russell's conviction that the *Paradiso* of the *Divine Comedy* "is the most sublime portrait of heaven from the Book of Revelation to the present."[31] The present author would disagree with the elevation of the presentation of heaven in the *Divine Comedy* above all others, but Russell acknowledges that Christians most often thought of heaven through what we call "here images," or what Russell terms "metaphors." He specifically mentions the metaphors of kingdom, garden, and city. Garden is the most common metaphor overall, while kingdom is more commonly found in the Eastern tradition and city more common in the West.[32] The third book is called *A Brief History of Heaven* by Alister McGrath.[33] He focuses not on theologians but on how Western literature and art have portrayed heaven. Here too, he shows that many of the images we derived from Scripture in the section above have been used throughout history by writers, poets, and artists in their depictions of heaven, particularly the images of city, garden, reunion, and homeland. However, there are some other images of heaven McGrath finds

---

[30] Colleen McDannell and Bernhard Lang, *Heaven: A History* (New Haven: Yale University Press, 1988), x.

[31] Jeffrey Burton Russell, *A History of Heaven: The Singing Silence* (Princeton: Princeton University Press, 1997), xiii, 151.

[32] Russell, 13.

[33] Alister E. McGrath, *A Brief History of Heaven* (Malden, MA: Blackwell, 2003).

in art that do not appear to have any scriptural support, such as some art from Romanticism and Transcendentalism and the idea of Feuerbach, Marx, and Freud that heaven is a dream or wishful thinking.

McDannell and Lang add an interesting overall note on the images for heaven: "Two major images dominate theology, pious literature, art, and popular ideas. Some Christians expect to spend heavenly life in 'eternal solitude with God alone.' Others cannot conceive of blessedness without being reunited with friends, spouse, children, or relatives."[34] They refer to the first image as theocentric views of heaven and the second as anthropocentric. These two models seem related to what we cited above from Craig Blaising, the spiritual vision and new creation models of heaven,[35] with the difference being that the anthropocentric views of McDannell and Lang are more focused on human relationships in heaven, while the model proposed by Blaising focuses more on the setting of heaven, the new creation. Still, there is some commonality. The theocentric view as described by McDannell and Lang resembles the spiritual vision model mentioned by Blaising and championed by Michael Allen. The anthropocentric view of McDannell and Lang seems to fit well within the new creation/restoration view advocated by Blaising, Randy Alcorn, N. T. Wright, and others.

We mention this to give a historical perspective on a recent development. While the spiritual vision model was dominant for most of church history,[36] the new creation model has enjoyed renewed popularity in recent years. We have mentioned the impact of Randy Alcorn's book on the popular level and the impact of the work of N. T. Wright on the academic level,

---

[34] McDannell and Lang, *Heaven*, 353.

[35] Blaising, "Premillennialism," 160n2. Blaising cites the work of McDannell and Lang and suggests comparing his categories with theirs.

[36] "The spiritual vision model was the dominant view of eternal life from roughly the third century to the early modern period." Blaising, "Premillennialism," 164. McDannell and Lang, *Heaven* (178, 345) see a theocentric view of heaven dominating from the Reformation through the eighteenth and nineteenth centuries, and a "theocentric minimalism" as "probably the most widely accepted orthodox version of heaven in twentieth century theology" (345).

along with the work of others like J. Richard Middleton and Blaising. We applaud the impact of the new creation model in making heaven literally imaginable for many, but it is an anthropocentric view. We also echo the concern of Michael Allen that we do not lose sight of what I think must be the most important feature of heaven: the presence of God. Let us not lose theocentric approaches.

For our purposes, the presence of both anthropocentric and theocentric approaches in Christian history encourages us to embrace all the images we found in Scripture. They include some that support an anthropocentric or new creation model of heaven and some that support a theocentric or spiritual vision model of heaven. Both approaches are biblically valid, and we are healthier spiritually when we retain both in our thinking about heaven, rather than overemphasizing one over the other.

Cross-cultural Insights

Most theology has been done from a Western perspective, but most Christians today are in what is called the Majority world.[37] Christians living in non-Western cultures often read the Bible in ways that we do not.[38] Thus it is helpful to check our interpretation of the Bible with the interpretation of those from other cultures, for sometimes aspects of other cultures are closer to the cultures found in the Bible and therefore can help us to understand the culture of the Bible better. Unfortunately, the number of works written and/or translated into English by scholars and theologians from Africa, Asia, and South America on heaven is few.[39] One insight

---

[37] "Majority world" is a term used for the areas where the majority of the world's population lives, the developing countries of South America, Africa, and Asia, as opposed to the countries of North America and Europe, called the West.

[38] See the fascinating insights in Randolph Richards and Brandon O'Brien, *Misreading Scripture with Western Eyes: Removing Cultural Blinders to Better Understand the Bible* (Downers Grove: IVP Books, 2012).

[39] Stephen Pardue, "Eschatology in the Majority World," in *Majority World Theology: Christian Doctrine in Global Context*, ed. Gene L. Green, Stephen T.

that confirms the importance of including anthropocentric elements in our view of heaven comes from the African worldview, which is "highly anthropocentric."[40] For Africans, "the living and the dead in fact stand in a permanent and ongoing relationship."[41] We noted that one of the images for heaven is of a family reunion. Such an image resonates well with African culture and is an image they would surely not want our theology of heaven to omit. Beyond this, we await further reflection from the global church on the nature of heaven to confirm or revise our understanding of biblical teaching on this topic.

Theological Response: Three Important Questions

Based upon biblical teaching, illuminated by insights from history and cross-cultural partners, we now turn to the task of giving a theological response to three important questions about heaven. To some degree, our answers will be speculative, because the questions we are asking are not answered completely and explicitly in Scripture. Yet, it is important to ask them because they are questions asked by many thoughtful Christians and the lack of answers to them can dull our desire for heaven. We may think that heaven will be wonderful, but we lack much detail. Heaven is just a bright blur. If heaven remains just a bright blur, it will be difficult to find it taking a hold on our hearts. Thus, we will ask questions and try to give theological answers that follow the directions we believe Scripture is pointing. And if to some degree our responses here are speculative, where they are wrong, they will err in being too small and unworthy; the reality will always be better (1 Cor 2:9).

Pardue, and K. K. Yeo (Downers Grove: IVP Academic, 2020), 596.

[40] James Henry Owino Kimbo, "The Past, the Present, and the Future of African Christianity: An Eschatological Vision for African Christianity," in Green, Pardue, Yeo, *Majority World Theology: Christian Doctrine in Global Context*, 616. Kimbo here draws on the work of the important African theologian, J. S. Mbiti, and his work, *African Religions and Philosophy* (London: Heinemann, 1969).

[41] Kimbo, 623.

What Will We Do?

One question that troubles many is, What will we do? Faced with the prospect of eternal life, some fear heaven must eventually involve boredom. From the book of Revelation, we can affirm that we will rest (14:13), we will worship (15:2–4), and we will serve (22:3). Worship can involve all of life (Rom 12:1–2), and serving can involve many activities. Scripture supplies some clues as to what some of those activities may be, and fleshing out those clues in some specific possibilities may help give us a fuller, more active vision of what heavenly life might involve and relieve the fear of boredom.

Randy Alcorn draws numerous implications from the idea that heaven will ultimately be the new creation. Why might there not be exploration of that new universe, use of the resources of that creation in technology, building, the production of works of art, even sports? Could it be that as we were given stewardship over the first creation, we will also be given stewardship over the new creation? Could that be part of the rule we are given (Rev 20:4)? If this is so, and if we consider all the developments that have occurred down through history, even in a fallen context, could we not expect far more exciting developments resulting from a holy stewardship of a new creation and full obedience to a new cultural imperative?[42]

But Peter Kreeft has suggested other stimulating possibilities. He asserts that we need heaven because "no one dies finished. . . . Our lives are incomplete in all three of their essential relationships: (1) to ourselves, (2) to others, and (3) to God."[43] Heaven is where these relationships can be completed. While there may be no verse specifically connecting these three incomplete

---

[42] Alcorn, *Heaven*, 409–51. These pages include chapters with the titles: "Will Heaven Ever Be Boring?" "Will There Be Arts, Entertainment, and Sports?" "Will Our Dreams Be Fulfilled and Missed Opportunities Regained?" and "Will We Design Crafts, Technology, and New Modes of Travel?" On some points, Alcorn goes well beyond Scripture into sheer speculation, but on many other points there is some implicit biblical support.

[43] Kreeft, *Everything You Ever Wanted to Know about Heaven*, 53–54. Kreeft cites the work of Richard L. Purtill, *Thinking about Religion* (Englewood Cliffs, NJ: Prentice-Hall, 1978), 136–52, as prompting his thinking. Purtill suggests three

tasks with activity in heaven, Kreeft believes these three incomplete relationships correspond to three traditional doctrines. As a Catholic, he understands these doctrines as purgatory, the communion of saints, and the beatific vision and sees heavenly activity implicit in each of these doctrines.

First, Kreeft suggests that purgatory may involve not punishment but "reading the already-written book of your life with total understanding and acceptance."[44] But one need not accept any idea of purgatory to believe that the first step into heaven could involve seeing all of one's own life from heaven's perspective. This will mean seeing exactly how Rom 8:28 was true in everything in our lives. We will have the answer to every nagging Why? we ever murmured. As a Catholic, Kreeft suggests this is a fitting idea of purgatory, a preparation for heavenly life. But why may we not appropriate it as the first event, or lesson, of heavenly life?

Still, what more might we do that would not eventually end in boredom? Kreeft says "getting to know people is in one way or another the only thing we find inexhaustible."[45] So the second suggestion Kreeft has as to what we will do in heaven is to get to know each other. He associates this with the doctrine of the communion of saints. Because in heaven no one will be misunderstood or rejected, in heaven we will be able to know each other and truly experience communion with others at a depth never before possible.[46] And as our life there will be ongoing, there will always be more to know of each other.

The third activity Kreeft identifies us doing in heaven is what is called the "Beatific Vision." He states, "The Beatific Vision is also not boring because it is dynamic rather than static, exploring rather than

---

human tasks in heaven: "(1) understanding our earthly life 'by Godlight,' (2) sharing all other human lives, and (3) exploration into God."

[44] Kreeft, *Everything You Ever Wanted to Know about Heaven*, 65.

[45] Kreeft, 53.

[46] Kreeft, 58. Kreeft takes this further than I think warranted in saying, "It seems likely, therefore, that we shall enter without limit fully into all the lives that ever were, are, or will be, not only on earth but also of non-earthly creatures on other planets" (78–79).

staring at God, endless beginnings rather than merely the end."[47] We will begin a never-ending journey into the knowledge of God, unending because it is the knowledge of an infinite and inexhaustible God. We will never tire of the contemplation of God because there will always be more to contemplate.

What of Earthly Life Will Be in Heaven?

The second question that troubles the hearts and minds of many is, Will there be animals, music, food, sports, etc. in heaven? Will there be anything truly good here on earth that is lost in heaven? I think Rev 21:24–27 provides the clearest hint here. Earthly kings will bring "their glory" into heaven; nations likewise will bring their "glory and honor" in. God is the giver of every good and perfect gift (Jas 1:17); if any of his gifts to this creation are truly good, why would they be missing in the new creation? God's character has not changed. If we affirm the new creation is this creation without all the effects of sin, only those things that manifest sin will be gone. Nothing truly good from the first creation is lost. We may need to be careful, since sin is so deeply intertwined with so many aspects of earthly life, but we may affirm that whatever is truly good on earth will appear in heaven, only in its purified and completely God-glorifying form.

How Can We Be Happy if Someone We Know Is in Hell?

The third and most difficult question of all is, how can we ever rejoice in heaven if we know that anyone is in torment in hell? This is a question every sensitive heart must take seriously, but I think there are some helpful suggestions we can offer.

Kreeft considers the question and says we will not grieve over those in hell because what ends up in hell is not persons, but something quite different. He quotes C. S. Lewis: "What is cast (or casts itself) into hell is not

[47] Kreeft, *Everything You Ever Wanted to Know about Heaven*, 53.

a man; it is remains."[48] They are no longer fully human; they are only what remains after humanity has been abused and trashed. After wood has been burned, ashes remain. When a human being chooses life apart from God, he or she loses all the good that he or she experienced because of common grace and becomes "remains," no longer what we remember as human. Randy Alcorn goes further and says that perhaps we will not feel toward them what we did earlier, because they will be radically changed. What we loved about them was something derived from their creation in God's image, some spark of God's creation still alive in them. But after death and judgment, that is all gone. They are no longer bearers of God's image; they have rejected that status.[49] N. T. Wright agrees, saying that those who finally reject God become after death and by their own choice, "beings that once were human but now are not;" as such they have passed "beyond hope but also beyond pity." They are "in an ex-human state" and can no longer excite sympathy in others.[50]

A second suggestion comes from C. S. Lewis, in his book *The Great Divorce*. The book describes an imaginary bus trip from hell to the outskirts of heaven. Some of the inhabitants of heaven come down the mountains to talk to the group who have made the trip. One of the blessed spirits is a woman whose husband meets her. He is disappointed that she is not sad that he went to hell rather than heaven. He tries to use her compassion for him to mar her blessedness in heaven. She tells him it will not work:

> "No, Frank, not *here*," said the Lady. "Listen to reason. Did you think joy was created to live always under that threat? Always defenseless against those who would rather be miserable than have their self-will crossed? For it was real misery. I know that now. You made yourself really wretched. That you can still do. But you can no longer communicate your wretchedness. Everything becomes

---

[48] Kreeft, *Everything You Ever Wanted to Know about Heaven*, 221, quoting C. S. Lewis, *The Problem of Pain* (New York: Macmillan, 1962), 125.

[49] Alcorn, *Heaven*, 362.

[50] Wright, *Surprised by Hope*, 182–83.

> more and more itself. Here is joy that cannot be shaken. Our light can swallow up your darkness; but your darkness cannot now infect our light. . . . Can you really have thought that love and joy would always be at the mercy of frowns and sighs? Did you not know that they were stronger than their opposites?"[51]

To read the whole book is very worthwhile, but the central point here is that it is not just, nor right, that the condemned, who freely and deliberately reject joy, should forever retain the power to veto the joy of others. Lewis says that those who live in perfect joy can no longer fall from that joy; it is too strong, and it is right that they should not be saddened by the condemned. I believe Lewis is right; it would not be just for the condemned to retain such power. I do not know exactly how God will break that power, but I can see that it is fair and just and necessary for God to do so.

A third provocative suggestion is that hell might be the kindest gift God can give to those for whom his presence would be torture. N. D. Wilson relates a conversation he had with an atheist friend who asked him if he thought she would go to hell. "I don't know," he said. "Don't you want to?" His friend replied, "Why would I want to go to hell?" He simply said, "God is who he is. Do you want to be with him?" He speaks of those who hate God, "Hell is for you because God is kind and reserves a place for those who loathe Him to the end, an eternal exile, a joyless haven for those who would eternally add to their guilt, a place where blasphemy will be new every morning. A place less painful and less terrible than the alternative."[52] We may wrongly think of lost people as wanting to go to heaven, but is this indeed the case? They have spent their lives avoiding God; why would they at death long to go to a place that is filled with the presence of God?

A final suggestion is that part of our difficulty may be that we are not yet fully sanctified and do not sufficiently understand the goodness of God's justice. It is worth noting the angels and those with them in heaven in the book

---

[51] C. S. Lewis, *The Great Divorce* (New York: Macmillan, 1946), 118.

[52] N. D. Wilson, *Notes from the Tilt-a-Whirl* (Nashville: Thomas Nelson, 2009), 175–76.

of Revelation seem to feel no uneasiness in seeing God's judgment fall on the wicked; rather, they praise him for it.[53] Certainly the diminution of God in contemporary secular thought could make hell seem more problematic. In an attempt to revise our traditional ideas of hell because of the difficulties they pose, some are moving toward an annihilationist view of hell or an inclusivistic view of salvation. But it is at least equally possible that contemporary cultural assumptions have prevented us from seeing and understanding rationales for hell that previous generations found at least somewhat cogent. J. I. Packer concludes his brief consideration of this question with this: "God will judge justly, and all angels, saints, and martyrs will praise him for it. So it seems inescapable that we shall, with them, approve the judgment of persons—rebels—whom we have known and loved." He acknowledges, "this sounds to us more like hard-heartedness than Christlikeness, yet Christlikeness is precisely what it will be." The difference is that "in heaven, our minds, hearts, motives and feelings will be sanctified, so that we are fully conformed to the character and outlook of Jesus our Lord."[54]

Practical Application

All theology in the end must lead to application or it is useless. The most obvious application of the doctrine of heaven is hope. Evil will not always triumph; death does not have the last word; we will dwell with God and know him intimately; we will see our loved ones again. Jesus will make all things new. The hope of heaven has been criticized by some as dulling the cry for justice in the here and now, by promising to those suffering "pie in the sky by and by when they die."[55] But the bigger question is, is it true? Is heaven real? If so, it should be the light of hope that shines upon our path

---

[53] See Rev 15:3–4; 16:5–7; 19:1–8.

[54] J. I. Packer, "Hell's Final Enigma," *Christianity Today* 46, no. 5 (April 2002): 84.

[55] This is a phrase coined by labor organizer Joe Hill in 1911 to ridicule the Christian notion of heaven. See "Pie in the sky," Phrase Finder, accessed August 12, 2024, https://www.phrases.org.uk/meanings/pie-in-the-sky.html.

in the darkest of times in our lives. Most of us reading this book will likely never face a situation in which we are called to follow Christ at the cost of our lives, but many brothers and sisters around the world face life-and-death choices on a regular basis. For them, if there is no heaven, choosing to follow Christ is utter foolishness. Even for us, in much less dangerous contexts, there are times when only the hope of heaven suffices. When our loved ones die, when we face death ourselves, when there is no more earthly hope, the reality of heaven matters intensely.

The doctrine of heaven is also a thermometer of our spiritual health. Paul said, "I long to depart and be with Christ" (Phil 1:23); can our hearts echo him? If our hearts are cold toward heaven, something is wrong with us. Have we become satisfied with earth, with a relationship with God still hindered by an environment filled with sin and a human nature still in process toward holiness? God is not satisfied; his purpose is to be personally present to us in a place where all the marks of sin are erased, in relationship with us as glorified humans. If that is his goal, it must be ours, and our vision of heaven must be clear enough to attract us onward. That is why it is important to ponder the images and deal with the questions that may trouble and cause us hesitations, until there is enough clarity in our vision of heaven for it to ignite in our hearts and produce a longing for heaven.

Finally, the hope of heaven, especially the hope of a new creation, should give direction to the church in its mission today. We pray, "Your kingdom come. Your will be done on earth as it is in heaven" (Matt 6:10). We affirm that God's kingdom was inaugurated in Jesus and will one day be consummated. But in the in-between time, the church acts as the agent or instrument through which the kingdom is furthered, such that God's will is done on earth as it is in heaven. What must guide us in our mission is our answer to what it looks like for God's will to be done on earth as in heaven. Here is where heaven as new creation may help. Can we imagine an earth without all the markings of sin? That would be a place where God's will is fully done. This gives us a goal toward which to work.

From this perspective, N. T. Wright draws out categories of justice, beauty, and evangelism as categories for the church's work in this world.

This work is nourished by the basic disciplines of Christian spirituality (prayer, Scripture, worship, etc.), but these disciplines are themselves best understood in the context of our ultimate hope.[56] Far from the criticism made that some people are so heavenly minded they are no earthly good, the more heavenly minded we are, the more prepared we are to do earthly good. True, we will never bring the kingdom by our efforts, but our work now is a participation in and an anticipation of God's work of making all things new. We are directed and sustained by that hope (1 Cor 15:58).

[56] See Wright, *Surprised by Hope*, 189–289.

CHAPTER 9

Hell: The Reality Almost Too Horrible to Contemplate

Introduction

One of the biggest barriers to Christian faith, especially since the Enlightenment, has been what is called the problem of pain. The existence of pain and suffering in this world has seemed to many incompatible with the existence of a God who is both all-powerful and benevolent. While that problem has traditionally received massive attention from apologists and philosophers of religion,[1] another problem is only beginning to receive similar attention—the problem of hell. Yet that problem may be even more severe. For all evil and suffering on earth is temporary and may be offset by future joy (2 Cor 4:17), but the pain and suffering of hell are eternal.

[1] While the number who have addressed this issue is legion, some see Alvin Plantinga, *God, Freedom, and Evil* (Grand Rapids: Eerdmans, 1989) as giving the best philosophical argument for the compatibility of the Christian God with evil and pain in this world.

Therefore, it is not surprising to find traditional formulations of hell being challenged, even from within evangelicalism. Speaking of the traditional formulation as involving eternal conscious torment, evangelical statesman John Stott said, "Emotionally, I find the concept intolerable and do not understand how people can live with it without either cauterizing their feelings or cracking under the strain."[2] Stott's words have given fuel to a growing movement challenging the traditional understanding of the nature of hell.[3] But there are also a number of positions that pose a challenge to traditional understandings of the occupants of hell. Universalism, pluralism, and several versions of inclusivism challenge the traditional notion that hell is for all those who live and die without placing personal faith in Christ.[4] Underlying these questions concerning the nature and occupants of hell, there is a third question: Why should there even be such a place as hell?

We will structure this chapter around these three questions:

1. Why should there be such a place as hell?
2. Who will go to hell?
3. What is the nature of hell?

In so doing, we will survey biblical teaching on this doctrine, consider the witness of history (including these recent challenges), examine key theological questions, and suggest how a right understanding of this doctrine

---

[2] David L. Edwards and John Stott, *Evangelical Essentials: A Liberal-Evangelical Dialogue* (Downers Grove: InterVarsity, 1988), 314.

[3] See the literature generated by those in this movement in Christopher M. Date, Gregory G. Stump, and Joshua W. Anderson, eds., *Rethinking Hell: Readings in Evangelical Conditionalism* (Eugene, OR: Cascade, 2014).

[4] Pluralism and inclusivism are among the views included in Dennis L. Ockholm and Timothy R. Phillips, eds., *Four Views on Salvation in a Pluralistic World* (Grand Rapids: Zondervan, 1995); rising interest in universalism is reflected in David W. Congdon, ed., *Varieties of Christian Universalism: Exploring Four Views* (Grand Rapids: Baker Academic, 2023). Less common but still drawing some interest is the possibility of salvation after death; see James Beilby, *Postmortem Opportunity: A Biblical and Theological Assessment of Salvation After Death* (Downers Grove: IVP Academic, 2021).

should impact the lives of Christians on a practical level. We will find that hell is indeed a reality almost too terrible to contemplate, but only almost. We must bring ourselves to contemplate it, painful though it is, because it is so prominently taught in Scripture, both in relationship to the nature of God and humans and in the teaching of Jesus.

Why Is There Even Such a Place as Hell?

The very reality of hell as a place is increasingly challenged in our day,[5] but Scripture is clear on that matter. The Gospels as well as the book of Revelation repeatedly describe lost persons as being "thrown into hell" (Matt 5:29; 18:9; Mark 9:45, 47; Luke 12:5) or thrown into "the blazing furnace" (Matt 13:50) or "eternal fire" (Matt 18:8) or "the lake of fire" (Rev 20:15), which all seem to require a place for them to be thrown into. Lost people are placed outside the Holy City (Rev 22:15) and the place they occupy before their final sentencing to hell (*hades*) is called a "place" (Luke 16:28). But even among those who agree on the reality of hell as a place there is some difference, at least differences of emphasis on why there must be such a place.

The most common idea in contemporary evangelical theology is that hell is the inevitable result of genuine human freedom. God, who chose to give us the tremendous and terrifying gift of freedom, allows us to use it, even to our eternal ruin, and respects it. God is only responsible insofar as he chooses to give us the gift of freedom; the major responsibility for the reality of hell is the human choice to reject God and all that God offers.

For example, in *The Problem of Pain*, C. S. Lewis considers several objections to the doctrine of hell but is emphatic in his response that God has already done all that is possible to save people; if they are condemned, it is their choice. He writes, "If the happiness of a creature lies in self-surrender,

[5] A 2014 Lifeway survey of 3,000 Americans found only 61 percent affirm belief in hell as a real place. See Bob Smietana, "Americans Believe in Heaven, Hell and a Little Bit of Heresy," Lifeway Research, October 28, 2014, https://research.lifeway.com/2014/10/28/americans-believe-in-heaven-hell-and-heresy/.

no one can make that surrender but himself . . . and he may refuse"; or, "forgiveness needs to be accepted as well as offered if it is to be complete: and a man who admits no guilt can accept no forgiveness"; or, "I willingly believe that the damned are, in one sense, successful, rebels to the end; that the doors of hell are locked on the *inside*."[6] No one is in hell who truly wants to be in heaven. He concludes:

> "What are you asking God to do?" To wipe out their past sins and, at all costs, to give them a fresh start, smoothing every difficulty and offering every miraculous help? But He has done so, on Calvary. To forgive them? They will not be forgiven. To leave them alone? Alas, I am afraid that is what He does.[7]

Millard Erickson, in the theology text most widely used in evangelical circles, follows Lewis's lead: "We should also observe that God does not send anyone to hell. . . . It is man's choice to experience the agony of hell. . . . It is God's leaving man to himself, as man has chosen."[8] As much as I like the arguments of Lewis and Erickson, and as much as I agree with much of what they say, it seems to me they downplay something that Scripture retains, namely a more active, judging, punishing role for God.

To be fair to Lewis, he begins with the conception of hell as "positive retributive punishment inflicted by God," and sees this as a manifestation of God's justice.[9] Michael Bird agrees: "Hell is about justice, not torture."[10] This gives God a much more active role in establishing a reason for hell's existence—it is the place where the Judge of all the earth sends those who reject him and choose their own way.

---

[6] C. S. Lewis, *The Problem of Pain* (New York: Macmillan, 1962), 118, 122, 127. Emphasis in original.

[7] Lewis, *Problem of Pain*, 128.

[8] Millard F. Erickson, *Christian Theology*, 3rd ed. (Grand Rapids: Baker Academic, 2013), 1138.

[9] Lewis, *Problem of Pain*, 120–21.

[10] Michael F. Bird, *Evangelical Theology: A Biblical and Systematic Introduction* (Grand Rapids: Zondervan, 2013), 335.

Scripture speaks of the Lord as the one who pronounces the horrifying words, "Depart from me, you lawbreakers!" (Matt 7:23). The Son of Man is the one who sends his angels to gather "all who cause sin and those guilty of lawlessness," and "throw them into the blazing furnace" (Matt 13:41–42). In Matt 25:31–46, Jesus himself judges all the nations and sends one group "into the eternal fire" (v. 41). Interestingly, the text says this "eternal fire" was prepared "for the devil and his angels," but it is also the destination of those who, to their surprise, are rejected by God. While the Gospels contain most of the teaching on hell, Paul also sees God's justice as manifested in the punishment of those "who don't know God" and "don't obey the gospel of our Lord Jesus" (2 Thess 1:8). In the book of Revelation, God's angels praise his just judgment of evil (Rev 16:5–6; 19:1–3), culminating in the solemn scene of judgment before the great white throne, where "anyone whose name was not found written in the Book of Life was thrown into the lake of fire" (Rev 20:15).

It is possible that these are simply descriptions of what happens when God leaves the lost to themselves and withdraws himself and with himself all goodness from them (Jas 1:17), but the language of Scripture suggests hell is not just being left alone by God. There is a measure of retributive punishment. Could it be that we are so sensitive to the objections to hell as vindictive and unreasonable that we may be omitting an inescapable element of biblical teaching? Part of the answer to the question—why hell exists—is that hell is the place God has designated for the just punishment of those who reject God. If there are many who feel no qualms of conscience when an earthly judge sentences a murderer to death, then why would they feel squeamish about God, the only righteous Judge, sentencing anyone to hell? The problem must be that we do not feel that anyone truly deserves it. This leads to our second question.

Who Will Go to Hell?

This question demands consideration because of the increasing presence of pluralistic and inclusivistic ideas of salvation in mainline Protestant, Catholic, Orthodox, and even some evangelical circles. A 2014 survey of

3,000 Americans found that just under half (45 percent) believe there are many ways to heaven.[11] Such ideas have a multiplicity of sources, but at least one source is the perceived difficulty of consigning huge segments of humanity to hell, especially segments which have had little exposure to Christianity but, according to some, have worshipped God as best they knew in their cultural context. In response to such ideas, the 2000 *Baptist Faith and Message* added a statement to clarify the position taken by Southern Baptists: "There is no salvation apart from personal faith in Jesus Christ as Lord."

In contrast to this view, called exclusivist, numerous views have emerged in recent years. In fact, there is a spectrum from exclusivism to universalism. The names and numbers of views within this spectrum differ among those who address this topic;[12] we will consider four main camps below, while acknowledging some sub-groupings within each and one additional minor view. The nature of this book and the limitations of space preclude an exhaustive treatment of these camps. Such a treatment would need at least one separate volume for itself. At the same time, the importance of this question for the doctrine of hell requires at least a brief consideration of the varying positions on it.

Before considering these perspectives, however, there is one group for which at least some in almost all camps, including exclusivists, make an exception. That is the group of those incapable of coming to personal faith in Jesus Christ as Lord due to being too young to understand and respond

---

[11] Smietana, "Americans Believe."

[12] John Sanders, *No Other Name: An Investigation into the Destiny of the Unevangelized* (Grand Rapids: Eerdmans, 1992), and Terrance L. Tiessen, *Who Can Be Saved? Reassessing Salvation in Christ and World Religions* (Downers Grove, IL: InterVarsity, 2004), 31–47, both give five views, but with different names and some with multiple sub-views; Millard J. Erickson, *How Shall They Be Saved? The Destiny of Those Who Do Not Hear of Jesus* (Grand Rapids: Baker, 1996), includes seven views; Christopher Morgan, "Inclusivisms and Exclusivisms," in *Faith Comes by Hearing: A Response to Inclusivism*, ed. Christopher W. Morgan and Robert A. Peterson (Downers Grove, IL: IVP Academic, 2008), 17–39, identifies nine views.

to the gospel message or due to mental inability to understand and respond to the gospel message.[13]

The majority position among evangelicals is that God will save all those who die in infancy; the question of the destiny of those with mental disabilities is not as prominent in the literature, but they seem to share the same inability to come to faith and perhaps they even "lack the capacity to commit sin"[14] and belong among those "who do not reach a stage of moral understanding and accountability."[15] The reasons for affirming the salvation of those who do not come to a position of moral accountability vary. Often cited are the just and merciful character of God, the attitude of Jesus toward infants (Luke 18:15–17), and the fact that judgment is "according to their works" (Rev 20:12) which those in this group cannot commit.[16]

There are still some who think the evidence is not strong enough to be dogmatic about the salvation of all within this group. Terrance Tiessen says, "Scripture is silent about how many of the infants who die in infancy are included among the elect, but we place our hope for their salvation in God's great mercy."[17] While some suspect that the position that all who die in infancy will be saved is "held for sentimental reasons,"[18]

[13] See the helpful book by Adam Harwood, *The Spiritual Condition of Infants: A Biblical-Historical Survey and Systematic Proposal* (Eugene, OR: Wipf & Stock, 2011).

[14] Kenneth Boa and Robert Bowman Jr., *Sense and Nonsense about Heaven and Hell* (Grand Rapids: Zondervan, 2007), 137.

[15] Daniel Akin, "Jesus Loves the Little Children: Why I Believe Children Who Die Go to Heaven," *Blog*, accessed March 19, 2024, https://www.danielakin.com/jesus-loves-the-little-children-why-i-believe-children-who-die-go-to-heaven mark-series/.

[16] See Akin, "Jesus Loves the Little Children"; Boa and Bowman, *Sense and Nonsense*, 135–37; Ronald H. Nash, *When a Baby Dies: Answers to Comfort Grieving Parents* (Grand Rapids: Zondervan, 1999); Erickson, *How Shall They Be Saved?*, 235–53; John MacArthur, *Safe in the Arms of God: Words from Heaven About the Death of a Child* (Nashville: Thomas Nelson, 2003).

[17] Tiessen, *Who Can Be Saved?*, 204.

[18] Tiessen, 212. He agrees here with the assessment of Sanders, *No Other Name*, 290, and David Clark, "Warfield, Infant Salvation and the Logic of Calvinism," *JETS* 27, no.4 (1984): 462.

Millard Erickson specifically denies that this position rests upon "a sentimental impulse," and makes a strong case from Scripture for the existence of an "age of accountability."[19] Even Roman Catholics, who for centuries held that unbaptized infants could not enter heaven, revised their position in 2007, when a Vatican Study Commission concluded there are "theological and liturgical reasons to hope that infants who die without baptism may be saved and brought into eternal happiness."[20] Thus, the position that argues for no salvation apart from personal faith in Jesus Christ (exclusivism) should be understood as making an exception for all those unable to understand and respond to the gospel due to age or mental disability.

There are numerous other groups involved in this debate. Some consider the fate of those who lived before Christ, both among the chosen people of Israel and all the other nations of the ancient world, and say that none of them heard the gospel and responded with faith in Christ. However, the New Testament certainly sees the faith of figures such as Abraham as saving faith, and most believe that those of the Old Testament who responded in faith to the revelation they received were granted salvation. What of those contemporaries of Abraham who lived in North and South America or China and India? Does it make a difference to the fate of the unevangelized whether they lived before or after Christ (see Acts 17:30–31)? Regardless of how God deals with those who lived before Christ, the more pressing question for us is the fate of the unevangelized in the world today. Can those who never hear the gospel today, at least not from any human messenger, be saved from sin and hell? Can a sincere follower of another religion go to heaven? The different answers given to these questions produce different responses to our question regarding who will go to hell.

---

[19] Erickson, *Christian Theology*, 581.

[20] "The Hope of Salvation for Infants Who Die Without Being Baptised," accessed March 25, 2024, https://www.vatican.va/roman_curia/congregations/cfaith/cti_documents/rc_con_cfaith_doc_20070419_un-baptised-infants_en.html#:~:text=Victor%3A%20infants%20who%20die%20unbaptised,would%20supply%20for%20the%20sacrament.

Universalism

While there have always been some on the popular level who believe that God is simply too loving and kind to send anyone to hell, this has always been an overwhelmingly minor view outside the bounds of Christian orthodoxy. However, some today see varieties of universalism developing with one form, Christian universalism, becoming a "genuine option within the theological landscape."[21] I think that is an overstatement of the viability of Christian universalism, but since there has been growing discussion of universalism in evangelical circles in recent years,[22] we include Christian universalism in this survey of views.

Contemporary Christian universalism has arisen from at least two impulses. One is the felt conflict between the triumph of God in the gospel and the lostness of untold millions. This perceived conflict has been a longstanding support for Christian universalism. Robin Parry contends, "To date, there has been no successful attempt to demonstrate the compatibility of eternal hell with the God of the gospel." By contrast, the view of hell which sees it as a place to which no one goes in the end seems to him a view which shows "the strongest view of divine love . . . the most powerful narrative of God's victory over evil" and "lifts the atoning efficacy of the cross of Christ to the greatest heights."[23] The second and more recent fuel for Christian universalism is the impact of the theology of Karl Barth. While

---

[21] Congdon, "Introduction," in Congdon, *Varieties of Christian Universalism,* xi.

[22] In addition to the book cited in the previous footnote, there have been chapters offering a universalist option in several recent evangelical multi-view books: Robin Parry offers such a chapter in *Four Views on Hell,* ed. Preston Sprinkle (Grand Rapids: Zondervan, 2016); Thomas Talbott argues for universal reconciliation in *Perspectives on Election: Five Views*, ed. Chad Owen Brand (Nashville: B&H Academic, 2006); and Thomas Greggs contributes a Barthian-universalist perspective in *Five Views on the Extent of the Atonement*, ed. Adam Johnson (Grand Rapids: Zondervan, 2019).

[23] Robin Parry, "Evangelical Universalism," in Congdon, *Varieties of Christian Universalism*, 37, 78–9.

Barth himself denied being a universalist,[24] his argument for "God's election of all people in Jesus Christ made it easy for those who followed him to take the next logical step."[25]

I respect the intention of universalists, especially Christian universalists. There are texts in Scripture that seem at first glance to support universal restoration (Rom 5:18; Col 1:20), but such texts are qualified, often in the immediate context (Rom 5:17; Col 1:23) and overwhelmingly in the larger context of the whole Bible. John Stackhouse believes that universalism cannot mount strong exegetical arguments and characterizes it as "the triumph of hope over exegesis."[26] In addition to the insuperable biblical teaching that all humans do not have the same destiny, there is also a problem with the universalist position on human free will. Evangelical universalists acknowledge the need for a personal faith response for salvation,[27] and Robin Parry states that universalists believe that God can "bring it about that all people freely accept the gospel."[28] But this seems contrary to the nature of genuine freedom: "With free will comes the possibility that humans may fail to receive God's grace but instead reject it. Because love cannot be forced, it is possible that some will reject it—even ultimately and finally."[29]

In the face of the empirical evidence for the reality of widespread human rejection of God and salvation in Christ, some universalists appeal to the possibility of postmortem salvation. Indeed, Parry says that the possibility

---

[24] Tom Greggs, "Post-Barthian Universalism," in Congdon, *Varieties of Christian Universalism*, 81, quotes Barth as having said regarding universal salvation, "I did not teach it, but I did not not teach it" (81).

[25] Congdon, "Introduction," xiii.

[26] John Stackhouse Jr., "A Terminal Punishment Response," in Sprinkle, *Four Views on Hell*, 134.

[27] For example, Parry says, "Evangelical universalists believe that apart from our loving trust in and surrender to God there is *no* participation in the salvation achieved in Christ." Parry, "Evangelical Universalism," 68.

[28] Parry, "A Universalist View," in Sprinkle, *Four Views on Hell*, 125.

[29] Clark Pinnock, "Responses to Thomas B. Talbott," in Brand, *Perspectives on Election: Five Views*, 263.

of salvation after death is "critical to most versions of universalism."[30] He claims the Bible does not directly address the issue but says that postmortem salvation is "highly consistent with the doctrine of divine holy love and the doctrine of God's eschatological victory over sin."[31] He acknowledges Heb 9:27, which says humans are to die once and then face judgment, but responds, "To insist that this judgment leads to irreversible punishment is to go beyond anything said in the text."[32] The note of irreversible punishment is present in other judgment texts (Matt 25:46; 2 Thess 1:9; Rev 20:11–15) and unmistakable in Luke 16:26, in which a great chasm is fixed between those in the differing destinations so that one may not pass from one destination to the other. Commenting on this text, I. Howard Marshall says, "The judgment is thus irrevocable."[33]

Moreover, John Stackhouse sees a "psychological deficiency in universalism," imagining that one who has begun to experience the sufferings of hell will be moved by that "to abandon one's resentment of God and instead develop soft, kind thoughts about him."[34] Despite the growing number of adherents to the various versions of Christian universalism, the case for it is weak, and the case against it is overwhelming. Universalism is inconsistent with the biblical evidence and the reality of human freedom in the answer it gives to our question of who will go to hell.

Pluralism

Pluralism may be the most popular view among the growing number of people who say their religion is "none." They would compare the different religions to different roads that lead to the same destination. A more technical definition of pluralism is the belief "that the major world religions

---

[30] Parry, "A Universalist View," 117.

[31] Parry, 116–17.

[32] Parry, 116.

[33] I. Howard Marshall, *The Gospel of Luke: A Commentary on the Greek Text*, NIGTC (Grand Rapids: Eerdmans, 1968), 638.

[34] Stackhouse, "A Terminal Punishment Response," 138.

provide independent salvific access to the divine Reality."[35] In terms of our question, who will go to hell, pluralism affirms that none need go there; there is a way of salvation available through every religion.

Arguments for pluralism include the claim that it is "the only way to promote justice in our intolerant and oppressive world" and religious experience is so transcendent and ineffable that no one religion can claim to be the only truth.[36] But John Hick says his path to pluralism was through "personal experience and observation." As he interacted with those from Hindu, Muslim, Sikh, and Buddhist backgrounds, he found that on a moral and spiritual level, "they seem on average to be neither better nor worse than are Christians." He believes that if Christianity were the one true religion, then its adherents should be in a closer relationship to God, and virtues like the fruit of the Spirit (Gal 5:22–23) "should be noticeably higher among Christians than among non-Christians."[37] His observation is that this is not the case.

Moreover, Hick observes that in a very high percentage of the cases, perhaps 98 or 99 percent, one's religion depends on where one is born. Hick says, "Any credible religious faith must be able to make sense of this circumstance," especially how it relates "to the universal sovereignty and fatherhood of God."[38] Surely something as important as one's eternal destiny should not turn on the accidental fact of one's birthplace.

Finally, Hick sees Christianity's lack of success in winning the adherents of other major religions as an argument in favor of pluralism. It is true that missionaries have made some progress, but they have found it easier to

---

[35] Dennis Ockholm and Timothy Phillips, "Introduction," in *Four Views on Salvation in a Pluralistic World*, 17. They say that pluralism is more accurately called "normative religious pluralism," but we will use the more common term of pluralism in our discussion.

[36] Ockholm and Phillips, "Introduction," 17.

[37] John Hick, "A Pluralist View," in Ockholm and Phillips, *Four Views on Salvation in a Pluralistic World*, 39, 41. It should be noted that although Hick is a recognized figure among pluralists, and writes in favor of it, he states that he has also argued elsewhere for universalism (45).

[38] John Hick, *God Has Many Names* (Philadelphia: Westminster, 1982), 61.

win converts from tribal religions than from the other major religions. If Christianity is the one true religion, should this be the case?[39]

Hick recognizes the immediate objection to pluralism. How can all these religions which differ significantly on the very nature of the divine reality (one being, a triune being, a pantheon, an impersonal reality) be paths to that same reality? Hick appeals to a distinction between "the Real/Ultimate/Divine in itself and that Reality as humanly perceived." Our limited perception of the divine Reality allows him to affirm that though the great religious traditions are quite different, they are "more or less equally salvific, human responses to the Ultimate."[40]

How should we evaluate pluralism? The first argument—that pluralism is necessary to promote justice and avoid intolerance and oppression—confuses persons and ideas as well as tolerance and agreement. Baptists have historically promoted full religious liberty and universal tolerance for all persons, while disagreeing with the truth or validity of the ideas or claims of other religions. The claim that the nature of religious experience prohibits one from judging such an experience as false is similarly confused. We would agree that what someone experiences in his or her religion is beyond our judgment, but a truth claim they make based on that experience can be a matter for discussion and evaluation.

Hick's argument from his personal experience and observation is, in my opinion, his strongest argument. The failure of Christians to show the reality of Christ in their character and conduct is a scandal and contrary to Christ's claim that others will know we are his disciples by our love for one another (John 13:35). At the same time, do we really think it is valid to judge the truth of a religion by the "moral development" of its adherents? This is "a thesis no world religion accepts."[41] Christianity accepts that its adherents are in process and still subject to sin and failure. That failure

[39] Hick, *God Has Many Names*, 60–61.

[40] Hick, "A Pluralist View," 46–47.

[41] Ockholm and Phillips, "Introduction," 18.

is lamentable and a hindrance to witness but does not in itself disqualify Christianity's claim to uniqueness.

His arguments regarding geography determining destiny and the supposed failure of Christianity to win adherents similarly need qualification. In its beginning Christianity was much more limited geographically than it has become. It has become the only truly global religion because people have in fact changed their religions and done so in the face of persecution and opposition. For example, Christianity is the predominant religion in 159 countries; the next closest, with fifty-two, is Muslim, predominant only in African and Asian countries; Christianity predominates in countries on every continent.[42] And while adherents of tribal religions have been the quickest to convert to Christianity, there are increasing numbers of converts from Muslim, Buddhist, and Hindu backgrounds.[43]

The weakest part of Hick's case is the supposed distinction between what is humanly perceived and "Reality" in itself. It is true, as Paul says, that now we know only "in part" (1 Cor 13:12), but the most important part of that statement is that there are some things we *know*. Those things that we know (about the nature of God and the uniqueness of Christ) are sufficient to ground Christianity's claim to be the only way to God and the only way to avoid going to hell. The real difference is at the level of presuppositions: Christians take the Bible to be authoritative in giving truth claims; Hick sees only the religious experiences described in the Bible as important. Christians affirm Jesus as the "one and only Son" (John 3:16), a claim validated by his life, death, and resurrection; Hick says there were "many human beings . . . called 'son of God' in the ancient world."[44] Hick does not note that only one is still called and recognized as Son of God by millions. The uniqueness of Jesus—in his incarnation, crucifixion, and resurrection—is still the strongest argument against pluralism.

---

[42] See Jason Mandryk, *Operation World*, 7th ed. (Colorado Springs: Biblica, 2010), 2.

[43] Mandryk, 8.

[44] Hick, "A Pluralist View," 33, 35.

Pluralism is an important and widely held position, especially among Catholics and liberal Protestants. The material above barely scratches the surface of the issues in this debate.[45] But among evangelicals, pluralism is an even more decided minority than universalism. It does not offer a trustworthy answer to the question, who will go to hell?

Inclusivism

Inclusivism comes in many varieties but is united in the affirmation that salvation extends beyond those who hear the gospel and place faith in Jesus Christ. It differs from pluralism in that it views salvation as rooted uniquely in the work of Jesus; it differs from universalism in its acceptance that some reject God and will go to hell. It differs most of all from the exclusivist claim that salvation is limited to those who hear the gospel and respond in faith. In the words of John Sanders, "Inclusivists affirm the particularity and finality of salvation only in Christ but deny that knowledge of his work is necessary for salvation."[46] Beyond this central affirmation, there is diversity on a number of issues.

For example, Roman Catholic inclusivism has had to attend to their historic belief in "no salvation outside the church" (*nulla salus extra ecclesiam*). Various documents of Vatican II opened the door to an expanded understanding of degrees of membership in the church, and with that Karl Rahner developed the doctrine of "anonymous Christians."[47] He wanted to accept the necessity of being a member of the church, but could not reconcile the resulting conclusion that the overwhelming majority of persons who have lived and are living now will go to hell with God's universal salvific will (1 Tim 2:4).

---

[45] For more see Gavin D'Costa, Paul Knitter, and Daniel Strange, *Only One Way? Three Christian Responses to the Uniqueness of Christ in a Religiously Plural World* (London: SCM, 2011).

[46] John Sanders, *No Other Name: An Investigation into the Destiny of the Unevangelized* (Grand Rapids: Eerdmans, 1992), 215.

[47] See Erickson, *How Shall They Be Saved?*, 103–20 for an overview of Roman Catholic inclusivism.

He developed the idea that all persons must be capable of becoming members of the church. They do so by responding to the "supernatural existential" which God places in every individual. Here is how Rahner describes a saving response to God: "If he does not suppress this truth but leaves it free play, then the grace of this truth by which he allows himself to be led is always already the grace of the Father in his Son. And anyone who has let himself be taken hold of by this grace can be called with every right an 'anonymous Christian.'"[48] Rahner goes further than some inclusivists in seeing other world religions themselves as possessing "a salvific status," through which "grace is mediated."[49] This seems to move Rahner close to pluralism, though he is still regarded by most as an inclusivist, indeed the most famous inclusivist.

Among Protestants, there have been a significant number of scholars who have been open to the possibility of salvation beyond the bounds of the evangelized, perhaps for some exceptional pagan responding to the revelation of God in creation and conscience. John Sanders names Ulrich Zwingli, Matthew Henry, John Wesley, William G. T. Shedd, A. H. Strong, and C. S. Lewis as having a place among inclusivists,[50] but it should be noted that in none of these did their inclusivism have a major place in their theology. That is not the case today. Inclusivism is being more and more widely embraced, with some calling it "the mainline model" or "the nearest approach to a consensus among Christian thinkers today."[51] My own interaction with students for the past thirty years indicates its growing popularity among young evangelicals. Its attractiveness seems to be in its ability to give an answer to the question regarding who goes to hell, one that does not include all the unevangelized and perhaps not all in other world religions.

---

[48] Karl Rahner, *Theological Investigations,* trans. Karl and Boniface Kruger (Baltimore: Helicon, 1969), 6:395.

[49] This is Clark Pinnock's assessment of Rahner in Clark Pinnock, "An Inclusivist View," Ockholm and Phillips, in *Four Views on Salvation in a Pluralistic World*, 99.

[50] Sanders, *No Other Name*, 269–76.

[51] Pinnock cites others as making such assessments, see Pinnock, "An Inclusivist View," 101.

The heart of inclusivism is the claim that God's universal salvific will (that is, his desire that all be saved) demands universal accessibility to salvation, even for those who never hear the gospel. They find a precedent for salvation without hearing the gospel in the case of Old Testament believers. It seems doubtful that many in the Old Testament era had explicit knowledge of the Messiah who was to be crucified and raised for them, yet his death was the basis for their salvation, applied retroactively to them. They were saved by trust in God and trust in the revelation they had of him.[52] It is true that the people of Israel were the recipients of special revelation, but it did not include the explicit message of the gospel until the coming of Jesus.

How then may salvation come to those today beyond the reach of the gospel? The most cogent argument given by inclusivists is that they respond to what is called by some "general revelation,"[53] the revelation given in creation and conscience. Romans 1:20 sees the universal availability of the revelation in creation as leaving all people "without excuse." The revelation of God's moral law written on our hearts and revealed to our consciences is said to lead our thoughts to "either accuse or even excuse" us on the day God judges us (Rom 2:15). Thus, what if someone responds positively to the revelation offered in creation and through conscience? While Michael Bird argues that sinful persons do not respond positively to universal revelation and thus it cannot be salvific,[54] inclusivists could argue that Rom 10:18 indicates that universal revelation may not always be suppressed. Concerning this verse, Millard Erickson says, "Paul appears to say that men have heard through this means [universal revelation in creation]. If that be

---

[52] J. N. D. Anderson, *Christianity and Comparative Religion* (Downers Grove: InterVarsity, 1970), 98–99.

[53] Sanders, *No Other Name*, 215. Saving grace is mediated to the unevangelized "through general revelation and God's providential workings in human history" (215).

[54] "Romans 1:18–25 explicitly states that knowledge of God through creation is suppressed and denied by unregenerate persons, which means that it is sufficient to illuminate our minds for accountability but inadequate to impart a saving knowledge of God because humans suppress the truth in unrighteousness and exchange it for a lie." Bird, *Evangelical Theology*, 71.

the case, then perhaps the essential nature of saving faith can be arrived at without the special revelation."[55]

What about the possibility of accessing the saving power of Christ through non-Christian religions? Clark Pinnock acknowledges that the most famous inclusivist, Karl Rahner, considers other religions to "possess a salvific status."[56] Pinnock himself sees inclusivism as calling for "a generous openness to the possibility of God's gracious presence" in world religions but calls for caution too. He says, "Inclusivism should not be rosy eyed about religion, which can contain noble truths as well as terrible errors and commend virtuous deeds as well as horrible atrocities." He adds, "Witchcraft and Nazism are not valid responses to the divine, according to the gospel."[57] When it comes to criteria for which religions or which aspects of a religion may lead one to salvation, Pinnock is less clear. He says, "As Lord of all, Jesus is the criterion of truth in religion."[58] But how to apply that criterion to religions, especially to some who have no conception of Jesus or a misconception of Jesus, is a slippery matter. J. N. D. Anderson believes there are "elements in non-Christian religions" that can lead their adherents to some grasp of "the righteousness and judgment of God . . . the sin and guilt of man, and . . . the need of men and women everywhere for expiation and forgiveness." He concludes, "The essential elements would seem to be a God-given sense of sin or need, and a self-abandonment to God's mercy."[59]

There are two other views that are on the margins of inclusivism. They share the concern of inclusivists that God desires the salvation of all and the conviction that some of those who never hear the gospel may nonetheless be saved. Yet, they qualify the idea that some may be saved without hearing the gospel. Terrance Tiessen in a view that he calls "accessibilism" affirms the following two theses: "All people meet Jesus Christ personally

---

[55] Millard Erickson, "Hope for Those Who Haven't Heard? Yes, But . . .," *Evangelical Missions Quarterly* 11 (August 1975): 124.

[56] Pinnock, "An Inclusivist View," 99.

[57] Pinnock, 112–13.

[58] Pinnock, 114.

[59] Anderson, *Christianity and Comparative Religion*, 110, 105.

at the moment of death, and they respond to him in a manner consistent with the response they had been giving to God and his revelation during their lifetime," and "God's saving grace is universally sufficient so that, on at least one occasion in each person's life, one is enabled to respond to God's self-revelation with a faith response that is acceptable to God as a means of justification."[60] Tiessen does accept that one may be saved without hearing the gospel *per se*, but believes there is also a sense in which we may say that "only those who believe in Jesus will be (finally) saved."[61]

The second view that could be seen as either inclusivist or exclusivist is that of James Beilby. He agrees with inclusivists in holding out hope for some who never hear the gospel during their lifetime but agrees with exclusivists that hearing the gospel and responding with explicit faith is required for salvation. He resolves the supposed problem by holding both inclusivist and exclusivist ideas through the concept of postmortem opportunity. He offers the following theological argument for his view: "God desires that all people be saved, some people do not have a premortem opportunity to be saved, and therefore, God will provide those people with a Postmortem Opportunity."[62] Beilby does not agree with the universalists that all will respond positively to a postmortem opportunity; he does not agree with the inclusivists that one can be saved without hearing and responding positively to the gospel. He simply extends the opportunity to hear the gospel beyond one's lifetime and so occupies a marginal place near inclusivism on this spectrum of answers to our question, who will go to hell.

Exclusivism

In our spectrum of answers to the question, who will go to hell, the last answer is exclusivism, though this term is problematic. It has a history of being associated with "arrogance, intolerance, dogmatism, and

---

[60] Tiessen, *Who Can Be Saved?*, 25. Emphasis in original.

[61] Tiessen, 25.

[62] Beilby, *Postmortem Opportunity*, 78–79.

closed-mindedness,"[63] and at times is used interchangeably with the even worse term "restrictivism."[64] Accordingly, some have suggested replacing the term with "particularism"[65] or "ecclesiocentrism,"[66] but neither of those terms has caught on in the literature on this topic or at the popular level, and exclusivism seems still the most widely used term. All the same, exclusivism seems a strange term for a view that focuses on a response to a gospel that is open to everyone who believes and which uses very inclusive language in describing those around the throne of God in heaven as including some "from every nation, tribe, people, and language" (Rev 7:9).

This view deserves to be called the traditional view of Christianity, for it is certainly the most widely held view throughout most of church history. It is still the most widely held view in theologically conservative circles but has been abandoned by many mainline groups and is questioned even in evangelical groups. Different advocates of exclusivism nuance it in slightly different ways,[67] so it is important to state here what the view of exclusivism adopted here does and does not claim.

The first claim addresses the issues raised thus far regarding Old Testament saints, infants who die, and those who suffer severe mental disabilities. It states: All those living after the time of Christ's life, death, resurrection, and ascension and who have the mental ability to understand the gospel message must hear and respond in faith to the preaching of the gospel in order to be saved. The reference to the time of Christ is important due to the fuller revelation that came through him. While Old Testament saints may have been saved by their faith response to the message they had received, Paul insists that after Christ's coming, Jews need to

---

[63] Ockholm and Phillips, "Introduction," 15.

[64] As, for example, in Sanders, *No Other Name*, 37.

[65] Ockholm and Phillips, "Introduction," 16.

[66] Tiessen, *Who Can Be Saved?*, 36.

[67] For example, see the slightly differing descriptions of inclusivism given by Sanders, *No Other Name*, 42–50, and Erickson, *How Shall They Be Saved?*, 61–62, including the differing terms for the view "restrictivism" by Sanders and "exclusivism" by Erickson.

believe the gospel message about Jesus (Acts 13:38–39), as do all people (Acts 17:30–31). And, as we argued earlier, there are grounds for making an exception for those unable to understand the message of the gospel from the requirement that one must hear and respond positively to the gospel for salvation. All the views we have examined thus far make such an exception, including most exclusivists.

But apart from these exceptional cases, the most important and distinctive exclusivist claim is that a positive, explicit response of faith to the preaching of the gospel is requisite for salvation. Does this lead to the related claim that all the unevangelized are lost? If so, this leaves exclusivists with the tremendous problem of seeing multitudes heading for hell through what seems to many to be no fault of their own. Indeed, Millard Erickson sees this as perhaps "the most serious problem with this view. . . . As the statement of the position usually stands, people are condemned for failing to do what they could not have possibly done."[68] But many exclusivists (including this author) respond with the claim that the unevangelized will not be judged and condemned because they are unevangelized; that is, no one will be lost due to a lack of information, only for a lack of righteousness. The former would be unjust, and the "Judge of all the earth [will] do right" (Gen 18:25 NIV). Rather, the unevangelized may and will be justly condemned for their willful rejection of the testimony of universal revelation in nature and in the moral law within (Rom. 1:20; 2:15).[69] God has spoken to all; thus, all are "without excuse" (Rom 1:20). No one in Scripture is exempt from judgment due to lack of information.

Further, there is biblical precedent for a view within exclusivism that any who respond positively to the revelation they have in creation and conscience will be given more revelation, enough to lead them to personal faith in Christ. James Beilby calls this the Universal Sending view and states that

---

[68] Erickson, *How Shall They Be Saved?*, 63–64.

[69] This argument has been made by exclusivists from Carl Henry, *Giving a Reason for Our Hope* (Boston: W. A. Wilde, 1949), 40, 42, to R. C. Sproul, *Reason to Believe* (Grand Rapids: Zondervan, 1982), 56.

it was "fairly popular in the Middle Ages," citing what Alexander of Hales (1180–1245) says of an unevangelized person: "If he does what is within his power, the Lord will enlighten him with a secret inspiration, by means of an angel or a man."[70] Thus, the idea that exclusivists believe that "general revelation does not provide a means to salvation"[71] is both true and false. By itself, general revelation is not salvific, but a positive response to general revelation may lead to the fuller revelation that is a means to salvation.

The biblical precedent for this is the Roman centurion Cornelius, called a "devout man" who feared God. An angel told him in a vision that his prayers and acts of charity had been pleasing to God and that he was to send men to Joppa to bring back a man named Peter, who was to tell him a message "by which you and all your household will be saved" (Acts 10:1–5; 11:14). Contrary to inclusivist views which see simply responding to the revelation one has as salvific, Cornelius was not saved until Peter came and preached the gospel message to him. Yet Cornelius's responsiveness to the revelation he had received was known by God and, I would add, was the work of the Spirit in the life of Cornelius. God would complete that work by giving Cornelius the further revelation he needed for salvation.

Moreover, exclusivists believe there is some evidence that some of those called unevangelized may be so only when we limit the preaching of the gospel to human agents. Another exclusivist claim that some make is that God is not limited to human agents in the preaching of the gospel. In recent years, there have been numerous reports of dreams and visons given to individuals within Islam. Alister McGrath states that "many Muslims become Christians through dreams and visions in which they are addressed by the risen Christ,"[72] or by angels, as suggested in the citation from Alexander of Hales. Some grant a role to such visions in the process of coming to faith in

---

[70] Beilby, *Postmortem Opportunity*, 28. The words of Alexander of Hales are from Ricardo Lombardi, *The Salvation of the Unbeliever*, trans. Dorothy White (Westminster, MD: Newman, 1956), 232.

[71] As Sanders, *No Other Name*, 45, claims.

[72] Alister McGrath, "A Particularist View," in Ockholm and Phillips, *Four Views on Salvation in a Pluralistic World*, 179.

Christ but question whether any come to full saving faith with no involvement of any human agent.[73] There may be no hard evidence of someone coming to faith through dreams and visions alone, but given the millions and millions of Muslims who live beyond the reach of the gospel, perhaps we should not expect to hear news of such individuals.

A final claim of most exclusivist positions is that a positive response to the gospel must occur during one's lifetime.[74] As we saw earlier, postmortem evangelization is an important part of the universalist position and that of some inclusivists,[75] and it is essential to the borderline inclusivist/exclusivist position of James Beilby.[76] But after devoting a full chapter to the biblical evidence for postmortem evangelization, Beilby acknowledges that nothing in Scripture gives "positive evidence for the theory of Postmortem Opportunity." The most he can claim is that "Scripture provides a counterexample to the claim that death is the end of opportunity to hear and respond to the gospel."[77] Even that is to claim more than is warranted. Far clearer are the implications of Heb 9:27 and Luke 16:26–27 that one's life on earth is the time allotted to respond to God and his revelation and time is ended by death.

Evaluation

Pondering the question, who will go to hell, is a painful, even heartbreaking experience. The answers of universalism and even pluralism are comforting, but, as to universalism, the testimony of Scripture to the reality and

[73] Douglas Geivett and Gary Phillips, "Response by Geivett/Phillips," in Ockholm and Phillips, *Four Views on Salvation in a Pluralistic World*, 196.

[74] Both Sanders, *No Other Name*, 46, and Erickson, *How Shall They Be Saved?*, 62, include this claim in their lists of exclusivist claims.

[75] Notably, it is the position defended by Clark Pinnock, *A Wideness in God's Mercy: The Finality of Jesus Christ in a World of Religions* (Grand Rapids: Zondervan, 1992), 169.

[76] Beilby, *Postmortem Opportunity*, is the most recent major presentation of the argument for the possibility of salvation after death.

[77] Beilby, 159.

permanence of lostness is so overwhelming that I cannot bring myself to see it as in any way a viable option. Adding the idea of postmortem evangelization as the way that all eventually come to faith only adds to its unlikeliness. Similarly, the option of pluralism misses the overwhelming importance of the uniqueness of Jesus. Many Christians, to our shame, may not be morally superior to those in other world religions. But the object of a Christian's faith, Jesus, is unique and superior to any other religious figure.

Inclusivism is an attractive option with a greater measure of biblical and theological support. The fact that some were saved in the Old Testament without full knowledge of the gospel we know argues that perhaps God saves those who respond in faith to the revelation of God they have. And we know that all have the revelation of God in creation and conscience. If that revelation is sufficient to leave them without excuse (Rom 1:20), can it not bring them to salvation by leading them to cast themselves on the mercy of the God they know is there and receive forgiveness through the Savior they sought without ever hearing his name?[78] Such arguments have led some to a position we have not yet mentioned, "reverent agnosticism." This position believes that Scripture does not answer some of our questions, such as the fate of the unevangelized. Some people are "pessimistic agnostics," arguing that salvation beyond those who hear the gospel and respond in faith is only an exceptional possibility under very special circumstances and that we have no warrant to expect that God will act to save anyone apart from faith in Christ,[79] while others are more optimistic, speculating on the possibility of special revelation being given to some beyond the reach of the gospel through dreams and visions.[80] Still, when all is said and done, I find myself constrained to maintain the exclusivist position, with the claims given above. I do so for five reasons.

---

[78] Perhaps nowhere is this more attractively presented than in the story of Emeth in *The Last Battle*, the final volume of *The Chronicles of Narnia* by C. S. Lewis.

[79] This seems to be the position of J. I. Packer and Douglas Geivett and Gary Phillips. See the discussion in Ockholm and Phillips, "Introduction," 22.

[80] McGrath, "A Particularist View," 179.

Five Reasons Why I Am an Exclusivist

1. A Biblical Reason. Exclusivism has by far the strongest biblical case. While other verses could be cited, John 14:6 and Acts 4:12 are among the clearest texts on the uniqueness of Christ. Coupled with biblical references to other religions as idolatrous (Pss 96:5; 97:7) and even Judaism as incomplete after the coming of Christ (Rom 10:1–3), pluralism is untenable. Likewise, Scripture passages which paint the reality and permanence of lostness (Matt 25:46; 2 Thess 1:9–10) render universalism implausible; its reliance on postmortem evangelization is weakened both by the lack of any clear biblical teaching in support of it and the prominence of clear biblical teaching which contradicts it (Heb 9:27; Luke 16:25–26).[81] The inclusivist suggestion that some may be saved by a positive response to the revelation they have seems to fit the case of Cornelius in the Bible, but he was not saved until he heard the gospel (Acts 11:14). His story encourages us to believe that if any respond to the revelation they have, God will give them more revelation, sufficient to hear and respond to the gospel. This leads to a second reason.

2. A Theological Reason. I am using the term "theological" to refer to ideas about God. A factor that lies in the background of many of the positions we have discussed is the idea that God owes everyone more of an equal opportunity, especially the unevangelized. Since God loves all (John 3:16) and wants all to be saved (2 Pet 3:9), he will do something to make salvation more accessible. He will accept some based on implicit faith in the light they have, or he will encounter them through their world religion, or evangelize them after their death.

Such people are echoing the question raised by Abraham long ago, "Won't the Judge of the whole earth do what is just?" (Gen 18:25). Indeed, he will. But while God is fair to all, I cannot see how we can possibly maintain that all are treated equally. To say that a child raised in a loving

[81] See the assessment of postmortem evangelism in Erickson, *How Shall They Be Saved?*, 159–75.

Christian home and one raised in a militantly Muslim home have equal chances of becoming a Christian strains credulity. Certainly, there are some raised in the former home who do not become a Christian and some raised in the latter home who do; humans make choices and grace is amazing. Yet such inequalities do not mean injustice. God can be fair and just to all and yet gracious to some because grace is by definition what no one has a right to. Grace is always beyond "fair." If God simply treated us all justly, none would be saved. If he chooses to extend grace to some who do not deserve it, he does no injustice to those to whom he does not extend it. Those who are lost "are condemned not because they are nonelect but because they spurn God's universal revelation in nature and history and in the human conscience and mind."[82]

Further, there is biblical teaching that God takes some of these inequalities into account, with differing standards of judgment for those with differing levels of knowledge (Luke 12:47–48; Matt 11:20–24). With his perfect knowledge of the obstacles and opportunities faced by individuals, only God can judge with perfect knowledge of all the facts. We have reason to trust his fairness.

3. An Anthropological Reason. A hidden assumption behind a number of the positions we considered in the discussion of this question (who will go to hell) is that the problem of lostness is a lack of information. Inclusivism, for example, assumes that there are many out there, honestly and sincerely seeking God; they simply lack the information they need to find him. But many missionaries have had the experience of sharing the gospel with followers of other religions who reject the message of Jesus and chose to live in darkness. The teaching of the Bible, though hard for modern people with a high view of humans to accept, is that there is "no one who seeks God" (Rom 3:11) and that "people loved darkness rather than light" (John 3:19). The problem of lostness is not due to lack of information for

---

[82] Carl Henry, "Is It Fair?" in *Through No Fault of Their Own: The Fate of Those Who Have Never Heard*, ed. William V. Crockett and James G. Sigountos (Grand Rapids: Baker, 1991), 254.

the human mind, but the perverseness of the human heart. Even the idea of postmortem evangelism assumes some will respond to the gospel then. Their problem during their earthly life was never the lack of information; they were sent to hell for their rejection of God and his revelation. Is there really reason to think that death will change their heart?

4. A Missiological Reason. There is much discussion regarding the impact of one's position on the lostness of the unevangelized on one's view of the missionary mandate.[83] Whether universalists, inclusivists, or exclusivists, evangelicals all agree that the primary basis for the missionary task comes from Christ's command, "rather than from any calculation of relative need."[84] Moreover, evangelism is not just due to the needs of the lost; it is also for the glory of Christ.[85] Yet, it is undeniable that "the strongest motivation for evangelism is attached logically to the exclusivist view."[86] Indeed, it is hard to believe that Christ would have given us the missionary mandate, which has led to a multitude of martyrs down through church history, if the communication of the gospel was not the way God has designed to save people. It is hard to believe Christians would have responded to the missionary call as they have and are still responding if salvation was accessible to all without hearing the gospel. Despite the disclaimers and caveats, the views other than exclusivism do seem to undercut missions. To be consistent with their view, exclusivists should therefore be marked by a zealous commitment to the missionary mandate of the church as given to us by Christ in the Great Commission (Matt 28:19–20).

---

[83] See Charles Van Engen, "The Effect of Universalism on Mission Effort," and John Ellenberger, "Is Hell a Proper Motivation for Missions," in *Through No Fault of Their Own*, 183–94 and 217–27; and Erickson, *How Shall They Be Saved?*, 255–69.

[84] Erickson, *How Shall They Be Saved?*, 269.

[85] John Piper has memorably said: "Missions is not the ultimate goal of the church. Worship is. Missions exists because worship doesn't. Worship is ultimate, because God is ultimate, not man." John Piper, *Let the Nations Be Glad! The Supremacy of God in Missions*, 3rd ed. (Grand Rapids: Baker Academic, 2010), 15.

[86] Erickson, *How Shall They Be Saved?*, 268.

5. A Practical Reason. If the other views are right and I am wrong, I will be overjoyed to find heaven much more populated than I think. I will be surprised, but not upset. But if the other views are wrong and I am right, then the supporters and advocates of the other views may have been guilty of encouraging views that weakened support for the preaching of the gospel or led people to think that they would be accepted by God on some basis other than receiving grace by faith in response to the gospel. This would be tragic.

We have spent a lot of time on the issue of who will go to hell because traditionally hell has been seen as an eternal destiny. However, some of the same pressures that have led some to reconsider who goes to hell have also led to controversy around our third question, the nature of hell.

What Is the Nature of Hell?

To be more specific, the question we will consider in this section is: What is the nature of the punishment those in hell will suffer? We want to consider the two major alternatives being debated today.

The Traditional View

The traditional answer to this question is that hell involves conscious eternal torment. It is the overwhelming view of theologians and Christians through the centuries, from Tertullian and Augustine to Aquinas, Luther, Calvin, Wesley, and Edwards to contemporaries such as J. I. Packer, Millard Erickson, and D. A. Carson.[87]

---

[87] The strong support from history is the first argument offered by Robert Peterson, "The Case for Traditionalism," in *Two Views of Hell: A Biblical and Theological Dialogue*, ed. Edward William Fudge and Robert A. Peterson (Downers Grove: InterVarsity, 2000), 118–28. He cites eleven figures from differing times, locales, and branches of the church and concludes that their "unified confession of traditionalism is impressive, and it is not to be set aside lightly" (128).

Some think support for the traditional position is due, in least in part, to a belief in the immortality of the soul. Philip Hughes says, "It has also commonly been argued either *a priori* that the immortality of the soul demands the everlasting punishment of the wicked as well as the everlasting blessedness of the redeemed, or *a posteriori* that the endless punishment of the wicked as well as the everlasting blessedness of the redeemed demands the immortality of the soul."[88] And while the immortality of the soul "has been generally accepted in the Christian church. . . . its compatibility with the biblical revelation" is widely questioned today.[89] Thus, opponents of the traditional view say that the idea of "everlasting conscious pain" was "an idea borrowed, no doubt, from the pagan Greek notion that souls are immortal and cannot die."[90] But this is not what the major proponents of traditionalism appeal to: "If we take their own words seriously, we must understand that they [the figures cited from church history] unanimously believe in everlasting punishment because they are convinced that the Bible teaches it."[91] Today some opponents of traditionalism concede that contemporary defenses of traditionalism do not appeal to the immortality of the soul.[92] The key issue, for those in church history and today, is the teaching of Scripture.

---

[88] Philip E. Hughes, "Is the Soul Immortal?" in Date, Stump, and Anderson, *Rethinking Hell*, 188. In support of his claim, he cites Augustine, *City of God*, 6.12 in *NPNF*1, 2:121.

[89] Hughes, "Is the Soul Immortal?," 188–81. See also the critique of the belief in the immortality of the soul by Anthony A. Hoekema, *The Bible and the Future* (Grand Rapids: Eerdmans, 1979), 86–91.

[90] Edward Fudge, "The Case for Conditionalism," in Date, Stump, and Anderson, *Rethinking Hell*, 35.

[91] Peterson, "The Case for Traditionalism," in Fudge and Peterson, *Two Views of Hell*, 128.

[92] John Stackhouse Jr., "A Terminal Punishment Response" in Sprinkle, *Four Views on Hell*, 47. In responding to the presentation of the traditional view by Denny Burk, Stackhouse says, "To his credit, we must note, Burk avoids the non-Christian idea of an 'immortal soul'" (47).

On this issue, the traditional position has claimed extensive support. Robert Peterson lists ten foundational biblical texts that he sees as teaching conscious eternal torment: Isa 66:22–24; Dan 12:1–2; Matt 18:6–9; Matt 25:31–46; Mark 9:42–48; 2 Thess 1:5–10; Jude 7; Jude 13; Rev 14:9–11; and Rev 20:10–15. Of these ten, he says, "All ten speak of hell and not just of temporal punishment as do many passages used in annihilationist arguments."[93] Further, nine of the ten explicitly use terms like "eternal," "everlasting," and "forever and ever" to describe the punishment of the wicked; the final text (Isa 66:22–24) implies an eternal destiny in speaking of a worm that will not die and a fire that will not be quenched.

Of these texts, Matt 25:31–46 deserves special consideration as "historically the most important biblical passage on hell."[94] The teaching of the passage seems clear: the wicked go away to "eternal punishment" and the righteous to "eternal life" (v. 46). Both are alike in pointing to a conscious everlasting experience. Of the other texts cited by Peterson, 2 Thess 1:5–10 and Rev 14:9–11 are equally strong and categorical in teaching conscious eternal punishment. It is not hard to understand why this is the traditional position.

Conditional Immortality

The view in opposition to the traditional view is called by most of its advocates "conditional immortality," and by others "annihilationism." It sees immortality as a gift God bestows only on those who are saved through Jesus Christ; it is thus conditional. Those who do not come to salvation are raised to face judgment but are not given immortality: "They are punished with permanent destruction, including any finite conscious torment."[95] This view is specifically contrasted with universalism and purgatory as well

---

[93] Peterson, "The Case for Traditionalism," 169.

[94] Peterson, 140.

[95] Peter Grice, "Igniting an Evangelical Conversation," in Date, Stump, and Anderson, *Rethinking Hell*, 7.

as the traditional view. In this view, there comes a time when the lost no longer exist.

While some contend that there is evidence of conditionalism in the early church,[96] it was the 1982 publication of Edward Fudge's *The Fire That Consumes* that began to introduce conditionalism to contemporary evangelicalism.[97] Now in its third edition, Fudge's work remains "the most highly regarded explanation and defense of this position in evangelical theology."[98] But conditionalism took a huge leap toward respectability within evangelicalism in 1988 when John Stott came out in favor of conditionalism in his dialogue with David Edwards, defending it as part of his evangelical theology.[99] Since then, there has been enough discussion of conditionalism that three scholars in 2014 gathered together "a collection of solid evangelical voices in support of conditionalism," in a book entitled *Rethinking Hell: Readings in Evangelical Conditionalism*, most of them chapters from volumes that would otherwise be difficult to find.[100] In that volume, Glenn Peoples offers four of the "principle arguments" for evangelical conditionalism.[101]

His first argument is a critique of what he sees as the unwarranted reliance of the defenders of the traditional view on the immortality of the soul.[102] In spite of denials by contemporary defenders of the traditional view, Peoples argues that historically, the case for the traditional view was derived from and

---

[96] LeRoy Froom, "Conditionalism in the Early Church," in Date, Stump, and Anderson, *Rethinking Hell*, 260–75.

[97] Edward William Fudge, *The Fire That Consumes: A Biblical and Historical Study of Final Punishment*, 1st ed. (Houston: Providential, 1982).

[98] Gregory Stump, introductory comments to Edward W. Fudge, "The Final End of the Wicked," in Date, Stump, and Anderson, *Rethinking Hell*, 29.

[99] Edwards and Stott, *Evangelical Essentials*, 312–20. According to Peter Grice, "Igniting an Evangelical Conversation" (4) Stott had held conditionalism tentatively for some fifty years, but only came out openly in favor of it in 1988.

[100] This is the volume already cited a number of times, *Rethinking Hell: Readings in Evangelical Conditionalism*. The quotation above is from Gregory Stump, "Preface," xviii.

[101] Glenn Peoples, "Introduction to Evangelical Conditionalism," in Date, Stump, and Anderson, *Rethinking Hell*, 11–24.

[102] Peoples, 11–17.

dependent on the belief in the immortality of the soul. As mentioned above, traditionalists argue otherwise—that the traditional belief was drawn from their study of Scripture. Historians may continue to dig into the evidence, but regardless of which conclusion they come to as to the origin historically, the traditional view does not at all depend on belief in the immortality of the soul. God can continue to sustain the disembodied existence of persons after their death as he does their embodied existence during their life on earth. The emphasis on the immortality of the soul seems misplaced.

The second argument Peoples offers is the vision offered in the Bible of "a world without evil," a world in which "everything that exists will be united under Christ." In such a world, "What room is left for evil?"[103] But is the manifestation of God's justice in the conquest and punishment of wickedness itself an evil thing? At any rate, the wicked are still present in the last chapter of the Bible (Rev 22:14–15), long after Christ has come, has promised to make all things new, and has declared, "It is done!" (Rev 21:5–6). The Bible does not seem to see their continued existence, outside the new Jerusalem and indeed, in "the lake that burns with fire and sulfur" (Rev 21:8), as contrary to a world "united under Christ." They are under his wrath.

The third argument is from the nature of the substitutionary atonement made by Christ. The point Peoples seeks to make from the substitutionary nature of the atonement is not developed very fully or clearly. He notes, correctly, that Christ died for sinners, in their place: "In Christ the consequences of sin are revealed as Jesus intervened in history and took them upon himself. Jesus died for sinners."[104] The relevance of this for conditionalism is unclear. Is he saying that because Jesus died for us, we are exempt from death? But the whole point of conditional immortality is that all do not live forever, that the lost do suffer death in that they are finally consumed. I cannot see the force of this argument.

Fourth, Peoples draws upon the common use of the language of "death" and "destruction" in Scripture to describe the end of those who die separated

[103] Peoples, "Introduction to Evangelical Conditionalism," 18–19.

[104] Peoples, 20.

from Christ.[105] John Stott observes, "It would seem strange, therefore, if people who are said to suffer destruction are in fact not destroyed; and . . . 'it is difficult to imagine a perpetually inconclusive process of perishing.'"[106] He makes a similar observation about the association of hell and fire: "The fire itself is termed 'eternal' and 'unquenchable,' but it would be very odd if what is thrown into it proves indestructible."[107] But texts like 2 Pet 3:6 use the verb *apóllumi*, which Stott calls the most common Greek word for destruction,[108] for the destruction of the world of Noah's day. It was destroyed but continued to exist. The following verse, 2 Pet 3:7, then uses the noun form (*apōleia*) for the end-time destruction of the ungodly; they too will be destroyed but not annihilated. As to the argument concerning fire, the only way the fire can be unquenchable and continue to smoke (Rev 14:11) is if its fuel is not consumed.

Surprisingly, Peoples does not include among his four principle arguments one that I think is central for Stott and many evangelical conditionalists: the biblical vision of the justice of God. Stott sees "a serious disproportion between sins consciously committed in time and torment consciously experienced throughout eternity," though he acknowledges that the argument that "the impenitence of the lost also continues throughout eternity" would make eternal punishment consistent with God's justice.[109] In responding to Stott, J. I. Packer makes that very point. We have every reason to think that "continued hostility, rebellion, and impenitence Godward on the part of unbelievers" will continue after their death, meaning that "there will be no moment at which it will be possible for either God or man to say that enough punishment has been inflicted, no more is deserved, and any more would be unjust."[110] Beyond this argument is the more common

[105] Peoples, "Introduction to Evangelical Conditionalism," 21–23.

[106] Edwards and Stott, *Evangelical Essentials*, 316.

[107] Edwards and Stott, 316.

[108] Edwards and Stott, 315.

[109] Edwards and Stott, 318–19.

[110] J. I. Packer, "Evangelical Annihilationism in Review," The Highway, accessed November 11, 2015, at http://www.the-highway.com/annihilationism_Packer.html.

response, made since at least the time of Aquinas,[111] that temporal sin justly merits eternal punishment, because sin is against an infinite person, God. Calvin also responds sharply to the supposed injustice of eternal punishment:

> Even a blind man can see what stupid nonsense these people talk who are afraid of attributing excessive cruelty to God if the wicked be consigned to eternal punishment! If the Lord deprives of his Kingdom those who through their ungratefulness have rendered themselves unworthy of it—that, forsooth, will be too unjust! Yet their sins, they say, are temporal. Granted. But God's majesty, and also his justice, which they have violated by sinning, are eternal. Therefore, it is right that the memory of their iniquity does not perish. Yet thus the punishment will not exceed the measure of the transgression. This blasphemy is not to be borne, when God's majesty is so little esteemed, when the concept of it is valued less than the loss of one soul. But let us pass over these triflers, lest, contrary to what we have previously said, we seem to judge their ravings worth refuting.[112]

Evaluation

The reader will have noted that I have somewhat anticipated this section in already giving what I see as cogent and adequate responses to the conditionalists' arguments. Yet we have not yet given the conditionalists' response to the key argument of the traditional view, the prominent use of the terms "eternal" and "everlasting" in referring to the punishment of unbelievers. To mention just a few of the strongest examples, Matt 25:46 uses "eternal" to

---

[111] "It is just that he who has sinned against God in his own eternity, should be punished in God's eternity." Thomas Aquinas, *Summa Theologiae*, First Half of the Second Part, Q. 87, Art 3 (1.2.87.3). Thomas cites Gregory the Great (540–604) as support, "Whether any sin incurs a debt of eternal punishment," "Summa Theologiae: Question 87. The debt of punishment," New Advent, accessed April 26, 2024, https://www.newadvent.org/summa/2087.htm#article3.

[112] Calvin, *Institutes*, III.xxv.5 (2:996).

refer equally to the punishment of the ungodly and the life of the righteous; 2 Thess 1:9 gives "eternal destruction" as the penalty to be paid by those who do not know God and do not obey the gospel; and Rev 14:11 describes the smoke from the punishment of those who worship the beast as going up "forever and ever." This time referent is repeated in the second half of the verse: "There is no rest day or night for those who worship the beast." What is the conditionalist response to the seemingly obvious implication that "eternal," "everlasting," and "forever and ever" lead to the view that hell involves eternal conscious torment?

The most common response seems to have been originated by B. F. C. Atkinson in a privately printed book in 1968. He asserted, "When the adjective *aiōnios* meaning 'everlasting' is used in Greek with nouns of *action*, it has reference to the *result* of that action, not the process. . . . the lost will not be passing through a process of punishment forever but will be punished once and for all with eternal results."[113] Fudge makes the application to the term in Matt 25:46 and 2 Thess 1:9. "Eternal punishment" or "eternal destruction" does not mean "that Christ will be forever in the process of destroying them but that their destruction, once accomplished, will be forever."[114]

If accurate, this interpretation of "eternal" or "everlasting" would remove from the traditionalist case their strongest argument. But the conditionalist claim on this point founders on several points. As Packer and Peterson both note, the claim lacks support from those with expertise in grammar and linguistics.[115] More obviously, such a meaning for "eternal" clashes with internal evidence from the texts. For example, the "eternal destruction" of the wicked in 2 Thess 1:9 is coupled with their exclusion from the Lord's

---

[113] Atkinson's original privately printed work is cited here from Basil F. C. Atkinson, "The Doom of the Lost," in Date, Stump, and Anderson, *Rethinking Hell*, 100.

[114] Fudge, "The Final End of the Wicked," 42.

[115] Packer, "Evangelical Annihilationism in Review"; Robert Peterson, "A Traditionalist Response to Conditionalism," in Fudge and Peterson, *Two Views of Hell*, 97–98.

presence. But "only those who exist can be excluded."[116] Therefore, eternal destruction does not mean the annihilation of the wicked. Moreover, the usage of "eternal" with the life of the righteous in Matt 25:46 does not fit the idea of eternal as referring to results. Eternal life there is not the result of a process that ends but is an unending experience as is the punishment of the unrighteous. Revelation 14:11 is even more difficult for the conditionalist. When the writer says, "The smoke of their torment will go up forever and ever," and then adds, "There is no rest day or night for those who worship the beast and its image," the traditional view seems unavoidable. If an author meant to teach "eternal conscious torment," what words could he use to make the meaning clearer?

Stott concludes his case for conditionalism with this plea:

> I do not dogmatize about the position to which I have come. I hold it tentatively. But I do plead for frank dialogue among evangelicals on the basis of Scripture. I also believe that the ultimate annihilation of the wicked should at least be accepted as a legitimate, biblically founded alternative to their eternal conscious torment.[117]

In the years since Stott asked for frank dialogue, dialogue has indeed occurred, reflected in many of the books cited in the preceding pages. In England, where numerous evangelical scholars have joined Stott in support for conditionalism, the Evangelical Alliance has granted conditionalism the status Stott requested. A 2000 meeting issued a statement recognizing "conditional immortality" as "a significant minority evangelical view," that "should be regarded as a secondary rather than a primary issue for evangelical theology."[118]

I admire John Stott and have benefited greatly from his life and ministry, but the very tentativeness with which he presents his view betrays its

---

[116] Packer, "Evangelical Annihilationism in Review."

[117] Edwards and Stott, *Evangelical Essentials*, 320.

[118] Evangelical Alliance, "Hell and Evangelical Unity," in Date, Stump, and Anderson, *Rethinking Hell*, 288.

weaknesses. I do believe it is possible to see the punishment of the wicked as largely consisting in the complete withdrawal of God and all good. But there also seems to be a further and more active retributive punishment administered by God, linked to God as the Just Judge of all the earth,[119] an idea out of fashion even in much of evangelical Christianity. It may be that words like "destruction" and "perishing" imply that what is left to be punished is less than human, simply remains, and part of the punishment of hell is being left with the small, mean soul one developed on earth. In the end, the key factor is that the major descriptions of fire, punishment, destruction, and torment all include the word "eternal," and the conditionalist argument that we should see "eternal" as referring to results rather than duration, is less than convincing. I echo the words and attitude of J. I. Packer: "When John Stott urges that 'the ultimate annihilation of the wicked should at least be accepted as a legitimate, biblically founded alternative to their eternal conscious torment,' he asks too much, for the biblical foundations of this view prove on inspection . . . to be inadequate."[120] I gladly recognize evangelical conditionalists as fellow evangelicals; this point of doctrine does not touch the gospel and is not what I call a level one doctrine. At the same time, neither is it on the same level as the differing views on the millennium or the relationship between the rapture and the tribulation. After doing my best to read widely on both sides with an open mind, the traditional view seems clearly more strongly supported from Scripture.

Conclusion

No Christian I know of enjoys speaking about, teaching on, or even contemplating hell. We may agree that hell is mostly due to the reality of human freedom being misused, but we cannot ignore the biblical teaching that not only do perverse humans choose hell, but God in his justice also sends people there. The reality of the millions of unreached and those of other

---

[119] "Hell is about justice, not torture." Bird, *Evangelical Theology*, 335.

[120] Packer, "Evangelical Annihilationism," 8.

religions makes the question of who will go to hell urgent and painful. We believe the Bible teaches that God speaks to all in universal revelation and that, if any respond positively to universal revelation, he may send further revelation, even the gospel. All are without excuse. The Bible also seems equally clear that salvation comes from hearing and responding to the gospel. I for one fear engendering false hopes about a possible wider way when Christ teaches explicitly of a narrow way (Matt 7:13–14). While I agree that the descriptions of the punishments of hell may be figurative and may consist largely in the withdrawal of God's presence and all that is good, I cannot avoid the biblical teaching that this punishment is eternal, everlasting, and forever and ever. The full horror of it may be beyond our comprehension, but the idea of eternal punishment cannot be excised from hell any more than eternal life and joy can be excised from heaven. It affirms the final seriousness of being a human being.

The title and theme of this volume is that eschatology is *The Source of Hope*, but where is that hope when we have to deal with the doctrine of hell? In Dante's vision of hell, he has over the entrance, "Abandon all hope, you who enter here."[121] N. T. Wright concurs, saying those in hell are "beyond hope."[122] The hope is found in the fact that no one reading these pages—no one we work with, no family members we see, no friends we hang out with—no one presently alive has entered there and none need go there. If there is life, there is hope in the great grace of God. Thus, this discussion of hell, like the discussions of hell in the New Testament,[123] cannot end without mentioning the gospel as the message of hope and the way that leads to life, not to hell.

---

[121] Dante Alighieri, *Divine Comedy*, Canto III (III.7).

[122] N. T. Wright, *Surprised by Hope: Rethinking Heaven, the Resurrection, and the Mission of the Church* (New York: HarperOne, 2008), 182.

[123] "Views about hell should not be discussed outside the frame of the Gospel. Why not? Because it is only in connection with the Gospel that Jesus and the New Testament writers speak of hell, and the biblical way of treating biblical themes is in the biblical connections as well as in their biblical substance." Packer, "Evangelical Annihilationism."

CHAPTER 10

Conclusion: Living in Hope

We mentioned in the opening chapter some of the factors that make hope essential to all human flourishing, especially in an age like ours. We live in a world of pandemics, of open wars and hidden terrorists, with senseless shootings and political unrest, with economic uncertainties and personal tragedies. Where is hope to be found?

We have argued that eschatology is uniquely purposed by God to provide hope for hurting hearts. It remains for us now to briefly show how hope is connected to all the topics we have addressed. We first spoke of death. For many, death may seem the most hopeless of all the realities we face on earth. Even Christians recognize death as an enemy (1 Cor 15:26). But for the Christian, death is transformed by the severe mercy of God into amazing hope. By sentencing us to death, God gives us the hope that we are not condemned to live forever in a broken and corrupt world, filled with all the evils we mentioned above.

That hope is magnified in the second topic we addressed, what lies beyond death. Though it was only revealed in the shadows in the Old Testament, the sure hope of real life beyond the grave is brought to light by Christ. The prospect set before the believer is a life in the presence of Christ which is "far better" than life on earth (Phil 1:23), being "at home with the Lord" (2 Cor 5:8), in a place called "paradise" (Luke 23:43).

In chapters 4 and 5, we dealt with the apex and heart of all hope; indeed, with what is called "the blessed hope" (Titus 2:13), the second coming of Jesus. We addressed, in chapter 4, the difficult issue of the relationship of the rapture and the tribulation, but the controversies over these issues should not blind us to the hope—whether before, during, or after tribulation, Jesus will return. He is the object of our hope.

His coming will be the time for judgment and resurrection. And while judgment may sound ominous to us, it is the fruition of our hope for God's justice to be vindicated, for right to triumph and evil to be definitively put down. It is paired with the resurrection of the body, a reminder that our hope is not for endless existence as a disembodied soul or spirit but life in a new and glorious body, one no longer racked by pain or limited by disability, one no longer pained by the confusion of gender dysphoria. It will be a body that is able to enjoy, explore, and experience the new creation.

Does the mystery of the millennium have any hope for us? We do have to acknowledge the controversies over this doctrine. Perhaps it has produced more division among Christians than hope. Yet all the major positions affirm that there is coming a time when Satan will be bound and Christ will reign; indeed, one major view thinks this is happening now. Likewise, all the views see earth as not under evil oppressors forever; for Jesus is King! He will reign.

Of all the eschatological promises that bring hope, perhaps none grip us more than the vision of our eternal home in which Christ has made all things new, where the old order of death, grief, crying, and pain are no more (Rev 21:4). The images through which heaven is portrayed are more than wishful thinking; they are the fuel for endless hope, until one day sight replaces faith and hope is no mere hope but reality. As we mentioned at the close of the previous chapter, even the horrors of hell do not obscure the hope we have. None need go there, for God's arms are open wide to all who come in penitent faith.

This then is eschatology, the source of hope. Ponder it well and live in hope!

BIBLIOGRAPHY

Akin, Daniel. "A Rapture You Can't Miss (1 Thessalonians 4:13–18), A Judgment You Must Face (2 Corinthians 5:10), A Supper You Will Want to Attend (Revelation 19:1–10)." In *The Return of Christ: A Premillennial Perspective*, 46–61. Edited by David L. Allen and Steve W. Lemke. Nashville: B&H Academic, 2011.

Alcorn, Randy. *Heaven*. Carol Stream, IL: Tyndale, 2004.

Allen, Michael. *Grounded in Heaven: Centering Christian Hope and Life on God*. Grand Rapids: Eerdmans, 2018.

Anderson, J. N. D. *Christianity and Comparative Religion*. Downers Grove: InterVarsity, 1970.

Beale, G. K. *The Book of Revelation*. NIGNT. Grand Rapids: Eerdmans, 1999.

Beilby, James. *Postmortem Opportunity: A Biblical and Theological Assessment of Salvation After Death*. Downers Grove: IVP Academic, 2021.

Berkouwer, G. C. *The Return of Christ*. Translated by James Van Oosterom. Edited by Marlin J. Van Elderen. Grand Rapids: Eerdmans, 1972.

Bingham, D. Jeffrey, and Glenn R. Kreider, eds. *Eschatology: Biblical, Historical, and Practical Approaches*. Grand Rapids: Kregel Academic, 2016.

Blomberg Craig L., and Sung Wook Chung, eds. *A Case for Historic Premillennialism: An Alternative to "Left Behind" Eschatology*. Grand Rapids: Baker Academic, 2009.

Boa, Kenneth, and Robert Bowman, Jr. *Sense and Nonsense about Heaven and Hell.* Grand Rapids: Zondervan, 2007.

Bock, Darrell L., ed. *Three Views on the Millennium and Beyond.* Grand Rapids: Zondervan, 1999.

Brand, Chad O., ed. *Perspectives on Israel and the Church: Four Views.* Nashville: B&H Academic, 2015.

Brannon, M. Jeff. *The Hope of Life After Death: A Biblical Theology of Resurrection.* Downers Grove: IVP Academic, 2022.

Clouse, Robert G., ed. *The Meaning of the Millennium: Four Views.* Downers Grove: InterVarsity, 1977.

Congdon, David W., ed. *Varieties of Christian Universalism: Exploring Four Views.* Grand Rapids: Baker Academic, 2023.

Conyers, A. J. *The Eclipse of Heaven: The Loss of Transcendence and Its Effect on Modern Life.* Downers Grove: InterVarsity, 1992.

Cooper, John W. *Body, Soul & Life Everlasting: Biblical Anthropology and the Monism-Dualism Debate*. Grand Rapids: Eerdmans, 2000.

Crockett, William V., and James G. Sigountos, eds. *Through No Fault of Their Own: The Fate of Those Who Have Never Heard.* Grand Rapids: Baker, 1991.

Date, Christopher M., Gregory G. Stump, and Joshua W. Anderson, eds. *Rethinking Hell: Readings in Evangelical Conditionalism.* Eugene, OR: Cascade, 2014.

Davis, Andrew M. *The Glory Now Revealed: What We'll Discover about God in Heaven.* Grand Rapids: Baker, 2021.

Davis, Chris. *Bright Hope for Tomorrow: How Anticipating Jesus' Return Gives Strength for Today*. Grand Rapids: Zondervan, 2022.

D'Costa, Gavin, Paul Knitter, and Daniel Strange. *Only One Way? Three Christian Responses to the Uniqueness of Christ in a Religiously Plural World.* London: SCM, 2011.

Edwards, David L., and John Stott. *Evangelical Essentials: A Liberal-Evangelical Dialogue*. Downers Grove: InterVarsity, 1988.

Emerson, Matthew Y. *"He Descended to the Dead": An Evangelical Theology of Holy Saturday*. Downers Grove: InterVarsity, 2019.

Erickson, Millard J. *How Shall They Be Saved? The Destiny of Those Who Do Not Hear of Jesus*. Grand Rapids: Baker, 1996.

Feinberg, John S., ed. *Continuity and Discontinuity: Perspectives on the Relationship Between the Old and New Testaments*. Wheaton: Crossway, 1988.

Fudge, Edward William. *The Fire That Consumes: A Biblical and Historical Study of Final Punishment*. 1st ed. Houston: Providential, 1982.

Fudge, Edward William, and Robert A. Peterson. *Two Views of Hell: A Biblical and Theological Dialogue*. Downers Grove: InterVarsity, 2000.

Groothuis, Douglas. *Deceived by the Light*. Eugene, OR: Wipf & Stock, 2002.

Gundry, Robert H. *The Church and the Tribulation*. Grand Rapids: Zondervan, 1973.

Gundry, S. N. "Judgment of Nations," *Evangelical Dictionary of Theology*, 3rd ed., Grand Rapids: Baker Academic, 2017.

Hammett, John S., and Katie J. McCoy. *Humanity*. Theology for the People of God. Edited by David S. Dockery, Nathan A. Finn, and Christopher W. Morgan. Brentwood, TN: B&H Academic, 2023.

Harris, Murray J. *Raised Immortal: Resurrection & Immortality in the New Testament*. Grand Rapids: Eerdmans, 1983.

Hays, J. Daniel, J. Scott Duvall, and C. Marvin Pate. *Dictionary of Biblical Prophecy and End Times*. Grand Rapids: Zondervan, 2007.

Hick, John. *God Has Many Names*. Philadelphia: Westminster, 1982.

Hoekema, Anthony A. *The Bible and the Future*. Grand Rapids: Eerdmans, 1979.

Hultberg, Alan, ed. *Three Views on the Rapture: Pretribulation, Prewrath, or Posttribulation*. Grand Rapids: Zondervan, 2010.

Johnston, Philip S. *Shades of Sheol: Death and Afterlife in the Old Testament*. Leicester, UK: Apollos, 2002.

Jones, David. "To Bury or Burn? Toward an Ethic of Cremation." *JETS* 53, no. 2 (June 2010): 335–47.

Keller, Timothy. *On Death*. New York: Penguin, 2020.

Kline, Meredith G. "The First Resurrection." *Westminster Theological Journal* 37, no. 3 (1975): 366–75.

Kreeft, Peter. *Everything You Ever Wanted to Know about Heaven: But Never Dreamed of Asking*. San Francisco: Ignatius, 1990.

———. *Heaven, the Heart's Deepest Longing*. New York: Harper Collins, 1980.

Kübler-Ross, Elisabeth. *On Death and Dying*. New York: Macmillan, 1969.

Ladd, G. E. *The Blessed Hope*. Grand Rapids: Eerdmans, 1956.

———. *The Presence of the Future*. Grand Rapids: Eerdmans, 1974.

Lewis, C. S. *The Great Divorce*. New York: Macmillan, 1946.

———. *The Problem of Pain*. New York: Macmillan, 1962.

MacArthur, John. *Safe in the Arms of God: Words from Heaven About the Death of a Child*. Nashville: Thomas Nelson, 2003.

Mason, Matthew. "The Wounded It Heals: Gender Dysphoria and the Resurrection of the Body." In *Beauty, Order, and Mystery: A Christian Vision of Human Sexuality*, 135–47. Edited by Gerald Hiestand and Todd Wilson. Downers Grove: IVP Academic, 2017.

Mathison, Keith. *Postmillennialism: An Eschatology of Hope*. Phillipsburg, PA: P & R, 1999.

McDannell, Colleen, and Bernhard Lang. *Heaven: A History*. New Haven: Yale University Press, 1988.

McGrath, Alister E. *A Brief History of Heaven*. Malden, MA: Blackwell, 2003.

Merkle, Benjamin L. "Could Jesus Return at any Moment? Rethinking the Imminence of the Second Coming." *Trinity Journal* 26, no. 2 (Fall 2005): 279–92.

Middleton, J. Richard. *A New Heaven and a New Earth: Reclaiming Biblical Eschatology*. Grand Rapids: Zondervan, 2004.

Morgan, Christopher W., and Robert A. Peterson, eds. *Faith Comes by Hearing: A Response to Inclusivism*. Downers Grove: IVP Academic, 2008.

———. *Heaven*. Theology in Community. Wheaton: Crossway, 2014.

Morris, Leon. *The Biblical Doctrine of Judgment*. Eugene, OR: Wipf & Stock, 2006.

Nash, Ronald H. *When a Baby Dies: Answers to Comfort Grieving Parents*. Grand Rapids: Zondervan, 1999.

Ockholm, Dennis L., and Timothy R. Phillips, eds. *Four Views on Salvation in a Pluralistic World*. Grand Rapids: Zondervan, 1995.

Packer, J. I. "Evangelical Annihilationism in Review." The Highway. Accessed November 11, 2015. http://www.the-highway.com/annihilationism_Packer.html.

———. "Hell's Final Enigma." *Christianity Today* 46, no. 5 (April 2002): 84.

Pate, C. Marvin, ed. *Four Views on the Book of Revelation*. Grand Rapids: Zondervan, 1998.

Pentecost, J. Dwight. *Things to Come: A Study in Biblical Eschatology*. Findlay, OH: Dunham, 1958.

Phelan, John E., Jr. *Essential Eschatology: Our Present and Future Hope*. Downers Grove: IVP Academic, 2013.

Pinnock, Clark. *A Wideness in God's Mercy: The Finality of Jesus Christ in a World of Religions*. Grand Rapids: Zondervan, 1992.

Piper, Don. *90 Minutes in Heaven: A True Story of Death and Life*. Grand Rapids: Revell, 2004.

Piper, John. *Let the Nations Be Glad! The Supremacy of God in Missions*, 3rd ed. Grand Rapids: Baker Academic, 2010.

Rahner, Karl. *Theological Investigations* Vol. 6, *Concerning Vatican Council II*. Translated by Karl and Boniface Kruger. Baltimore: Helicon, 1969.

Ramm, Bernard. *Them He Glorified: A Systematic Study of the Doctrine of Glorification*. Grand Rapids: Eerdmans, 1963.

Rawlings, Maurice. *Beyond Death's Door*. Nashville: Thomas Nelson, 1978.

Reiter, Richard R., ed. *Three Views on the Rapture: Pre-, Mid-, or Post-Tribulation?* Grand Rapids: Zondervan, 1984.

Rosenthal, Marvin. *The Prewrath Rapture of the Church*. Nashville: Thomas Nelson, 1990.

Russell, Jeffrey Burton. *A History of Heaven: The Singing Silence*. Princeton: Princeton University Press, 1997.

Sanders, John. *No Other Name: An Investigation into the Destiny of the Unevangelized*. Grand Rapids: Eerdmans, 1992.

Schnabel, Eckhard. *40 Questions about the End Times*. Grand Rapids: Kregel Academic, 2011.

Schreiner, Thomas R. *Revelation*. BECNT. Grand Rapids: Baker Academic, 2023.

Shatzer, Jacob. *Transhumanism and the Image of God: Today's Technology and the Future of Christian Discipleship*. Downers Grove: IVP Academic, 2019.

Sprinkle, Preston. *Four Views on Hell*. Grand Rapids: Zondervan, 2016.

Storms, Sam. *Kingdom Come: The Amillennial Alternative*. Christian Focus: Ross-shire, Scotland, 2012.

Thiselton, Anthony C. *Life after Death: A New Approach to the Last Things*. Grand Rapids: Eerdmans, 2012.

Tiessen, Terrance L. *Who Can Be Saved? Reassessing Salvation in Christ and World Religions*. Downers Grove: IVP Academic, 2004.

Walls, Jerry L. *Heaven, Hell, and Purgatory: Rethinking the Things That Matter Most*. Grand Rapids: Brazos, 2015.

Walls, Jerry L., ed. *The Oxford Handbook of Eschatology*. New York: Oxford University Press, 2008.

Walvoord, John F. *The Blessed Hope and the Tribulation: A Study of Posttribulationism*. Grand Rapids: Zondervan, 1976.

———. *The Millennial Kingdom*. Grand Rapids: Zondervan, 1959.

———. *The Rapture Question*. Rev. ed. Grand Rapids: Zondervan, 1979.

Williamson, Paul R. *Death and the Afterlife: Biblical Perspectives on Ultimate Questions*. New Studies in Biblical Theology 44. London: Apollos, 2018.

Wittmer, Michael E. *Heaven Is a Place on Earth: Why Everything You Do Matters to God*. Grand Rapids: Zondervan, 2004.

———, ed. *Four Views on Heaven*. Grand Rapids: Zondervan, 2022.

Wright, N. T. *Surprised by Hope: Rethinking Heaven, the Resurrection, and the Mission of the Church*. New York: HarperOne, 2008.

GENERAL INDEX

T

U

V

SCRIPTURE INDEX

John

Acts

Romans

1 Corinthians

2 Corinthians

Galatians

Ephesians